Lloyd George and Churchill

Lloyd George and Churchill

How Friendship Changed Politics

Marvin Rintala

Madison Books

Published by Madison Books
4720 Boston Way, Lanham, Maryland 20706

3 Henrietta Street
London, WC2E 8LU, England

Distributed by National Book Network

The paper used in this publication meets the minimum requirements of American National Standard for Information Sciences—Permanence of Paper for Printed Library Materials, ANSI Z39.48–1984.

An earlier version of chapter 2 appeared in *Biography: An Interdisciplinary Quarterly* 11, Spring, 1988. © 1988 by the Biographical Research Center.
An earlier version of chapter 5 appeared in *Biography* 8 (Summer 1985): 248–64.
An earlier version of chapter 8 appeared as "The Love of Power and the Power of Love: Churchill's Childhood" in *Political Psychology* 5 (1984): 375–90.

Library of Congress Cataloging-in-Publication Data

Rintala, Marvin.
Lloyd George and Churchill : how friendship changed politics / Marvin Rintala.
p. cm.
Includes bibliographical references and index.
1. Lloyd George, David, 1863–1945—Friends and associates.
2. Churchill, Winston, Sir, 1874–1965—Friends and associates.
3. Great Britain—Politics and government—1901–1936. 4. Great Britain—Politics and Government—1936–1945. 5. Friendship—Great Britain—History—20th century. 6. Prime ministers—Great Britain—Biography. I. Title
DA566.9.L5R5   1994   941.083'092'2—dc20   94–27342   CIP

ISBN 1–56833–031–6 (cloth : alk. paper)

British Cataloging in Publication Information Available

To the memory of
Todd Homer Callihan
who taught me too briefly about friendship

Contents

Preface

When David Lloyd George and Winston Churchill began their long friendship, which was so distasteful to their numerous enemies, one of those enemies—which one is no longer known—described the new friends as "the Heavenly Twins." This far from complimentary term caught on and was widely used at least until the beginning of the First World War. The term was borrowed from the title of a late Victorian novel written by Sarah Grand, the pen name of Frances Elizabeth Clarke McFall, whose books had at least brief popularity, and who was to serve late in life as mayor of Bath.[1]

A visitor to the mayor's house in Bath later found it tastelessly decorated.[2] This seems appropriate for there was little that was tasteful about McFall. *The Heavenly Twins* was a ponderous and grotesque novel, whose publication needed financial subsidy from its author.[3] McFall's Heavenly Twins were not Castor and Pollux lighting up the firmament of British literature, or even connecting everyday life with myth.[4] McFall's Heavenly Twins, who appear also in her autobiographical novel *The Beth Book*, are gifted, irresponsible, and inseparable children.[5] The title characters of *The Heavenly Twins* are so named in derision by an adult character.[6]

There is no evidence that either Lloyd George or Churchill ever read McFall, but Lloyd George, at least, would have been enormously amused by the literary counterparts. Like Lloyd George and Churchill, McFall's twins are utterly unconventional and unself-conscious, and their fame is widespread.[7] The term of derision becomes a description of reality in the novel. Such might also have been the case with Lloyd George and Churchill. After both were dead, the earl of Swinton, who had known them, wrote that the term was apt.[8] In reality, both Lloyd George and Churchill stood out clearly above all their rivals in British politics.[9]

Unlike Lloyd George, Churchill would hardly have appreciated McFall's irony, for he liked to be told of his stellar qualities. When the relatively young Churchill first reached cabinet rank, Lord Curzon, ever servile before those who might prove helpful, congratulated him, "*Sic itur ad astra.*"[10] The recipient, who had problems with Virgil in any language, might have needed a translation, but he had no problem in understanding his wife's message, "you fly from one scene to another thro' space like a glorious star shedding comet."[11] Churchill agreed. When he first met Violet Asquith, he told her, "We are all worms. But I do believe that I am a glowworm."[12] He was, but so was Lloyd George, who let others say it of him, but preferred it not be in his presence. Lloyd George ridiculed fawners like Curzon to their faces. However, he did not censor, or censure, biographers who wrote of him, "And in the midst shines one star, so much the brighter in the clouded heavens that the others seem by its side small and colourless and faint."[13]

Unlike some of their admirers, I see no need to choose between the Heavenly Twins of British politics. Both of them, and their friendship, deserve and need to be understood. A prefatory note of caution may nevertheless be appropriate. Not all friendships are made in heaven.[14] Even if a particular friendship were angelic, much humility, as C. S. Lewis saw, is needed if one is to eat the bread of angels without risk.[15] Neither Lloyd George nor Churchill had much humility. Certainly neither tolerated fools gladly. The state of their souls aside, together they could escalate the risks not only for their rivals for power, but for millions of other human beings as well. High politics does not exist in a vacuum. The decisions made by the most powerful have important, sometimes fatal, consequences for the powerless. These consequences, which flow from the distinctively coercive nature of the state as a social institution, must be part of the understanding of the powerful. Those looking up at the heavens may be hurt by a falling star. So may those many who are not even looking up.

Their rivals certainly envied Lloyd George and Churchill their many gifts, among the chief of which was their friendship. The Heavenly Twins were widely, deeply, and persistently hated by other members of the British political elite, who were ever alert for any possible descent to earth. As Richard Pryor put it, when the earthbound catch those who fly resting on a rock, the earthbound will pull off the wings of the fliers.[16] That is what almost happened to Lloyd George in the Marconi affair and to Churchill with Gallipoli. That is what happened to both during the last decade before the Second World War, when British government was dominated by three men: Ramsay MacDonald, Stanley Baldwin, and Neville Chamberlain. The first and third of these hated both Lloyd George and Churchill.[17] Baldwin also hated Churchill, enough to deny him ministerial office, including minister for the coordination of defence, but his obsession with keeping Lloyd George out of ministerial office became the primary goal of his political life.[18] To block an emerging coalition between Lloyd George and the Labor party in 1931, Baldwin led the Conservative party into coalition with MacDonald.[19] Some believe the ultimate source of all this hatred of Lloyd George and Churchill was envy.[20] MacDonald felt so inferior that he had Lloyd George's portrait removed from display at Chequers.[21] In rejecting ministerial office for Churchill, Baldwin made his envy plain: "But where would I then stand when Churchill comes along with his hundred horsepower brain?"[22]

It is not my intention to pull off any wings. Some might fall off of their own weight. Each reader of this book will doubtless decide, perhaps on the basis of whether peace or social justice is seen as more important, what meaning there is in the Heavenly Twins appellation. That is as it should be. Each reader should at least begin with a light heart, recalling the report by McFall:

Preface

There was no fun for the Heavenly Twins apart, so they decided to sit together at the wedding breakfast, and nobody dared to separate them, lest worse should come of it.[23]

Introduction:
Friendship in Politics

What precisely did "friends" mean?
—Sarah Grand

Many poets and novelists have celebrated friendship. Many
journalists have observed, sometimes in an exaggerated
manner, the significance of particular friendships in politics. However, scholarly inquiries into friendship are relatively rare. As a field of study, friendship is distinctly
underdeveloped. Apart from a few essays, heavily normative rather than empirical, philosophers have given little con-
sideration to friendship.[1] Psychologists have been no more
helpful. Freud did not say much about friendship, and,
perhaps consequently, there are few psychoanalytic papers
on the subject. Psychological studies of any methodological
persuasion are surprisingly few.[2] Friendship does not appear in a standard psychological dictionary, nor is it a
specialized field of inquiry among sociologists.[3] It has been
largely ignored by most social scientists, from whose research the importance of friendship as a human relationship is hardly apparent. Even when friendship is discussed
in sophisticated scholarly studies, it is not defined with
sufficient clarity, so that its meaning from study to study
could remain constant.[4]

Political scientists, in particular, have not paid much

attention to the relationship between friendship and politics. One significant political scientist, Carl Schmitt, did
argue that politics flows from the ability to distinguish
friend from foe.[5] Schmitt's argument is strikingly similar to
that made by Henry David Thoreau, who observed that the
state "did not know its friends from its foes and I lost all
my remaining respect for it, and pitied it."[6] Schmitt's hypothesis has been ignored by most political scientists, perhaps because of his suspected role as an intellectual
predecessor of national socialism; there are few scholarly
resonances, or refutations, of his argument.[7] One of the few
intellectual echoes of Schmitt is heard in José Ortega's
pronouncement "that Man may be friend or enemy, that he
may *be for* us or *be against* us, is the root of everything
social."[8] Ortega's broadening of Schmitt's argument to all
social relationships, not merely those which are political,
appears not even to have been noticed by social, including
political, scientists. Even Schmitt's narrower claim was
broader than his own practical application of his argument,
which came down to the proposition that what is political
is determined by enmity.[9] In practice, Schmitt concentrat-
ed on foes and ignored friendship. His perception of politics, therefore, excluded cooperation among friends, and saw
all of politics in terms of conflict among foes. This perception has been deservedly rejected as far too narrow. Consensual power is just as much power as is coercive power.
Power can best be defined as the social relationship that
occurs whenever one or more persons act as another person wishes.[10] Hatred is certainly present in politics, but
people act out of love, as well.

Possible explanations for the widespread scholarly silence
about friendship are varied. It has been suggested, for instance, that friendship is uncommon among university pro-
fessors. Academic career decisions are seldom motivated
explicitly by either friendship or enmity, although more often
by the latter.[11] Possibly scholars seldom study friendship
among other people because they so seldom encounter it in
their own lives. This may not be an excessively cynical
observation about people who often forget the names of
distant friends, but never their institutional affiliation.

Even more pessimistic is the possible explanation that
friendship is uncommon in human relationships generally.[12]

If that were true, the paucity of scholarly studies of friendship would not only be excusable, but appropriate. What does not matter much in social, including political, life ought not to matter much in social, including political, science. The assumptions that friendship exists, and should therefore be studied, are probably tolerable assumptions, nevertheless.

There are probably some other reasons why friendship, especially in politics, is so little studied. For some people friendship is possible only "when no business is afoot."[13] Thus, it cannot exist among people who work together or share the same field of work. This would preclude friendships between politicians. Work undeniably makes a difference in friendships. Competition does in fact affect friendships. In highly competitive careers, including business and the military, career competition can severely minimize friendship possibilities.[14]

Examining the impact of competition on friendship, one social scientist distinguished between two mutually exclusive kinds of friendship—one of practical utility and another of emotional fulfillment.[15] Such a distinction possesses analytical clarity, which may not exist within human motivation. In social relationships rational calculation and emotional attraction are so closely connected as to be practically inseparable. Furthermore, emotional fulfillment is as much a human need as is practical utility. A friendship based solely on emotional fulfillment has utility for human beings, who need to be loved.

Political careers are among the most competitive of careers. Even friends who are not career politicians can be separated by political differences, although for such followers friendships can certainly cross party lines.[16] It has been suggested that political deviants can form friendships with each other more readily than can political conformers, but the general fate of political deviants is political defeat.[17] As an expert observer of the corridors of power noted, defeat can bite deeply into friendships.[18] Joseph Chamberlain, who had much experience of his friends becoming his foes and little of his foes becoming his friends, sadly related to Lord Randolph Churchill his own conclusion that "no private friendship can long resist the effect of political contest."[19] Chamberlain's experience supported Cicero's prophecies that desire of high office would lead to the most bitter enmities between the dearest friends and that friendship would be found least often among the powerful.[20]

To some, any friend in power is a friend lost. Those who gain power, in turn, discover the loss of former friends, appearing to confirm at least part of the scenario of *Prometheus Unbound*: "to be Omnipotent but friendless is to reign."[21] In one variation of this position, there are few friends in politics, mostly only allies in a cause. In another variation, in politics the law of the jungle prevails, with alliances, but not friendships, possible.[22] To listen to politicians, they alone are burdened, and they are alone while burdened.

If it is lonely at the top, according to some persons including politicians as well as observers of politics, it should be. Many persons believe that personal relationships should not affect decisions of state. As one member of this school put it, the job comes before all else, even friendship.[23] This view flows from an ethical perspective that assumes that personal influence is partial influence, and therefore improper. Charles de Gaulle, who perhaps both articulated and exemplified this perspective at least as well as any other politician, proudly proclaimed; "Where I am, a man must have neither friends nor enemies."[24] Not many politicians, at least in democratic political cultures, are aloof enough to keep the social distance de Gaulle undoubtedly kept between his fellow human beings and himself. His goal, which at first glance seems intensely impersonal, may actually result in the personalization of power. Other members of the political elite may find themselves locked out of power possibilities. The unapproachable leader does as he or she chooses. "Reason of state" leads fairly easily to "I am the state." This norm can be applied to justify the most arbitrary action. Winston Churchill icily observed to a distinguished admiral of the fleet whom he was demoting; "I have to consider my duty to the State which ranks above personal friendship."[25] Isolation of a leader may mean that he or she hears no voices, certainly not of equals, other than his or her own. Even *vox populi* needs to be articulated by someone to be heard.

Churchill's apparent rejection of the propriety of friendship in politics was typical of many of his statements to others, especially in his old age. The elderly Churchill, who had outlived all his political peers, loved to pontificate, "there are no friends at the top."[26] This theme was repeated by him in numerous variations, but it was not original with Churchill.[27] He had learned it, like many other things, from David Lloyd George. It was Lloyd George who made famous the proposition, also in numerous variations, that there is no friendship at the top. But this formulation was no more original with Lloyd George than it was, later, with Churchill. Lloyd George, ever alert for a good line, had been given this advice early in his political career by Stuart, later Lord, Rendel.[28] Where Rendel got the line is unknown, and perhaps does not much matter. As Plato puts it in the *Phaedrus*, what matters is not what country it comes from, but what the truth of the matter is.[29]

The matter—whether there is friendship at the top—does matter. If politicians are incapable of friendship with each other, not only would the love of power be incompatible with the power of love, but the former would be stronger than the latter. It is a common human feeling that no one could be friends with a power maniac and that power corrupts love. The dichotomy of power and love is easy to see. It is not unusual to assume that power and love are wholly incompatible sources of human motivation.[30] This assumption may itself not be compatible, for instance, with the exercise of power, and the action of obedience, between those parents and those children who love each other.

Not all observers, let alone all practitioners, of politics accept the incompatibility of power and love. Some see love as the foundation, not the negation, of power. For these persons, love need not always be powerless and power need not always be loveless.[31] It may be that power can be exercised within a friendship. Aristotle thought that the powerful care more for friendship than for justice.[32] Harold Lasswell apparently agreed, for he pointedly asked: "what, indeed, is the constitution among friends?"[33]

More clinically, a supremely political novelist argued that "power sprang as much from intimacy as from anything."[34] It was no accident that this novelist was British. It may be that in British political culture friendships among the powerful are of special significance. Even at the level of members of the House of Commons, friendships cross party lines.[35] A leading member of that House proudly reported "Men of opposite parties meet on most friendly and amiable terms, a condition of things which very few countries can compete in."[36] The author of this political statement not only had no old school tie, but was the chief opponent of the power of old school tie-wearers in British politics. He was, indeed, the person from whom Churchill learned the expression: "there is no friendship at the top."

It is of secondary significance whether Lloyd George, or Churchill, or anyone else, was always internally consistent in reporting the relationship between friendship and politics. What is more important is: What do the actions of politicians reveal about the relationship? The actions, not the words, of politicians define the empirical relationship between friendship and politics. The verbal assertions of Lloyd George and Churchill articulate the question at hand. Those assertions do not answer the question, but they provide convenient, and appropriate, hypotheses for examination in this book. The relationship between Lloyd George and Churchill will here be drawn upon to provide at least a preliminary partial answer to the question they raised. Study of one human relationship will not provide a full answer to the question. If, however, the relationship between Lloyd George and Churchill was one of friendship, at least the possibility of friendship at the top will be demonstrated. Many other scholars will have to determine how large the room is.

This is not a book about the concept of friendship, let alone about whether the study of friendship should be called amicology or something a bit less pretentious.[37] This book is a description of the political consequences of a particular human relationship. This book is therefore biographical, but is in no way intended as a full-scale biography of either Lloyd George or Churchill. There are already many conventional biographies of each. It is unhelpful, however, to suggest that the last word has been written on either Lloyd George or Churchill. Certainly the last word will never be written on the former. This book is hardly the last word on either, but it might be an early word on their relationship.[38]

What is needed now is social scientific use of those vast conventional biographical resources about Lloyd George and

Churchill which already exist and which will continue to come into existence, without, alas, any assistance from social scientists. This book, however, may reveal some important facets of the personalities of Lloyd George and Churchill. Friendship is a voluntary relationship, and therefore reveals much about the selves involved in that relationship. In friendship, one wears no mask but is psychologically naked.[39] Perhaps that is why the powerful, who wear and need so many masks, often fear friendship.

In friendship human beings may reach their highest level of individuality.[40] Marcel Proust was surely wrong when he argued that friendship involves abdication of self.[41] The selves of Lloyd George and Churchill existed, of course, before they met, although they may have been altered by their relationship.

To determine whether Lloyd George and Churchill were friends, an explicit minimal operational definition of friendship is needed. Without such explicitness, the internal consistency of this, or any, book on a particular human relationship would suffer. With such explicitness, this book, limited though its scope may be, can perhaps make a contribution to comparative studies of friendship, as well as to much more limited, but nevertheless appropriate, questions about British politics, such as the political consequences of friendship within the cabinet, and about international politics.

That any definition of friendship is possible would be denied by some. It has been argued, for instance, that each friendship is unique, "and can be compared only with itself."[42] Some writers have declared an inability to formulate a definition of friendship that covers all the conditions, because friendship is neither a formality nor a mode. Undeniably, friendship is less institutionalized than some other social relationships such as marriage.[43] These kinds of difficulties are met, however, in all comparative studies, and in the case of a particular cultural context, there may in fact be some degree of institutionalization of friendship.[44]

There are other procedural problems in studying friendship. There may be certain qualities in friendship that everyone knows but no one can define.[45] Some aspects of friendship may be ineffable. If these aspects cannot be articulated by participants in a particular friendship, it becomes even more difficult for others to understand that relationship. The task of social science is, nevertheless, to understand the relationships of human beings whether or not they understand their own relationships. This book assumes that friendship can and should be studied, and that friendship can and should be understood. While regretting the present absence of an accepted general theory of friendship, this author assumes that the most urgent present need in studies of friendship is "descriptive patience" about particular friendships.[46] This descriptive patience should be made useful for students of other particular friendships by a definition of friendship that is minimally, but intentionally no more than minimally, explicit in articulating that understanding. I do not claim that all friendships in politics are like the relationship of Lloyd George and Churchill, or that they should, or must, be like that relationship. This is a Weberian study, not normative preaching. I do not presume to tell other people whether, or how, they ought to love one another.

This book is, nevertheless, a study of one kind of love. Whatever else friendship is, it is a kind of love. It is no accident that, in Latin, friendship takes its name from love. Whenever we speak of friendship, we must also speak of love.[47] To equate friendship with love is, however, an oversimplification, even if less serious an error than to assume that friendship is not a kind of love.[48] This latter error is more common in modern society.[49] Friendship is sometimes regarded as involving the giving and at other times as involving the receiving of love.[50] Each of these perceptions is one-sided. More accurately, friendship involves the sharing of one kind of love.[51] It has been argued that this sharing must produce a "mirrored doubleness of life."[52] This is an exaggerated argument. The sharing of love in friendship need not be symmetrical, but it must have a substantial element of mutuality.[53] Nicholas Berdyaev was mistaken when he argued that only erotic love demands mutuality.[54] Friendship is a living as well as loving relationship between two human beings, not some kind of aloof, unreciprocated feeling of cordiality. Unrequited friendship is a contradiction in terms.

The definition assumed here is that friendship is nonfamilial, nonsexual love. Most of the chapters that follow examine, explicitly or implicitly, whether Lloyd George and Churchill loved each other. The adjectives in this simple, inelegant definition of friendship also matter, however, and the questions raised by those adjectives about the present case need to be articulated and, insofar as possible, answered.

Lloyd George and Churchill were not related to each other by birth or, at any time, by marriage. This simple declarative statement is more important than might be thought. Many senior members of the British political elite were, and are, related to other, sometimes many other, members of that elite. Family ties were especially significant in the British cabinet when Lloyd George and Churchill started their political careers. For instance, sometimes it was difficult to distinguish the Conservative party from the House of Cecil. One member of the Cecil family, A. J. Balfour, succeeded his uncle, Lord Salisbury, as prime minister in 1902. Nepotism in the literal sense was not always so nakedly practiced, but family ties mattered in many political careers. The Cecil family was hardly alone in this. In 1952, when his eventual succession to Churchill as leader of the Conservative party and hence as possible prime minister seemed uncertain, Anthony Eden married Churchill's niece.[55] Since being Churchill's sons-in-law had not harmed Duncan Sandys or Christopher Soames in their political careers, this was good strategy. Three years later, Eden finally succeeded Churchill in both offices. Lloyd George served in the House of Commons with his daughter Megan, his son Gwilym, and Gwilym's brother-in-law, Goronwy Owen.

Lloyd George and Churchill, however, were never tied together by family necessity. Each chose the other. If they were brotherly, it was only in the sense of friendship as brotherhood by amity. Such brotherhood, of course, may be more important than family ties, because it reveals more of the self.[56]

To characterize friendship as nonsexual love is to raise more complex problems than does characterizing friendship as nonfamilial. Family ties are readily visible; sexual ties may not be. For some students of friendship, all friendship is sexual in nature. For others, there is at least an element of libido even in the most spiritualized friendship. This position has been rejected by other students of friendship,

probably for valid reasons.[57] Sexual love is only one kind
of love; Eros is only one of humanity's many gods. Erotic
love can easily enough be distinguished conceptually from
friendship, but applying this distinction to a particular case
is less easy. To see the present case more clearly, a few
eyebrows perhaps need to be raised.

Lloyd George's sexual activity reached legendary propor-
tions. Probably not since Palmerston had a British prime
minister shown so few inhibitions in his sex life. Ironically,
one of his leading competitors in the contest of mighty lovers was H. H. Asquith, his great, and initially successful,
rival for leadership of the Liberal Party. Lloyd George was
a lecher whose degree of promiscuity suggests a compul-
sive need for genital gratification.[58] One of his lieutenants,
writing of his septuagenarian leader, described this need in
unforgettable but here probably unprintable terms.[59] Lloyd
George, whose vocabulary was never vulgar, used more
romantic language to make the same point about himself,
writing as a teenager into his diary.[60]

Lloyd George understood his sexual appetites, but the
British electorate did not. His sex life appears essentially
to have escaped mention in the British press during his
lifetime, and was probably unknown to those many Protestant nonconformist clergymen who were politically close to
him.[61] Editorial reluctance to refer to the topic was encouraged by the fact that on the rare occasions when it was
raised, Lloyd George brought libel actions, successfully.[62]
Veiled references to his sexual appetite did appear in a few
contemporary novels.[63] The author of one of those novels,
Arnold Bennett, disliked Lloyd George, probably because the
prime minister had overruled him during the First World
War when he was a minor government functionary. Lloyd
George, who seldom held a grudge for long, soon took his
mistress to Sunday dinner at a home where Bennett was
staying.[64] Perhaps Lloyd George thought people who read
Bennett's novels were less censorious; if so, he was probably correct. After Lloyd George's death, when he could no
longer fight back, novelistic references to his sexual activities became ever more explicit.[65]

If most Britishers were not informed about Lloyd George's
amorousness, the British political elite was. His numerous
enemies in that elite discussed the topic among themselves

to the point of obsession. They generally referred to him privately as "the Goat," a term first used by Sir Robert Chalmers, permanent secretary to the treasury.[66] This term was especially commonly used by Stanley Baldwin and his entourage, few of whom could be accused of leading interesting personal lives.[67] A bitter critic of Lloyd George suggested, during the First World War, that once the war had ended the prime minister should be publicly castrated.[68] Even for such critics, however, a stay of execution was apparently in order. John Maynard Keynes translated the private imagery of Lloyd George's enemies into a public reference to "this goat-footed bard."[69] None of these critics apparently recalled William Blake's "Proverbs of Hell," which included the insight; "the lust of the goat is the bounty of God."[70]

Lloyd George was surely fleet, if not always firm, of foot in his sexual travels. He married Margaret Owen in 1888, and remained married to her until her death in 1941. For the last three decades of that marriage, his mistress was Frances Stevenson, his private secretary, who became the second Mrs. Lloyd George in 1943, and the first Countess Lloyd George of Dwyfor in 1945. For those three decades, Lloyd George maintained two homes, one with his wife in Wales, and the other, generally in the London area, with Stevenson. Sometimes Lloyd George went on holiday with both his wife and his mistress.[71] He would have seen no reason not to do so, since he loved both.[72] Late in his adulterous relationship with Stevenson, he behaved jealously toward her, probably with some reason, since she also was capable of unfaithfulness.[73] There is no doubt, however, that Lloyd George was the father of Stevenson's daughter, born when the father was sixty-six and the mother forty.[74] The generally liberated nature of their relationship was indicated by Lloyd George's unsuccessful urging that Stevenson marry another man while continuing her relationship with Lloyd George. They laughed together at Margaret Lloyd George, as well as at his other mistresses.[75] There were plenty of the latter. Lloyd George was faithful neither to his wife nor to his mistress.

In his home with Stevenson, Lloyd George was a sultan with his harem, with numerous concubines, many of them his employees.[76] He much preferred female to male household servants.[77] He was, nevertheless, capable of charming women outside his circle of influence. He possessed aphrodisiacs other than power; he was handsome, vital, and genial, and without pomposity.[78] Lloyd George liked to be surrounded and fussed over by women of all social classes, with the notable exception of aristocrats.[79] He was one of the few British politicians of his generation who did not frequent all-male clubs. He did not think a man and a woman could be friends without having sexual intercourse.[80] Generally, he was more interested in the conquest than in a continuing relationship.[81]

Lloyd George's one-night stands posed the greatest danger to his political career. More than once his name was dragged through the divorce courts. In the most threatening of these cases, Catherine Edwards, wife of David Edwards, claimed that Lloyd George was the father of her child.[82] Lloyd George's alibi, that he had been at the distant House of Commons on the night in question, was false, since on that date Parliament was not in session.[83] Perhaps not surprisingly, the lawyers in the case arranged matters to Lloyd George's benefit. While an affair had probably occurred, nevertheless he was probably not the father of the child.[84]

All of Lloyd George's sexual activity was heterosexual. The detailed record of his endless affairs reveals no hint of any homosexual activity. Many male observers, however, identified what they characterized as a feminine component in Lloyd George's personality. Keynes described Lloyd George as a vampire, a *femme fatale*, and "the lady from Wales" with "the feminine enticements, sharpness, quickness, sympathy."[85] Thomas Jones saw Lloyd George as a great actress.[86] Lloyd George appeared to have a feminine element at the center of him, a strain of gentleness and tenderness, according to Frank Owen, "almost that of woman."[87] Oswald Mosley found in Lloyd George a sensitivity to others that Mosley claimed was wrongly attributed to gifted women rather than to outstanding men.[88]

That male and female attributes could be interchanged would not have surprised Lloyd George, who had discussed "interchangeability" with Stevenson even before reading, shortly after its publication, Virginia Woolf's *Orlando*. By letter, he urged Stevenson to notice a particular passage in that novel. Stevenson responded that she understood what he meant.[89] The editor of their correspondence found Lloyd George's enthusiasm for this passage "strange," and concluded, "It is difficult to think of Lloyd George as a transvestite."[90] This conclusion seems correct but simplistic. Woolf's novel argues that clothes do not make a man or a woman. *Orlando* is not about transvestites, but about androgyny, a more complex phenomenon. The exchange between Lloyd George and Stevenson about *Orlando* reveals nothing about Lloyd George's sexual preference, but it is an illustration of the fact that nothing human was alien to Lloyd George, who quickly became part of all he saw and felt.[91]

Churchill also read *Orlando*, according to his son Randolph,[92] but Churchill was no more a transvestite than Lloyd George. He once dressed as a woman when he played "Lady Bertha" in a school play at the age of ten.[93] Much later, he had a horror of looking effeminate in newsreels, and insisted that no makeup be applied to him.[94] After he had made what turned out to be his last House of Commons speech, he yearned to speak there once more, to warn about "the loss of masculinity, of virility" in Britain.[95]

Churchill had not always been so concerned. The sybaritic life he led provided no Spartan model for others. Throughout his adult life he wore astonishingly expensive pink silk underwear.[96] Upon his marriage, his mother-in-law presented him, entirely usefully, with three perfume bottles. When told that only women could visit a harem in Morocco, Churchill fluffed up his hair, wrapped a scarf around his head, and asked if he could go as his mother-in-law.[97] Again in North Africa, at the Cairo Conference, Churchill successfully invited "Pa" Watson, military aide to Franklin Roosevelt, to dance with him.[98]

Unlike Lloyd George, Churchill was hardly a ladies' man, and generally ignored women socially.[99] By his own statement, he was "stupid and clumsy" in his relations with women.[100] He seldom conversed with or about them. When he wanted to be cordial, he would ask a woman her age.[101] According to his doctor, when Churchill did notice another person, he was usually attracted by male good looks and by a cheerful demeanor.[102]

After he married Clementine Hozier when he was thirty-three, Churchill surely did not commit adultery with another woman.[103] Since his wife survived him, and since there is no credible evidence that before his marriage he had sexual relations with any woman, it is likely that Clementine Churchill was the only woman with whom he was sexually intimate. He loved his wife, and she was one of only two women who loved him as an adult. The other was Violet Bonham Carter, H. H. Asquith's daughter, who faithfully presented Churchill with a posy of violets on his birthdays, and after his death, when he could no longer smell the flowers, published the most loving, and perhaps the most understanding, of all appreciations of the object of her chaste love.[104]

It would probably be correct to describe Churchill as without strong sexual desires. The nature of those desires, however strong or weak, has been the subject of considerable heat, if less light. Lord Beaverbrook is reported to have claimed that Churchill once said he had gone to bed with a man to see what it was like. Less disputably, Churchill observed of Prince Eugene of Savoy, who was certainly unattractive and who may have been homosexual, that he was very ugly, and so were his habits.[105] If this was indeed Churchill's attitude, it is difficult to understand the major role played, in his personal life and in his political career, by Edward Marsh, who was homosexual.[106]

In his first ministerial office, as under-secretary of state for the colonies, Churchill hired Marsh to be his private secretary. Marsh was then an obscure clerk in the West African Department of the Colonial Office, and Churchill's initiative came after a chance social encounter, apparently only their second meeting. For three decades, until Marsh's retirement in 1937, Marsh was Churchill's principal assistant in most of Churchill's numerous ministerial offices. Where Churchill led, Marsh followed. Marsh served Churchill like a knight-errant serving his king, declining more prestigious jobs because he couldn't face separation from Churchill.[107] When they were temporarily separated, Marsh, reporting on official matters, signed his letter "Love from E."[108] Marsh adored Churchill and was his constant companion.[109] Churchill, who was two years younger, wrote to Marsh, "You are a good little boy, and I am very fond of you."[110] Both sometimes played the role of little British boys, birching each other.[111] Early in their relationship Churchill promised he would "cherish and hold to" Marsh all his life, and he did.[112] When Marsh died, Churchill told the press truthfully, "we have always been the closest of friends."[113] Except for his love for Rupert Brooke, the central fact of Marsh's life was his love for Churchill.[114]

Some years before he met Marsh, Churchill, at the age of twenty-one, had been involved in a legal case that was mentioned soon afterwards in a House of Commons debate. The barrister father of a former officer in the British army wrote to another officer that while Churchill was a student at Sandhurst, the British military academy, someone there had been court-martialed "for acts of gross immorality of the Oscar Wilde type with Mr. Churchill."[115] Churchill sued the author of this letter for £20,000 damages for libel. The author withdrew, and apologized for, his statement, and paid £500 damages.[116] This legal case has never raised much curiosity among Churchill's biographers. The offending letter, for instance, asserted there had been a court-martial at Sandhurst. There seems to have been no scholarly examination of the Sandhurst court-martial records, if any, for the appropriate years.

Whatever the facts of such legal cases, there is no evidence that Lloyd George and Churchill had in any respect a sexual relationship with each other. The assumption that their relationship was nonsexual is consistent with the known data, and the nonsexual character of friendship is clearly met in their relationship. That relationship, as this book will clarify, was intimate, but not sexually intimate.

If friendship is a kind of love, there is still one unanswered definitional question: What is love? To answer that enormous question comprehensively is far beyond the scope of this study. But it is necessary to clarify a few of the operational assumptions about love present in this book. All kinds of love, not merely friendship, can be intellectually understood. Love including friendship is not ineffable. Any kind of love involves an encounter between two persons, creative of unity but also of individuality.[117] That is a paradox, but it is also true. Lloyd George and Churchill were, and worked, together for forty-four years, but they were also most truly themselves while they were, and worked, together. Whether or not love is the moving power of life, it might be the moving power of two particular persons' lives, even when those persons are both superbly gifted and supremely ambitious politicians. This moving power is by nature in constant change. The relationship of Lloyd George and Churchill was always there, but always changing. Their friendship was, as are all friendships, a voyage of discovery.[118]

Both travelers enjoyed that voyage. Both understood that all love involves delight in the beloved, and that particular love called friendship involves mutual delight.[119] Both delighted in the presence of the other. They had great fun together. They sometimes angered, but never bored, each other. May the reader discover the novelist's truth: "Not that there was ever much monotony in the neighborhood of the Heavenly Twins; they managed to introduce variety into everything."[120]

Chapter One

Roots of a British Oak

> Lloyd George is rooted in nothing;
> he is void and without content.
> —John Maynard Keynes

In the early 1920s, William Halse Rivers Rivers, a distinguished British neurologist and social scientist, joined the Labor party in the hope of becoming a member of Parliament for the express purpose of psychoanalyzing David Lloyd George.[1] Rivers died suddenly, before either his immediate or ultimate goal could be realized. A few years earlier, Wilfred Owen, the most gifted of the many British war poets of 1914–1918, had drafted the text of a play answering the question "who *was* Lloyd George?"[2] Shortly before the armistice, Owen was killed in battle, and the text of his play remains unknown. Winston Churchill, who survived Lloyd George by two decades and who wrote about so many of his contemporaries, never wrote at length about Lloyd George.[3]

Such potentially interesting lacunae may be one reason for scholarly complaints about the unsatisfactory quality of biographical studies of Lloyd George.[4] Such complaints could hardly derive from the quantity of those studies. More has been published about Lloyd George than about any other British politician except Churchill. To many of the many observers, Lloyd George remains an enigma.[5] Little about him was straightforward. He was probably indirectly responsible for the famous and bitter criticism of his own policies in John Maynard Keynes's *The Economic Consequences of the Peace*.[6] Lloyd George was almost always up to something, and often only he understood what it was. To conclude that he was a "man of straw" is too easy.[7] There was too much, not too little, substance in him for easy understanding.

Some observers have simply thrown up their hands and concluded, "he is really too complex for analysis."[8] Such a surrender is understandable but inappropriate. Precisely because Lloyd George was so complex, he needs analysis. No other British politician is seen as so "baffling to a fair judgment."[9] This surrender is appropriate. Scholars are not judges, of politicians or of anyone else, except perhaps in scholars' own minds. No one has appointed us to judge Lloyd George or any other politician, and in any event, few will listen to any judgments we make. The British electorate, and later the highest Elector, had many opportunities to judge this man. That is surely enough opportunities for judgment of any human being, even Lloyd George. The task of students of Lloyd George is to understand, not to judge, him.

Even understanding is undeniably difficult. With many other politicians, relatively simple analytical tools, ranging from Freudian to Weberian to Marxian, alone or in combination, have sufficient explanatory value. With Lloyd George, no one of these tools is sufficient, and even in combination, they do not seem to provide full understanding. This may be more of a reflection on the adequacy of those tools than on the object. Since Lloyd George was an artist, it may be no accident that the most incisive depictions of his personality are found in novels. He has, perhaps, to be taken more on his own terms than he has been taken so far by most scholars. Starting so much as is possible from scratch, without preconceptions, might be helpful. Such an attitude was certainly helpful for those who met him. Many people who encountered him in person simply did not know what to make of him. Sometimes the language of their confusion was not far wrong, however.

Lloyd George was *sui generis*, and those who met him understood that in some significant way, or ways, they were encountering a distinctively individual human being. Americans, living in a relatively individualistic culture, often grasped that better than Britishers. Roy Howard, head of the United Press, writing to E. M. House, described Lloyd George as "an intensely human individual."[10] Nicholas Murray Butler introduced Lloyd George to an American audience simply as "David Lloyd George, human being."[11] That was enough, at least for a beginning. Lloyd George could take it from there, especially with an audience. He did not need a recitation of his accomplishments to impress other people. His ease in and enjoyment of a wide variety of human situations were impressive. Very little that was human frightened him.

At a dinner party hosted by the duke of Westminster, Churchill's suspenders were once removed by a hired pickpocket entertainer. Churchill, enraged, demanded an apology.[12] It is difficult to imagine Lloyd George reacting that way. He liked a good joke at his own expense; Churchill did not.[13] Had he witnessed Churchill's suspenders being removed, he would have laughed uproariously at the performer's skill. Deft hands were certainly needed to fool Lloyd George, whose hands were even defter. By the end of the evening, he would have mastered the trick himself, and would probably have succeeded in removing the duke's suspenders, and probably something from the duchess as well, before leaving the party with one of the less-exalted female dinner guests.

Lloyd George would probably, however, not have been present at the duke's dinner party. Lloyd George disliked dining out, and no duke would have been likely to invite the worst political enemy of British dukedom to his table.[14] If he had been invited, Lloyd George would probably have declined, graciously. Among the few places he disliked visiting were stately homes, and he seldom went. He detested making official visits to George V at Balmoral.[15] Contrary to the claim of a cynical observer, he was never "much softened" by the courtesies of noble houses.[16] He regularly rejected invitations from the social leaders and the social climbers in London's West End. He did not care to go into high society, for which he had only contempt. He never felt at home in the drawing rooms of Mayfair, but not because he did not feel good enough to be there.[17] He thought they were artificial places, and he sought reality. He was free of the snobbish desire to hobnob with peers, which has afflicted some other leaders of the British left, perhaps most notably Ramsay MacDonald. Lloyd George did not collect aristocrats socially. He wanted to destroy them politically.

Churchill, a politician of relative simplicity, did not understand himself.[18] Lloyd George, a politician of enormous complexity, did understand himself. He had an "almost diabolical" knowledge of human beings and their motivations.[19] He confessed all in letters to the women in his life. Before he married Margaret Owen he wrote to her: "It comes to this, my supreme idea is to get on. To this idea I shall sacrifice everything—except I trust honesty. I am prepared to thrust even love itself under the wheels of my Juggernaut if it obstructs the way."[20] Ten years later, lonely in London, he wrote to Margaret Lloyd George, who preferred to, and did, live in Wales[21] while her husband was at the House of Commons: "I am not the nature either physically or morally that I ought to have been left thus."[22] In 1922, he wrote to Frances Stevenson from the European conference in Genoa, which was failing to reach his goal of integrating a peaceful, democratic Germany into the European system: "I am working as I never worked in my life to save it. Every art & device my simple nature is capable of."[23]

Lloyd George was full of contradictions, but those contradictions reveal something of his inner self. He was fatherless as an infant but blessed with a happy childhood, which included fatherly love; he had little formal education but was an intellectual, though he never pretended to be such; he was from but not of Wales; he was the political voice of British Nonconformist Protestantism but not a sectarian.[24]

Lloyd George's father, William George, died when Lloyd George was seventeen months old. Lloyd George's mother, Elizabeth Lloyd George, died when her elder son was thirty-three years old. The claim that she "only outlived her husband by a short period, and David was left an orphan" is patently false.[25] Few children have been the center of so much loving attention as David. There was not only his mother, but his grandmother, Rebecca Samuel George, who died when Lloyd George was five years old, and his maternal uncle, Richard Lloyd, with whom Elizabeth Lloyd George and her children lived after William George's death. David Lloyd George was, as he later understood, the pampered pet of an entire family.[26] He was spoiled by his mother, grandmother, uncle, and even by his older sister, Mary Ellen, and younger brother, William. The latter two probably performed their ministrations less enthusiastically than did their elders, for his siblings paid some of the cost of all the love lavished on Lloyd George. Mary Ellen, being female, was expected to cater to her brother. The entire family assumed it would be William's lot in life to be literally his brother's keeper. This assumption was realized when William George joined his brother in a solicitors' firm in Wales while his brother was pursuing his political career in London.[27] Lloyd George attracted the clients, and let George do the work. Lloyd George depended on his brother for practical support, but did not ordinarily seek his company for social purposes. This inequity eventually distanced the brothers, although Lloyd George, at least, continued to speak well of his brother.[28]

As a child, then, Lloyd George was in fact much loved, including by his uncle. For more than five decades, Richard Lloyd was probably a better father to his nephew than are most fathers, and as good a father as William George likely would have been had he lived.[29] To call Richard Lloyd a saintly genius is excessive, but he willingly accepted and ably met substantial financial, intellectual, and ethical obligations to his sister's children, especially, but not only, Lloyd George.[30] Richard Lloyd was one of life's worthies. In a culture in which corporal punishment of children was common, he never lifted a hand against David, whose childhood behavior must occasionally have sorely tempted his uncle. Throughout his childhood, David was rarely criticized and hardly ever punished.[31] Within the family, only his mother applied physical punishment, which, given her general gentleness, is hard to imagine as being brutal.

Lloyd George's good fortune continued in school. He enjoyed his school days. This was understandable. At school he was well taught and well treated. He was not punished by his schoolmaster, David Evans.[32] Bright and articulate, Lloyd George became teacher's pet as well as his own family's pet, all without losing face among his peers. Not surprisingly, as a child Lloyd George developed a rather good opinion of himself.[33]

Lloyd George may have enjoyed his school days, but they were undeniably short. His formal education began and ended in a village schoolhouse. He had no secondary, let alone tertiary, education. That he did not go to secondary school did not mean lack of motivation. Secondary schools were almost nonexistent in Wales in Lloyd George's adolescence. The limited duration of his formal education caused some observers to conclude that he was ill educated, and lacked breeding. To his critics Lloyd George was not only a shallow lowbrow, but "a howling yahoo" of no intellectual accomplishments and little knowledge, at home only with equally uneducated persons. John Buchan made it explicit: because Lloyd George lacked the "normal" education of British politicians he had "large gaps in his mental furniture."[34]

No doubt Lloyd George's education differed substantially from that of the British political elite of his time; most members of the House of Commons had more formal education than he had. Of seven cabinet members between 1918 and 1959 who were neither Conservative nor Labor, he was the only one without either public school or university education. Many of his most powerful Liberal Party colleagues looked down on him because of his minimal formal education. To Lord Haldane, for instance, Lloyd George was "an illiterate with an untrained mind." H. H. Asquith, fatally outwitted by Lloyd George in 1916, contemptuously claimed that his rival, who could "neither read nor write," was "totally devoid of either perspective or judgement."[35]

It has been argued that Lloyd George was particularly disadvantaged by gaps in his formal education in dealing with complex issues at the Paris Peace Conference in 1919. Georges Clemenceau, who found Lloyd George totally lacking in cosmopolitan general culture, would have agreed.[36] Nevertheless, Keynes, so critical of Lloyd George's policies at the peace conference, conceded that he was "intellectually the subtlest" of the Big Four.[37] Americans who were also critical of his policies agreed that Lloyd George had the quickest mind of the Big Four.[38] The professorial president of the United States may not have heard this judgment, so favorable to his antagonist, but he had had glimpses of it already. Before Lloyd George became prime minister, Walter Hines Page, American ambassador in London, wrote to Woodrow Wilson that Lloyd George was "quick as lightning" and that "his wit and nimbleness have their due relation to a matured philosophy."[39] After Lloyd George became prime minister, Page wrote, again to Wilson, that, in addition to being entirely approachable, Lloyd George had "as quick a mind and as ready speech as any man that I ever encountered."[40] Even some of Lloyd George's British enemies saw him as "superlatively intelligent."[41]

In fact, Lloyd George thought hard and quickly about problems. While serving, well into his seventies, as a judge, as chairman of Carnarvonshire Quarter Sessions, Lloyd George, without taking notes, missed nothing material in witnesses' statements when he gave his judgments.[42] Basil Liddell Hart, who was perhaps the most intellectually distinguished participant in British policy discussions in the first half of the twentieth century, considered Lloyd George to have one of the quickest minds he had encountered. Liddell Hart, who also respected Churchill's intelligence highly, "always" found Lloyd George "much the quicker in uptake" of the two. Indeed, Liddell Hart concluded that of all the people he had known personally, only T. E. Lawrence was on Lloyd George's intellectual level.[43] That Lloyd George was not one of their own did not prevent numerous British universities, beginning with Oxford University in 1908, from giving him honorary doctorates.

Those who assumed that Lloyd George's limited formal education indicated limited intelligence were wrong. So were those who assumed he was only functionally literate. Far from detesting reading, as has been argued, Lloyd George used books to educate himself, by wide, continuous reading. His reading experiences began in his childhood home, which had a well-stocked library, much of it left by his schoolmaster father. Lloyd George's last learning experience with books, shortly before his death, came when he reread Charles Dickens's novels, which he loved. His reading was more catholic than that of most British politicians, including those with public school and university education, and it was certainly broader than Churchill's. In old age, with little else to do, Churchill read more than before, but did not buy books, preferring the economy of borrowing them from public libraries.[44]

Lloyd George could read French and Latin, and he read French-language newspapers as well as Prince Kropotkin on the French Revolution. He also read widely in the serious fictional literature of his time. The claim that he had "no knowledge of contemporary literature" is entirely unjustified. His careful attention to Virginia Woolf was noted above. In conversation, he could draw appropriately on a fund of stories from Anatole France's novels.[45]

Lloyd George learned more than table talk from his wide reading. He also learned a lot about the human condition, including how to improve it. In 1913 he praised Henrik Ibsen, who "converted me to women's suffrage."[46] For Lloyd George, Ibsen may have been a better teacher than was Margaret Lloyd George, who opposed suffrage for women. Ibsen was also a better teacher on women's suffrage for Lloyd George than was Churchill, who was far from committed to the women's cause. Already in 1913, Lloyd George was the strongest advocate of women's suffrage within the cabinet. His new house on Walton Heath was nevertheless damaged by a suffragette's bomb. When the cabinet tergiversated on suffrage expansion, Lloyd George voted for, and Churchill voted against, an unsuccessful private member's bill for women's suffrage. Lloyd George continued to support women's suffrage within the cabinet. When in late 1916 he became prime minister, as suffragettes realized, women's suffrage in some form was virtually certain. That expectation was met. Prime Minister Lloyd George was responsible for the first British installment of women's suffrage in 1918. A year later, his personal introduction to the House of Commons of the first woman to serve as a member of Parliament was entirely fitting. He had pushed for women as candidates in the 1918 general election, and in that campaign he was the only leading politician to speak to a rally of new women voters.[47]

As his position on women's suffrage demonstrated, Lloyd George was free of the inhibitions encouraged by the traditional, and traditionalist, British educational system. His mind ranged widely, without conventional preconceptions, picking up information many other British politicians would have disregarded.[48] He never considered himself fully educated, so he never stopped learning.

While Lloyd George learned much as an adult, his lack of knowledge as a young adult should not be exaggerated. Before he qualified as a solicitor, for instance, he had to pass standardized examinations dealing with general knowledge as well as specialized legal knowledge. The specialized legal examinations were taken by a significant number of Oxford and Cambridge graduates. It is worth noting that in this competitive situation Lloyd George passed his final qualifying examination "with Honours."[49]

In his continuing education, Lloyd George did not confine himself to learning from books. He read and understood other human beings, and he was interested in everything and everyone. He did not always derive his knowledge through the ear more than the eye, as has been claimed, but he certainly preferred to learn from people rather than from, say, official papers. He may have been one of the prettiest talkers who ever lived, and words came to him like Ariel to Prospero. Churchill may have been correct in suggesting that at his conversational best Lloyd George could talk a bird out of a tree, but Lloyd George seldom monopolized conversation. Contrary to the claim that he seldom let other people talk, he was one of the most attentive of listeners. Those who met him left their meetings feeling themselves more important than when they had arrived.[50]

Lloyd George listened enthusiastically to other people regardless of their station in life. He was especially fond of listening to the views of young people.[51] One of the many young persons to whom he listened, Harold Macmillan, later gratefully recalled, "he was unlike a beech tree, under which nothing grows, but was a great and splendid oak, which fosters the flowers and undergrowth beneath it."[52] In this capacity for encouraging the growth of younger persons, Lloyd George was unlike his Liberal predecessor, William Gladstone, in whose shadow nothing grew, but resembled more his Conservative predecessor, Benjamin Disraeli, one of the great parliamentary listeners. Lloyd George listened, interested, to the dullest House of Commons speeches, because, as he put it, he learned something of substance from even the least effectively presented speech.[53]

Lloyd George preferred, nevertheless, conversational listening, in which he could, and did, ask frequent questions. When he asked those questions, he "made you feel that everything you said mattered."[54] That feeling was appropriate, for he really wanted to know the answers to the questions he asked. Meeting Fyodor Chaliapin at dinner, Lloyd George quizzed him on conditions in Russia. After seeing *Birth of a Nation,* Lloyd George wanted to hear E. M. House's account of reconstruction in the American South. As minister of munitions Lloyd George invited Bertrand Russell to lunch, assigning his own motorcar to fetch and return his pacifist guest.[55] He tried to enter into other people's thoughts and feelings. To Frances Stevenson he wrote: "I am always interested in people—wondering who they are—what they are thinking about—what their lives are like—whether they are enjoying life or finding it a bore."[56] His interest in other people, and his quick grasp of what they thought and felt, were crucial elements in his distinctive capacity to build a consensus for common action in a particular political situation.[57]

Lloyd George thought best when in genuine communication with other people. Churchill thought best when he was alone. It has been argued that Churchill was also a good listener, or, less flatteringly, that he listened to everyone, though he could not grasp all that was said to him. Least flatteringly, it has been argued that Churchill, enslaved by his own words, was often unable to follow someone else's argument. The least flattering argument is closest to the truth, although it needs qualification. It is at least premature to assume that Churchill could not follow other people's arguments. He often failed to do so, for the simple but sufficient reason that he did not hear those arguments. He was a poor listener in a wide variety of contexts. Nature had formed him of the giving rather than the receiving tribe and he was incapable of true discussion. His conversational contribution was always a monologue. Never off stage, he addressed the smallest audience as he would the largest audience.[58]

Many other persons, including other powerful persons, did not care to be lectured constantly by Churchill. His inattention to others irked politicians from Asquith to Harry Truman, and soldiers from Alan Brooke to George Marshall. Even his relatives were exasperated. Since he did not listen to his allies, it was unlikely he would try to understand what potential allies might be thinking and feeling.

Churchill was impervious to his atmosphere.[59] When, in old age, he was told by his doctor that he lacked antennae, he reacted: "What do you mean by antennae?"[60] This question was doubtless sincere. He had never had antennae.[61] What he never had, he never missed—or understood.

It is an overstatement to conclude that Churchill was incapable of mutual understanding, but with most people that was painfully close to the truth.[62] Lloyd George was a rare exception, and even he was often sorely tried. During the Second World War, Lloyd George, in a meditative mood, observed, "Winston has never been much inclined to listen. I fear that now he will listen even less."[63] Lloyd George's tone had not always been so gentle. In April 1915, after Churchill impatiently interrupted Lloyd George with "I don't see . . . ," the latter responded: "You will see the point when you begin to understand that conversation is not a monologue!"[64] Later the same day, typically, Lloyd George apologized, and was, typically, quickly forgiven by Churchill, who, untypically, added: "It was *I* who was churlish and difficult."[65] It was highly unusual for Churchill to apologize for his rudeness, but he never learned Lloyd George's lesson.[66]

Churchill simply was not interested in what other people thought or felt. He never paid compliments. He never acknowledged failure. He lived in his own self-contained world. He heard only his own message. Communication was for him a one-way street. As prime minister he seldom lingered in the House of Commons after his own wartime speeches to hear other members' speeches. That had long been his practice while in ministerial office. While first lord of the admiralty three decades earlier, he attended Commons infrequently and only as a matter of form. Out of ministerial office, when he could hardly plead the pressure of official business, he continued to be inattentive to the speeches of others.[67] In 1932, George Lansbury, perhaps the kindest person ever to serve as leader of the opposition, attacked Churchill, to widespread approval: "He usurps a position in this House as if he had a right to walk in, make his speech, walk out, and leave the whole place as if God Almighty had spoken. . . . He never listens to any other man's speech but his own."[68]

Lansbury's attack was entirely understandable: Churchill

was totally self-centered. Even after he retired from ministerial office, he subscribed to the services of a newspaper
clipping agency, and read the most trivial press references
to himself. He gave autographed copies of his books as gifts
to his servants, who might have preferred something more
substantial, and to his hosts, even those hardly likely to
read those books. For variety he presented Toby jugs
adorned with his likeness. Obsessed by self, he could not
assess a situation dispassionately. That is why he left no
completed work. Even the Second World War he helped win
was never officially ended. He left no heirs in British political leadership, and, in the judgment of the editor of his
speeches, no message for the future. He was a beech tree,
not an oak, even though he was mistakenly identified as
the latter.[69]

Lloyd George's intellectual talents were also exemplified
by his writing. He wrote many books and almost endless
journalism. His writings certainly sold well. In the first
twelve months after he left 10 Downing Street in 1922, he
earned £30,000 as a newspaper columnist.[70] The enormous
payments he regularly received for his journalism were at
least partially justified. Not only did his articles sell newspapers and magazines, but his journalistic writings were
much more interesting than his books, probably because in
journalism he revealed more of himself and of others.

Lloyd George's gifts as a writer were fewer than
Churchill's gifts as a writer. Lloyd George's books are still
worth reading, however, even if more for their substance
than for their style. Their intellectual content is substantial. Lloyd George was not a great writer, although it is too
much to say that he was not a good writer. George V may
have been the only reader to find all six volumes of Lloyd
George's war memoirs "very interesting."[71] Those volumes
nevertheless reveal much about the First World War, if much
less about their author. This was in distinct contrast to
Churchill's memoirs of that war, which A. J. Balfour described as "Winston's brilliant Autobiography, disguised as
a history of the universe."[72] Lloyd George's response to *The
World Crisis* was essentially similar to Balfour's. That response was justified, for *The World Crisis* was so overwhelmingly concerned with its author that it became his *apologia
pro vita sua.* In this respect, *The World Crisis* was no differ-

ent from most of Churchill's writings. Most of the eight million words he wrote were about himself. Lloyd George could be casual about his own role in dramatic events, while Churchill could not.[73]

Lloyd George was never a pamphleteer. He could compose effective official memoranda when he chose to do so, but he did not often so choose. He did not read all official memoranda addressed to him. He wrote sparingly to colleagues. He preferred face-to-face discussions with his fellow politicians and even with his angry wife. He often failed to answer letters.[74] What letters he wrote were spontaneous. They were not all written in English. All letters addressed to him in Welsh were answered in Welsh. He was that rarity, a genuinely bilingual politician. He was equally fluent in English and "classical Welsh."[75]

Lloyd George may have entered the House of Commons without the advantages of a university education. He also entered a political career without any of the disadvantages of a university education. Not having been to university, where debating clubs were so influential as training grounds for aspiring politicians, he had no respect for a debating-club style of politics. Policy, not pedantry, mattered for him. He used his gift of speech to get power to do things, not to score debating points.[76]

The same kind of balance sheet may apply to Lloyd George's lack of a public school education. He had not acquired a team spirit at public school or probably anywhere.[77] If he had been a team player, however, he might well have ended up one of the minor luminaries of British politics, always one of the ministrables, perhaps even in the most prestigious ministry, without ever leaving a lasting mark on British society, becoming one of the unknown prime ministers. It is also possible that the intellectual value of a public school education was minimal. Not all schools are educational institutions. Lloyd George may not have missed much of genuine worth. Churchill, who had gone to Harrow, was later forced to ask, "Who's Matthew Arnold?" When told, he shook his fist and thundered, "Oh, this public school education. If I ever get my chance at it!"[78] He was similarly uninformed about William Blake.[79]

There were other advantages to Lloyd George of lacking an old school tie. He never judged other people, including other politicians, by where they had been educated. Such considerations were for him irrelevant. He had open contempt for Gladstone and Asquith, both of whom so judged. Proudly, and accurately, Lloyd George related, "I judge by what a man can do and has done rather than by his old school tie."[80]

Lloyd George, knowing his education was imperfect, was not afraid to ask basic questions. He was ridiculed for asking, at the Paris Peace Conference, where Teschen, disputed by Poland and Czechoslovakia, was located. T. E. Lawrence was probably correct in asserting that only Lloyd George would have asked that question, instead of pretending that he knew the answer.[81] Lloyd George was also not afraid to admit that his spoken French was imperfect. As prime minister, he initiated use of interpreters at conferences with French politicians and generals.[82]

Lloyd George understood, and worked hard to correct, the gaps in his knowledge; he did not resent having been denied much formal education, however. As a young man he asked, "Does education alone, apart from other qualifications, make men good citizens?" His answer was: "That is not so."[83] Understanding that common sense is not necessarily produced by formal education, he did not think his education had been inferior.[84] On St. David's Eve 1903, he observed, "Personally, I should be ungrateful if I did not say that I owe nothing to the University—I speak in all modesty and humility—I owe nothing to secondary schools. Whatever I do owe, it is to the little Bethel."[85] This was true. Not all educational institutions are schools. Lloyd George's real education started in the Bethels of his childhood and youth. The Protestant Nonconformist chapel was his secondary school.[86] He learned to read and write in the village schoolhouse, but he learned to think and to feel and to listen and to speak in Nonconformist chapels. By far the most important source of both his political style and his political values was religious Nonconformity.

That Lloyd George grew up in Wales was a lesser part of his origins. He may have become the most famous Welshman of all time, at least among British politicians, and perhaps even the greatest Welshman of modern times or, alternatively, the greatest Welshman yet born. He was certainly greeted in song, by Welsh constituents, as "Cambria's uncrowned King." It is, nevertheless, a serious error to argue that throughout his political career his values were Welsh values and that his devotion to Wales was the one fixed principle of his political career.[87]

Lloyd George did declare, early in 1889, in accepting the Liberal party nomination as a candidate for the House of Commons, that he was "a Welsh Nationalist first and a Liberal afterwards."[88] During his first decade in the House of Commons, he often seemed less Liberal than Welsh. He was eventually instrumental in the disestablishment of the Anglican Church of Wales, and in the creation of the Welsh Department of the Board of Education.[89] Both of these campaigns, however, may have resulted more from Lloyd George's Nonconformity than from Welshness. He did not do much else of significance solely for Wales. His major contribution to Wales was himself, not his policies, even in the opinion of those who emphasize his Welshness.[90] That Lloyd George was from Wales seemed to many Britishers sufficient explanation, however, of what they saw as his personal weaknesses. Anti-Welsh sentiments were and are not uncommon in the rest of Britain, even among creative artists, and it is sometimes difficult to distinguish whether Wales was or is being criticized for having produced Lloyd George, or he was or is being criticized for being Welsh.[91]

To view the essential Lloyd George as Welsh is nevertheless mistaken. In Wales, Lloyd George was originally an outsider. His father had known little Welsh, and had left Wales to seek work in England as a schoolteacher. Lloyd George privately stressed that he had been born in England, not Wales, and that his mother tongue was English, not Welsh. To describe him as a "native Welshman" is to ignore the facts. His real language was the language of British politics, not of Welsh culture. He preferred living in, or near, the center of national power. People in Wales criticized him for living as an adult in England, not Wales.[92] Being so located was certainly his preference. As he wrote to Frances Stevenson: "I have *always* disliked Criccieth."[93] That was where Margaret Lloyd George lived. Her husband returned to live in Wales only when she was dead and he was himself dying.

Lloyd George may have started out as a Welsh Nationalist, but he did not remain so for long. Once in the House

of Commons, his attention soon turned to wider causes.[94]
By 1898 he was speaking for "British Members" against
Irish members. Lloyd George's terminology here was significant. To him, unlike to Churchill, the term "British" came
naturally. He never called himself, or thought of himself,
as "English." A Welsh critic who described him as an "English radical—nothing more" was only half right.[95] In 1930,
Lloyd George described himself as "for my country every
time, and I stand up for it."[96] That country was all of Britain, not merely Wales. Lloyd George became, and remained,
a British nationalist. The Parnell of Wales had become the
Chamberlain of Britain, although Lloyd George's British
nationalism, unlike Joseph Chamberlain's, never became
jingoistic imperialism.[97] Lloyd George certainly changed from
a regional advocate to a national politician. It did not take
long for him to start paying only lip-service to exclusively
Welsh causes. His eventual view was that Welsh national-
ists were "a lot of second-rate cranks."[98] Unlike some of
them, he never advocated a separate national Welsh state.[99]
The Welsh language was still useful, however, for by using
it Lloyd George could frequently hide his thoughts from
curious Britishers and others who did not know Welsh.[100]

Wales was also still useful to Lloyd George. Throughout
his parliamentary career (from 1890 to 1945) he represented only one constituency, in North Wales, which included
his childhood home. The Carnarvon District of Boroughs had
been created by the Reform Act of 1832, and it survived,
slightly enlarged, the major redistricting of British parliamentary constituencies before the 1918 general election,
when, not accidentally, Lloyd George was prime minister.
Although most Welsh seats were then held by Liberals,
Carnarvon Boroughs was not a safe Liberal seat when Lloyd
George first won it in 1890. His predecessor, who died in
midterm, was a Conservative. In the fifty-five years that
Lloyd George represented it, Carnarvon Boroughs was a safe
Liberal seat. To say that he had to fight hard to retain it
throughout thirteen general elections is exaggerated, at the
very least.[101] His smallest margin of victory was his first.
The only election in which he was unopposed was in 1922,
but only once, in 1929, did he have both Conservative and
Labor opponents, and even then he received a majority of
the votes cast. In 1931, he was reelected without appear-

ing in his constituency during the campaign. In his last general election contest, in 1935, he got twice as many votes as his only opponent, a Conservative. Most politicians in democratic political systems would be happy to occupy a seat with that degree of security.

His safe seat in North Wales gave Lloyd George political longevity of the highest degree. Upon entering the House of Commons, he was its youngest member.[102] With the death of T. P. O'Connor in 1929, Lloyd George became Father of the House of Commons.[103] He never experienced, as did many senior British politicians including Churchill, the indignity of losing his parliamentary seat. Not only was Lloyd George's fifty-five years of uninterrupted membership from one constituency a record for the House of Commons, it placed him in contention for seniority among legislators in all parliamentary systems.[104] Relatively free for most of his career from worries about reelection, he was able to focus his attention on matters of national policy. As Lloyd George recognized, one of Churchill's persistent problems was that, without a bond to a particular local constituency, he had no safe seat. Much of Churchill's career was spent in search of such a safe seat. In a larger sense, Churchill had no national constituency among British electors.[105] Rootless among followers, he had to be much more ruthless than Lloyd George needed to be merely to survive in politics.

Lloyd George had precisely the kind of national constituency Churchill lacked, as the latter realized. Lloyd George's true constituency appeared to be, but was not, Wales. In 1920–1921, for instance, only in Wales did Lloyd George dominate regional federations of the Liberal party; everywhere else in Britain, Asquithians were predominant. The Welsh connection was nevertheless deceptive. Lloyd George was a Free Church politician, not a Welsh politician. His natural national constituency throughout his political career was the Nonconformist Protestant community throughout Britain, not merely in Wales.[106] That community, significantly overrepresented in Wales, was Lloyd George's lifelong power base. He became a national political leader because he articulated Nonconformist political values, and he remained a national political leader long after he left the prime ministership in 1922 because he continued to articulate those political values.

Lose Rosebery referred to the young Lloyd George as "the great protagonist of Nonconformity."[107] That Lloyd George was, and remained. He was the most powerful parliamentary champion of Nonconformity. He may even have been one of the modern British apostles of the Nonconformist conscience. Leon Trotsky acidly asserted that for Lloyd George the Church was the central source of energy for all the major British parties.[108] Although Trotsky's assertion contained a solid grain of truth, in that Lloyd George gladly saw religious consciousness as a major social force in British politics, Lloyd George would not have capitalized the source of his own political values.

For Lloyd George, the Church was the Church of England, intertwined inextricably with the Conservative party. His own politics originated not in the Church, but in the chapels of Protestant Nonconformism. When he became prime minister, the *Christian World* proudly reported that he was the first member of a free church to hold that office.[109] In view of Lloyd George's earlier political services to Nonconformity, this pointing with pride was understandable. In 1898, he had helped found the Free Church Parliamentary Council, as a Nonconformist pressure group within the House of Commons. Four years later, when Nonconformists were vigorously opposed to the Education Bill of 1902, he made 160 speeches in the House of Commons attacking that bill.[110] At the beginning of the First World War, he had persuaded a reluctant Lord Kitchener, secretary of state for war, to provide, for the first time, Nonconformist chaplains for British army personnel. This was a more challenging task than one might think. After hearing from Lloyd George on the matter, Kitchener instructed his staff, "Find out what these Baptists are."[111]

In one particular policy area, Lloyd George's contribution to the political causes of Nonconformity was particularly noteworthy. Throughout his political career, he articulated the Nonconformist opposition to alcohol. He drank very little, although he did not advocate prohibition. His maiden speech in the House of Commons was an attack on governmental compensation for publicans whose licenses were not renewed. In 1915, convinced that excessive drinking by war workers was damaging the British war effort, he made a major effort to control consumption of alcohol. This effort was, at the time and later, severely criticized, including by Asquith and Churchill. The most famous consequence of Lloyd George's wartime efforts against alcohol was the public pledge by George V and Kitchener to abstain from alcohol consumption until victory was achieved. Kitchener kept his pledge, but George V privately resented his pledge and even more privately obtained medical advice that he needed whiskey. Indeed, George V later claimed that Lloyd George's public announcement of the king's pledge was a "scurvy trick." Lloyd George did not take the king's pledge, nor did he claim publicly to have done so.[112]

In view of Lloyd George's devotion to Nonconformist causes, it may not be surprising that before he became prime minister, the Reverend Dr. John Clifford, perhaps the most influential Baptist clergyman in Britain, proclaimed that Lloyd George was in politics to serve God in politics.[113] Nonconformist support of Lloyd George was not withdrawn during his prime ministership. Late in his occupancy of that office, he received strong endorsement from the Reverend Dr. J. H. Shakespeare, widely known as "John the Baptist."[114] Writing in *The Lloyd George Liberal Magazine*, Shakespeare revealed: "When the maladies of the body politic seem to threaten a fatal end, I can yet sleep at nights as soon as I hear that he has been called in."[115] This Nonconformist confidence in Lloyd George never died. The *Baptist Times* wrote in 1935, "Mr Lloyd George is still the greatest Parliamentarian of the day. He is perhaps the only one of our statesmen with the sacred spark of genius."[116]

One scholar described Lloyd George's political style as a mixture of Wesley and Rousseau, of the Nonconformist conscience and the general will.[117] The Wesleyan element was surely there, but the strain of Rousseau was at least muted. Lloyd George's perception of democracy did not come from the general will but from a religious source. Lloyd George saw Martin Luther as the father of democracy.[118] The aspect of Luther's thought that most attracted Lloyd George was the proposition that each man is his own priest. Lloyd George was distinctly anticlerical in his politics. He grew up in a religious tradition that rejected a paid ministry. He confessed, "I hate a priest . . . whenever I find him."[119] This confession was puzzling, since Lloyd George did not in fact hate priests, whether Anglican or Roman Catholic.[120] Nor was he narrowly sectarian in his religious practices.

Lloyd George was open to religious experiences in a wide variety of settings, and his behavior was distinctly ecumenical. He took communion from the Anglican bishop of St. Asaph, A. G. Edwards, whose houseguest he had been, and whose friend he remained.[121] While in France he attended Sunday morning mass at the turn of 1906–1907 at the Roman Catholic Cathedral of Bayonne and in 1917 at Amiens Cathedral. These were not the first masses he had enjoyed attending. On Christmas Day 1897 he attended mass in the pope's private chapel at the Vatican. This mass was, he later judged, the most impressive religious service he had ever attended, and it was no accident that Lloyd George was so impressed. The pope was Leo XIII, author of *Rerum Novarum*, the most important papal encyclical on social justice in Lloyd George's lifetime. Their conceptions of social justice had much in common. The memory of his meeting with Leo XIII stayed with Lloyd George until his death. Shortly before that death, he told a visiting Nonconformist clergyman of his admiration for the "blind faith" he attributed to Roman Catholics.[122] Among his last words was a cry that was decidedly not Nonconformist: "The Sign of the Cross! The Sign of the Cross!"[123]

Whatever Lloyd George was, he was not a sectarian bigot. His origins were solidly in the dissenting sects of Britain, but not in one such sect. His father was Unitarian. His mother and her brother were Baptists, of the Disciples of Christ sect, and Lloyd George's childhood home was strictly Baptist. That home was, in fact, saturated in Nonconformist traditions. Richard Lloyd was a lay preacher of considerable reputation, to whom his favorite nephew sometimes referred, in Welsh, as the bishop. That nephew married Margaret Owen in a Methodist chapel. She was a Calvinistic Methodist. Some of the children of Margaret and David Lloyd George were raised as Baptists and others as Presbyterians. Their father was during most of his adult years a member of the Disciples of Christ congregation at Criccieth, and served as President of the Welsh Baptist Union.[124]

Nonconformity is difficult to define. At its origin it meant dissent from the Act of Uniformity of 1662, which completed the legal process of reestablishing the Anglican Church of England as the state church. For dissenters, common citizenship should not presuppose one common religious faith. They believed one could be a good citizen without accepting the state church. They began with a conviction that religious and national communities need not be identical. Religious freedom did not remain their only goal, however. They gradually came to share a conviction that British society needed to be reformed to a more nearly egalitarian society. They did not like the shape of the British national community, which was too hierarchical for them. They were, of course, not often found at or near the top of that hierarchy, and the Church of England was a solid part of the national establishment. Whatever their motives, religious dissenters became social Nonconformists, part of a social movement with a political as well as a religious message. They became, as an Anglican bishop of London was to put it, largely responsible for the democratic spirit in Britain.[125] Nonconformity was the seed-bed of political radicalism in Britain.[126]

Nonconformists did not conform among themselves on religious beliefs and practices. Lively, and sometimes deadly, disagreements on theological matters divided them from each other. These disagreements were still significant in Lloyd George's lifetime. These sectarian differences, however, bored him. He was not bored but angered by the puritanical lifestyles to which diverse theologies led many British Nonconformists. Among the puritans were members of his own family. His sister's puritanism seriously alienated both of her brothers, although Lloyd George at least wept at her death. Margaret Lloyd George was also undeniably puritanical. Her husband urged her to "drop that infernal Methodism." She did not. She remained active in chapel circles, and eventually became president of the Women's Section of the British Free Church Council.[127]

The adult Lloyd George did not adhere to the narrow creed of his childhood home. To conclude that he was a secularist who lacked religious consciousness is, however, unjustified. It is misleading to conclude that Lloyd George was a pagan, even if he may have suggested as much, which is by no means certain. He viewed the Passion Play at Oberammergau without emotion, but that may have been an aesthetic, not a religious, judgment. Lloyd George was in fact saturated with religious feeling. Not only did he not have a special dislike for Nonconformity, as has been argued, he nursed a genuine reverence for the free churches. He attended endless chapel services with enthusiasm. He delighted in hymn singing in chapel and elsewhere and he made his houseguests sing hymns.[128]

Lloyd George loved good sermons, and he recited long passages from his favorite sermons at the drop of a hat, even at supper, with oysters, at the most fashionable of restaurants. His political speeches drew on the technique and poetic imagery of Welsh narrative preachers, as he realized. His most memorable speeches used the *hwyl*, the rapt, half-chanting ecstasy near the end of a sermon, common among Welsh Nonconformist preachers. His best political speeches were, in fact, passionate sermons about right and wrong. They did not appeal to all listeners, for some found him to have an "unpleasant Nonconformist voice" with a "Little Bethel mentality." The sermonic quality of Lloyd George's speeches was no accident, for his first formal public speaking, as a teenager, was in chapel meetings, and he sought judgment of his first political speeches from Nonconformist clergymen. This was not surprising, since in Nonconformist circles it was difficult to distinguish between the pulpit and the political platform.[129]

Lloyd George's religious consciousness was genuine but not otherworldly. It was distinctly a feeling for the Gospel of good works in this world. In not being otherworldly, Lloyd George was being a good Britisher. In preaching good works in this world, Lloyd George was being a good Nonconformist Britisher. In his youth, he had contemplated writing a novel demonstrating how the poor are neglected in religion and politics, and inculcating a principle of religion and politics for the poor.[130] Churchill's youthful, and only, novel, *Savrola*, was about the powerful of this earth. Lloyd George never wrote his novel, but his political career was perhaps a worthy substitute. His political course was determined by his religious origins, and he followed this course with singularly little deviation.[131]

One of the great social divisions within Britain was, and is, that between the established Anglican Church and the Nonconformist Protestant chapel. Lloyd George made it crystal clear on which side of this barrier he would be found. In Queen's Hall in 1909 he asserted, "Those little chapels are there to fight for the rights of the people, and they do it."[132] In the conflict between Nonconformists and what he called, in Welsh, the church snobs, Lloyd George's commitment was fully engaged.[133] He openly attacked the privileges, which were denied to the Nonconformist chapels, of the established Church. In this attack, he had solid support from Nonconformists and, even in Wales, solid opposition from Churchmen and Churchwomen. When Lloyd George started his political career, most Nonconformists were Liberals, and one of Gladstone's many sins, in Lloyd George's eyes, had been being too much a Churchman.[134]

Lloyd George was the greatest political champion of British Nonconformity. It is exaggerated, nevertheless, to equate the political fortunes of British Nonconformity with the political fortunes of Lloyd George.[135] His was its dominant political voice throughout his political career, but he had a great predecessor, Joseph Chamberlain, in that role. Chamberlain, originally Unitarian, lost his faith.[136] If Chamberlain had not renounced Nonconformist causes for imperialism shortly before Lloyd George entered national politics, at least the young Lloyd George would have had to accept a concertmastership in Chamberlain's radical orchestra. As a radical Nonconformist politician, Lloyd George was to have many successors, sooner perhaps than he wanted. Most of these successors were not in the Liberal party, but in the Labor party. Among his political heirs, Aneurin Bevan was not only Welsh but a Baptist, and Anthony Wedgewood Benn, a Congregationalist.[137]

Just as they had earlier given a dynamic moral content to the Liberal party, the Nonconformist chapels gave a dynamic moral content to the Labor party. Many Labor pioneers were Nonconformists, and political careers did not alter their faith. As Ellen Wilkinson put it in middle-age, "I am still a Methodist, you can never get its special glow out of your blood."[138] The Reverend Dr. Clifford, who was to proclaim Lloyd George God's servant, had written an early Fabian Society tract stressing the parallels between socialism and the teachings of Jesus Christ.[139] Clifford was not lone in drawing such parallels. Victor Grayson, who had started training for the Unitarian ministry before becoming a Labor party crusader, preached "Socialism—God's Gospel for Today."[140] The Reverend Dr. J. Lewis asked his audi-

ence: "Who was their Saviour but a Labour man?"[141] The
spiritual father of the Labor party agreed. Keir Hardie's
personal roots were in the Scots Morrisonian sect, and his
political leadership was distinctly evangelical. Campaigning
successfully for a seat in the House of Commons, Hardie
proclaimed: "My cause is the cause of Labor—the cause of
Humanity—the cause of God."[142] These were not isolated
cases.

Nonconformity was a powerful force in shaping the ideology of the Labor party. Among both Labor and Liberal
members of Parliament elected in the 1906 general election,
the Nonconformist ethic was important. This may have been
to the political benefit of Nonconformity, but it was not to
the long-term benefit of the Liberal party, which had for
decades enjoyed the support of Nonconformists.[143] Indeed,
after the 1906 general election, the victorious prime minister, Henry Campbell-Bannerman, correctly observed, "We
have been put into power by the Nonconformists."[144] The
growing significance of the Labor party, still committed to
Nonconformist equalitarian ethics, meant that the overwhelming Liberal victory of 1906 would remain the high
watermark of the Liberal party. In 1918, with Lloyd George
as prime minister, manhood suffrage was finally realized in
Britain. Even the poor, that is if they were male, could now
vote; working-class women were not enfranchised until 1928.

As prime minister, Lloyd George presided over the official disestablishment in 1920 of the Anglican Church of
Wales, which had been accepted by Parliament in 1914 but
delayed in implementation because of the First World War.
Nonconformist resentment at the privileges of the Church
of Wales had been the crucial element in sustaining a Liberal Wales. Disestablishment of that church was one significant way by which the Liberal party legislated itself out of
Cabinet power and office. Middle class Welsh Nonconformists could now safely drift to the Conservative party, and
working-class Nonconformists to the Labor party.

The competition between the Liberal and Labor parties
was particularly intense. Both were essentially eating out
of the same electoral bowl. Lloyd George's vigor in appealing for workers' votes did not endear him to all Labor party leaders. Ernest Bevin expressed this rivalry when he
observed, "Of all the men in politics that man does not

represent the sane portion of the citizens of this country."[145] This statement reflected accurately Bevin's long-term distrust of Lloyd George.[146] Bevin's animosity revealed more about him than about Lloyd George. In attacking Lloyd George, Bevin was in effect attacking his own origins. Bevin was raised as a Methodist by his mother and then his elder sister, and he had been, as a young adult, not only a regular chapel-goer but an active Baptist lay preacher. The British Socialist Society he joined in his political baptism was not a clear break with his chapel activities.[147] To Labor party leaders like Bevin, Lloyd George was dangerous precisely because he was, and remained, a radical Nonconformist.

The crucial stage in the migration of working-class Nonconformists from the Liberal party to the Labor party was the 1924 general election.[148] In that election the Liberal party was still led by Asquith, who lost his own seat to his only opponent, a Liberal solicitor who had converted to the Labor party. Equally appropriately, Asquith had long before converted from his original Congregationalism to the Church of England. This conversion did not flow from a deep religious consciousness.[149] Disraeli, who would have approved of Asquith's conversion, probably also explained it: "Going to church was held to be more genteel than going to [chapel] meeting."[150] Asquith's second marriage to Margot Tennant, who was even more assiduous a social climber than her new husband, took place in one of the most fashionable Anglican churches in London.[151] Unlike Asquith, Lloyd George never renounced his Nonconformist heritage. Entirely appropriately, his last public appearance was at a children's party at the Baptist chapel in Criccieth.[152] He never lost an opportunity to chide the Church of England for what he viewed as a comfortable acceptance of social inequality. He also never lost an opportunity to chide that church on any possible matter. As a young politician, he described an Anglican Church congress that had met in Wales as having "floated on barrels of beer."[153] Late in life he derided as inflated figures for Church of England membership claimed by the Archbishop of Canterbury: "If a businessman put that in his prospectus, he would be sent to gaol."[154]

Remaining true to his cultural origins was surely one of Lloyd George's most remarkable achievements. In this task he was not alone. To assist him he had the constant vigilance of his uncle, Richard Lloyd, who lived to see him reach the prime ministership. Lloyd applied himself with unflagging energy to the education of his favorite nephew. This education included political socialization. Like many nineteenth-century tailors and shoemakers throughout Europe, who had both time for reflection and opportunity to meet many other people in their work, Lloyd was a political activist with a progressive message. He saw no reason why his gifted nephew should not be trained to think as he did. As a five-year-old, that nephew had already carried a flag with the Liberal colors in the 1868 general election campaign.[155] Lloyd George was, thereby, however prematurely, present at the birth of the British party system, which came into being as a result of the suffrage expansion of 1867.

Strong-willed and innocent of self-doubt, Lloyd saw himself until the end of his long life as his nephew's political mentor. The barrage of avuncular advice Lloyd George received, generally in writing, was almost uninterrupted. It is therefore easy to overestimate Lloyd's impact on his nephew's political career. The argument that, but for Lloyd, his nephew might also have ended up a shoemaker is unpersuasive. The argument that, but for Lloyd, his nephew might never have been more than a village Lothario and a parlor politician is only slightly more credible.[156] Lloyd George chose a political career not because his uncle wanted him to, but because he wanted to change the world he lived in. He succeeded in that career because of his enormous talent. Lloyd's contribution to that career was one of encouragement, not of creation. Lloyd may have lived vicariously through his nephew's career, but the dominant will was Lloyd George's. It is even possible that the most important personal influence in making the young Lloyd George a radical critic of British society may not have been his uncle, but John Roberts, a candlemaker Lloyd George met while a teenager.[157]

The adult nephew always listened courteously to his uncle's advice, because he still loved his uncle, who had given him a secure and happy childhood. Lloyd George was not only grateful for that gift but psychologically strong enough to resist his uncle's advice without alienating, or wanting to alienate, the older man. The adult Lloyd George affectionately flattered his uncle in frequent letters, but he did not obey him. The claim that he did so is entirely off the mark. Lloyd George gave much to his uncle, but never his will. Like many other of life's worthies, Lloyd could be annoying to those he loved. Whenever Lloyd George's patience was tried by the persistent insistence of his uncle's advice, he would angrily complain about that advice in letters to his wife and to his brother.[158] The therapeutic value of such explosions seems to have been sufficient. There is no evidence he ever spoke, or wrote, to his uncle in real anger. The bond of love between uncle and nephew was never broken.

One of Richard Lloyd's teachings was to stay always with his nephew, molding his perception of the world and revealing his personal and political values with great clarity. Lloyd had a hero: Abraham Lincoln. When his hero was assassinated, Lloyd bought a large picture of him and hung it in a place of honor in his home. There it remained as long as Lloyd lived. It had first appeared in his home a few months after his nephew, who had been born sixteen days after the Emancipation Proclamation, came to live with Lloyd. When the nephew learned to read, biographies of Lincoln became one of his favorite childhood experiences. Lincoln became Lloyd George's hero as well as his uncle's. The hero worship of the uncle had been catching. The young Lloyd George eventually chose Lincoln's profession, the law, as his own, believing that Lincoln had made lawyers respectable in the eyes of the common people.[159] Lincoln had certainly made lawyers respectable in Lloyd George's eyes.

Lloyd George saw Lincoln as a champion of the oppressed with loyalties deep in the culture and traditions of his own nation. This perception was the basis for Lloyd George's abiding belief in the heroic quality of Lincoln's life. To Lloyd George, who was preparing as prime minister to unveil a statue of Lincoln in London, the subject of the statue was the biggest man ever thrown up by American politics, and, therefore, the standard for judging other American politicians, including those others whom he also respected. Even though Lloyd George understood that Lincoln was profoundly American, he saw Lincoln as having an exemplary extra-

American significance as the greatest statesman of the nineteenth century. In this evaluation, Lloyd George pointedly
passed over the creator of the British Liberal party, Gladstone. For Lloyd George, Lincoln was the inspiration of
democracy in all nations, including Britain where his impact was deep and permanent.[160] But in fact, any impact
Lincoln had on British politics was indirect, through Lloyd
George's own accomplishments. No other major British politician revered Lincoln as Lloyd George did. Churchill, for
instance, was unmoved by Lincoln, whose decisions he criticized severely, and to whom he preferred Robert E. Lee.[161]

To Lloyd George, however, Lincoln was America's greatest achievement. Lloyd George regarded America as the
greatest nation in the world, probably because it had produced Lincoln. He thought the equalitarian America was the
real America. Lincoln-connected stops were the highlight of
his 1923 tour of the United States, which was for him a
pilgrimage, and his most prized gifts were Lincoln memora-
bilia. At Gettysburg, he observed sincerely that Lincoln's
speech there was the world's greatest oration. Even in Rich-
mond, Virginia, Lloyd George praised Lincoln, without men-
tioning Thomas Jefferson.[162]

In his first speech as prime minister to the House of
Commons, Lloyd George quoted Lincoln. This was appropriate acknowledgment for the inspiration Lincoln had given
him. To Lloyd George, Lincoln was the greatest human being
who ever lived. Lloyd George was not cynical about the
possibility of human greatness.[163] He was capable of hero
worship and Lincoln was the correct hero for him. Perhaps
he should have been a bit more skeptical, about his hero
and about himself. Perhaps his education should have included Friedrich Nietzsche's admonition to beware lest one's
hero prove to be a statue that will fall, fatally, upon one-
self.[164] As prime minister Lloyd George, entirely without
irony, justified use of military force to keep Ireland within
the United Kingdom by referring to Lincoln's willingness to
use military force to preserve the unity of the United
States.[165] The great emancipator was also the great conquer-
or, and Lloyd George eventually appeared eager to emulate
his hero in both respects. He had learned well and never
forgot the Nonconformist lesson of social justice, but he

eventually appeared to forget the other Nonconformist lesson: peace. Since that second lesson was imperfectly learned, his education was as incomplete as that of his fellow Disciple of Christ, Lyndon B. Johnson. For a time, nevertheless, it seemed that Lloyd George was learning that second lesson.

Chapter Two

Made in Birmingham

In the late summer of 1899, David Lloyd George, always exhilarated by being in new places, was traveling in some of the newest of places—in western Canada. While in this outpost of the empire, he realized that to expand another such outpost the Conservative cabinet in Britain was about to make war on the Dutch-speaking Afrikaaners of southernmost Africa. During his first decade as a Liberal member of Parliament, South African matters had never been of much interest to Lloyd George.[1] He was deeply involved with social justice and the empowerment of Wales within Britain, but war and imperialism had remained mostly outside his policy concerns.

Now, however, Lloyd George's response was instant, and his feelings were intense. As alone as he would ever be in a gregarious life, there were no distractions to his personal decision making. He had access to neither advisors nor audience. The sensitive ear and the silver tongue were temporarily useless. He had only his intelligence and his conscience as guides. Having taken counsel with them, he immediately communicated his reaction to the impending war to his brother, William George: "The prospect oppresses me with a deep sense of horror. If I have the courage, I shall protest with all the vehemence at my command against the outrage which is perpetrated in the name of human

freedom."[2] Lloyd George interrupted his travels to return to
Britain to protest war and to test himself. On the way home,
he wrote to his wife, Margaret Lloyd George, from Winnipeg:
"It is wicked."[3]

Because Lloyd George acted consistently and persistently in accordance with his initial reaction to the Boer War,
that war became more than yet another exercise of colonial
expansion by the greatest of all colonial powers.[4] Britain
became deeply divided by the Boer War, and it was Lloyd
George who divided Britain. He made the war one of the
lasting moral issues of British politics. Even the politics of
conscience needs a leader. The ethical integrity of political
action does not become an issue unless someone makes it
an issue. Such articulation was incisively effected by Lloyd
George. His passionate speeches cut to the heart of the
matter. His became the most important British voice raised
against the Boer War both inside and outside the House of
Commons.[5]

Winston Churchill's later claim that Lloyd George was
merely following in the train of senior Liberal party leaders
was not only contradicted elsewhere by Churchill, but far
off the mark.[6] The Liberal party was deeply divided by the
Boer War. This division never really healed in much the
same way as those who supported and those who opposed
appeasement in the Conservative party never fully trusted
each other after Munich. H.H. Asquith, Edward Grey, and
Lord Rosebery (the most recent Liberal prime minister) all
supported the Boer War. They did their best to assure that,
as Asquith put it, the Liberal party would not "be captured
by Lloyd George and his friends."[7] Conservative supporters
of the Boer War also feared Lloyd George more than other
Liberal opponents of the war.[8]

It is equally inaccurate to claim that Lloyd George argued only that the Boer War was unnecessary. To him the
war was unjust as well as unnecessary. His public statements matched his private reaction. Privately he referred
to the war as "damnable." Publicly he spoke of it as "an
infamy." Also publicly he argued that it was "unjust" for
Britain to fight the less-powerful Boers.[9] The disparity between Boer and British military resources was certainly
substantial. Not only was Britain a great power, but the British troops sent to South Africa formed the largest overseas

expedition yet in British history.[10] To Lloyd George, greater British power should have brought a greater sense of responsibility: "Have you the right to be unjust to a man because he is poor and weak and insignificant? Every honest man would say you should treat him with more generosity. There is an unpleasant flavour of Panama about this."[11]

Lloyd George used arguments of utility to urge a speedy end to the war, but he was also outspoken in his attack on what he saw, doubtless correctly, as the economic motivation for Britain's going to war.[12] He said, "I thank Heaven for the spectacle of one little nation of peasants standing against the mightiest Empire in the world, preferring to die rather than prostrate itself with the other nations of the earth at the feet of the vulgar priesthood of Mammon."[13] He did not thank heaven for a British desire for South African gold mines. Instead, he saw the British policy that led to the war as "diabolical in its malignity."[14]

Lloyd George's attack on the British conduct of the war was, if anything, even more fierce than on the origins of the war. When the British army forced Boer children and their mothers into concentration camps, he responded, "If I were to despair for the future of this country it would not be because of trade competition from either America or Germany, or the ineffectiveness of its army, or anything that might happen to its ships; but rather because it used its great, hulking strength to torture the little child."[15] The hands of the British government were "stained with the blood" of Boer children.[16]

These were strong words. They were not intended to increase the speaker's popularity, and they did not do so. Because of them Lloyd George became the most hated politician in Britain. Although it was later difficult for some to comprehend the intensity of that hatred, he was viewed by many of his fellow Britishers as a "pro-Boer" and an "anti-Briton" who was in fact a traitor to Britain. This antipathy long outlived the Boer War.[17] Sympathize with the enemy Lloyd George certainly did, because he was human, and ashamed of British behavior in South Africa he certainly was. Anti-British he was not. He merely expected more from the Britain he loved. The British flag was not, in his view, Joseph Chamberlain's pocket-handkerchief.[18]

Lloyd George later said that he risked his life to oppose the Boer War. This is true. His attack on the war exposed him to a degree of animosity unusual in British political culture. He was burned in effigy at prowar demonstrations in his own North Wales constituency. He was bludgeoned on the head as he finished a speech in that same constituency. But he did not confine his speeches to his home constituency. Speaking in Glasgow, he was also in substantial physical danger. The greatest peril came, however, when he was scheduled to speak in Birmingham in 1901. That appearance revealed much about the Boer War, and even more about David Lloyd George.[19]

As a city (a status it achieved only in 1889), Birmingham was a creation of the industrial revolution in the nineteenth century. It was best known as the home of a multitude of manufacturing plants producing an almost infinite variety of goods, some of them of questionable quality. "Brummagem ware," as they were often called, was not a persuasive advertising slogan. Birmingham was also known as the home of Joseph Chamberlain, who had been the most powerful advocate of social justice in Britain before he left the Liberal party when William Gladstone embraced home rule for Ireland. When Chamberlain became technically a Liberal unionist and practically a Conservative, he kept his local power base in Birmingham. He was that rarity in British politics, a major national leader who was also a municipal boss. Even though no longer mayor of Birmingham, at the time of the Boer War he still dominated Birmingham at least as much as he dominated, while secretary of state for the colonies, the Conservative Cabinet.

Lord Salisbury, the aging and distracted prime minister, privately called the Boer War "Joe's War."[20] Publicly Lloyd George, more restrained with first names, let alone nicknames, referred to "Chamberlain's war."[21] Salisbury and Lloyd George were right, as was Churchill, who publicly identified Chamberlain as "the *fons et origo*" of British policy in South Africa.[22] This was the colonial secretary's war. British Imperialism was now identified with the political career of Joseph Chamberlain, who spoke for imperialism. He was Britain's empire-builder-in-chief. At the turn of the twentieth century, the British Empire had become Chamberlain's baby, as it had once been Benjamin Disraeli's.[23]

Lloyd George, but not Salisbury, meant something more by identifying the Boer War as Chamberlain's war. One of the many manufacturing firms in Birmingham was Kynoch's, which made munitions. During the Boer War, it was the principal private firm selling small arms ammunition to the British army. Kynoch's success in selling to the War Office was not diminished by the questionable quality of its ammunition. From 1889 to his death in 1913, the chairman of Kynoch's was Arthur Chamberlain, brother of the colonial secretary. Arthur Chamberlain's position was hardly surprising, for Kynoch's was a family-owned firm, and the family was the Chamberlains of Birmingham. By his own admission, Joseph Chamberlain had directly owned Kynoch shares sometime prior to December 1900. When and if those shares had been sold remained imprecise, and in any event, if sold they were sold to other members of the Chamberlain family. Some of the Chamberlain family shares in Kynoch's were owned indirectly, through the Birmingham Trust Company, of which Joseph Chamberlain was still a beneficiary.[24] All this ammunition was used by Lloyd George to attack the Boer War, but perhaps he should have referred to "the Chamberlains' war." Joseph Chamberlain's conflicts of interest were hardly likely to move committed imperialists, since the British Empire had been created by precisely such intermingling of national power and personal wealth.

Such conflicts of interest were hardly confined to the Chamberlains. Later, Kynoch's became, appropriately, part of Imperial Chemical Industries. In Birmingham, what was good for Kynoch's was also good for the British Empire. This was no surprise, for the empire was Joseph Chamberlain's Birmingham writ large.[25] In the House of Commons, Lloyd George's revelations about Kynoch's were more effective. Had Lloyd George known even more about Kynoch's, he would have slain Joseph Chamberlain in the House of Commons in 1900 as he was to slay Neville Chamberlain there in May 1940. During the Boer War, Beckett and Company of Pretoria, the Transvaal agents of Kynoch's, sold twelve million rounds of ammunition to the Boer army.[26] Bullets made in Birmingham killed British soldiers in South Africa.

The Boer War became, in many respects, a duel between Chamberlain and Lloyd George. This was ironic, for in his radical days before his conversion to imperialism, the former

had been a major inspiration to the latter. In many ways
Lloyd George was Chamberlain's political son, much more
than Chamberlain's biological sons, Austen and Neville.
Lloyd George may have had no hero other than Abraham
Lincoln, but Joseph Chamberlain was the most important
British model for Lloyd George's political career, as Lloyd
George realized. That career certainly derived more inspi-
ration from the example of Chamberlain than from that of
Gladstone. Even if he was no longer able to follow Chamberlain's policies, Lloyd George retained his respect for
Chamberlain's courage and gifts as a speaker, which often
seemed to resemble his own gifts as a speaker. These were
not all he had in common with Chamberlain. Churchill was
so struck by these similarities that he wrote about them to
Edward VII. Lloyd George's manner in his first ministerial
post was to resemble Chamberlain's, and he seemed to have
confidence in Chamberlain's continuing devotion to social
justice long after the facts should have suggested otherwise.[27]

Lloyd George's admiration for Chamberlain was sorely
tested when he arrived in Birmingham to speak against the
Boer War. Somewhere between 30,000 and 200,000 supporters of the war surrounded the hall where Lloyd George was
to speak, with, as he later put it, "intent to kill me."[28]
Whether or not the members of the crowd actually shouted
"Kill 'im,"[29] their behavior was consistent with that goal. The
angry crowd became a murderous mob. Every window in the
building was broken and those many supporters of the war
already in the hall rushed the speaker's platform. They were
prepared with sticks, bricks, hammers, and knives. Lloyd
George was able to escape out the back way by donning a
policeman's uniform as disguise. His escape from Birmingham, as well as his earlier safe arrival in the city and at
the speaking site, may have been aided by the fact that
many of Chamberlain's most vigorous Birmingham followers did not recognize Lloyd George when they saw him. If
Lloyd George was David and Chamberlain was Goliath, there
were some advantages to being David. Lloyd George risked
his life and narrowly escaped being lynched. Chamberlain
took a grim pleasure in the riot and openly regretted Lloyd
George's escape, but not all those present were so fortunate as Lloyd George. Forty persons were injured and two
were killed.[30]

Churchill was much less pleased by the events in Birmingham than was Chamberlain. His immediate reaction was to write to a prominent Conservative there that he was "disgusted," warning, "I hope the Conservative Party have kept their hands clean." A few days later he told the same correspondent that Birmingham would be blamed for the treatment of Lloyd George while he was there, adding, "Personally, I think Lloyd George a vulgar, chattering little cad, but he will have gained a hundred thousand sympathizers in England by the late proceedings."[31]

Lloyd George paid other costs for his opposition to the Boer War. He risked not only his life but his political career. His seat in the House of Commons was endangered, for even in Liberal North Wales, opponents of the Boer War were in a minority.[32] Lloyd George fully understood the political danger. Of his own rebellious constituents, he observed: "I must go down there and say a word to them, but do as they will, I shall continue to protest, even if they turn me out."[33] The word proved prolonged but narrowly sufficient.

Lloyd George also risked his financial means of support. Members of Parliament were still, before 1911, unsalaried. Ministers of the Crown were already handsomely compensated, but he had not yet held ministerial office. Since he, unlike many other British politicians, did not have independent means, he was for all practical purposes financially dependent on his solicitor's practice. Propertied clients were hardly likely to be attracted to the leading "pro-Boer" British solicitor. Lloyd George later stated that his opposition to the Boer War "ruined" his solicitor's practice. There is no doubt that his legal practice suffered. When, in 1905, he first assumed ministerial office, as president of the Board of Trade, he was still overdrawn £400 at the bank.[34]

The most painful cost was probably that paid by Lloyd George's still-growing family. Not only did they have to tighten their belts substantially, but they were ostracized socially by imperialists. There is no reason to assume that either David or Margaret Lloyd George felt deprived by not being asked to Margot Asquith's dinner parties, but their four children were another matter. Coached at home, the peers of the Lloyd George children taunted them with the purported political sins of their father. The oldest child, Richard, suffered so intensely that he had to be transferred from a school in the London area to one in Wales where family influence would provide at least some shelter.[35]

That son, who hated his father and was eventually disowned, nevertheless granted, "Great guts he always had."[36] This was so. Robert Boothby's argument that Lloyd George had infinite moral courage but was a physical coward is untrue as well as unkind. Birmingham took physical as well as moral courage. It was entirely typical of Lloyd George that his courage there rose to meet seeming disaster. Chamberlain's sympathetic biographer was correct, although not as he intended, in judging that Lloyd George was imprudent to attempt to speak in Birmingham.[37] Lloyd George would have considered this judgment to be the highest praise. He neither preached nor practiced prudence.

Lloyd George did, however, preach. His conscience had molded his initial response to the Boer War. His courage had molded the fidelity with which he maintained that initial response in the face of high costs. Both his conscience and his courage flowed from his religious consciousness. His speeches attacking the Boer War sounded like sermons because that is what they were. Those speeches sounded like the most famous of sermons because that was the origin of their content. He had entered politics to fight for social justice within Britain. The Boer War forced him to grapple with the foreign policy implications of Nonconformity. This world, he saw, included the entire human race, not merely the Welsh or even the British. If the poor were blessed, so also would be the peacemakers. If the costs of being a peacemaker were high, Matthew 5:9 was followed by Matthew 5:10–11.

The rewards to Lloyd George of his courageous opposition to the Boer War were also substantial. Wise or not, it did him honor.[38] He had been tested against the high standard that alone in Vancouver, he had set for himself. He had not been found wanting. Of this he was proud, and he said so. In September 1900, he addressed the Criccieth Liberal executive in his constituency. His real audience here was those Liberal imperialists who wanted to deny him renomination for the forthcoming "khaki" general election of October 1900. This audience heard the proudest personal statement Lloyd George ever made in public:

Five years ago the electors of the Carnarvon Boroughs handed
me a strip of blue paper, the certificate of my election, to hand
to the speaker as their accredited representative. If I never again
represent the Carnarvon Boroughs in the House of Commons, I
shall at least have the satisfaction of handing them back that
blue paper with no stain of human blood upon it.[39]

During the Boer War, while he was still in his thirties,
Lloyd George came to national and international fame. After Birmingham, his face was known even to his enemies.
The spotlight was on him and would never darken until he
died. During the Boer War he became a leading personality
of his time. He indelibly impressed himself on the imagina-
tion of his contemporaries by speaking as the voice of
humanity for the Boers.[40] The personal prestige he earned
would last a long time, especially if carefully husbanded.
Such caution, however, was not in Lloyd George.

If the Boer War reduced his wealth and increased his
prestige, its most important personal consequence was
something much closer to Lloyd George's heart. It made him
a lifelong member of the highest political elite in Britain.
He would never again, even when he was alone, be a backbencher. His voice would be heard, even if it did not carry
the day, on every significant issue, domestic and foreign,
of British politics. To his previous Welsh and Nonconformist followers, he added the British peace movement. The
latter gained a gifted and dynamic new leader, but it also
became partially a prisoner of its leader, just as British
imperialists were partially prisoners of their leader, Chamberlain. His opponents and enemies learned that Lloyd
George's aim could be painfully accurate. No one had ever
wounded Chamberlain as Lloyd George did over Kynoch's.

Lloyd George's was the only British political reputation
made by the Boer War. That war made Lloyd George. But it
was his courage, not his overwhelming charm, that made
Lloyd George.[41] Most precisely, it was his courage in Birmingham that made Lloyd George.

That war did not make Britain, however. Though Lloyd
George's political career was not among them, there were
many casualties. During the Boer War, South Africa became
a graveyard for British soldiers. Subduing 71,000 Boer

soldiers fighting a guerrilla war required almost 450,000 British and colonial troops and cost 22,000 British and colonial lives and at least £223,000,000. The British-Boer power disparity drew censure from the rest of the world, including Europe.[42] Criticism from Germany was the most serious. As Churchill saw, 1899 helped lead to 1914.[43] This was not merely hindsight on Churchill's part. In 1902 he warned of a "dragging, draining, dangerous war."[44] The military difficulties of the British Army in South Africa made Britain an international laughingstock.[45] Even Rudyard Kipling told "The Islanders" of this: "then was your shame revealed,/At the hands of a little people, few but apt in the field."

Shame comes in many sizes. Laughter at the incompetence of the British Army in dealing with a small guerrilla army turned into tears over the methods used by British military commanders to pacify the Boer territories. When Boer soldiers proved difficult to defeat, they turned their attention to Boer civilians. Prodded by those commanders, St. John Brodrick, secretary of state for war, wanted the Boer territories cleared of food. Lord Kitchener, now British commander-in-chief in South Africa, ordered the Boer earth to be scorched and the farmers' homes to be burned. That was done.[46] In a mostly agrarian society, this left many civilians homeless as well as hungry. These civilians were herded into concentration camps. At least 26,000 Boer women and children died in these camps, whose creation Churchill defended in a letter to *The Times*. The war was between the British and the Boers, but more than 13,000 blacks, whose war it was not, also died in British concentration camps.[47]

Given his treatment of Boer civilians, it is not surprising that Kitchener viewed Boer soldiers as less than human. Of his military opponents, he wrote to Brodrick, "Like wild animals they have to be got into enclosures before they can be captured." To capture this elusive game, Kitchener became an obsessed hunter, leaving professional military considerations of achieving strategic or even tactical objectives far behind. To Lord Roberts, his predecessor in South Africa, he wrote, "I look more to the numbers I kill or capture than anything else." To Brodrick, Kitchener reported that "the real criterion of the war is my weekly bag."[48] At this remove, Kitchener's personal preoccupation with a weekly body count may sound all too ominous. The first cracks in the British imperial wall appeared in South Africa during the Boer War.[49] These cracks were so broad and so deep they could be seen even at great distance. The British army needed the assistance of troops from several colonies, and some seeds of colonial independence were sown by the war. Frederick Borden, Canadian minister of defense, told Sir Edward Hutton, British commander of the Canadian militia: "General, I ask myself this question. Is it worth Canada's while to remain part of an Empire which can suffer disasters such as those of Methuen, Gatacre and Buller?"[50] The Boer War proved to be Britain's Vietnam, with the major difference that eventually, in 1902, Britain militarily subdued the Boers.[51] But in the longer run, this British military victory, like most military victories, proved Pyrrhic. The Boer guerrillas in South Africa lost the war, but won the peace. It was black South Africans who eventually paid the heaviest price for the Boer War and its aftermath. If that war was unworthy of Britain, the shame was relieved essentially only by one man's war against that war.[52]

In that smaller war, Lloyd George, who was exhilarated even more by learning new things than by being in new places, learned that he was a fighter. He also learned more about what he was a fighter for. He had always been a fighter for social justice. Through the Boer War, his consciousness about war and imperialism, which had not earlier been high, was raised substantially. He learned that peace and the rights of small peoples besides the Welsh mattered to him. Most importantly, he learned that peace and social justice are connected, that guns and butter are different priorities. Being Lloyd George, he wanted to talk about what he had learned, off the political platform. He chose as his classroom a gathering of the Welsh community in London in January 1901. Here he shared the first new lesson he had learned from the Boer War: imperialism meant lust for the lands of others.[53]

Chapter Three

The Meeting

He had music, the divine gift, in his soul,
and the voice of an angel to utter it.
                                        —Sarah Grand

In the first weeks of the twentieth century, properly counted, a month after the Victorian Age had finally expired, the
House of Commons was crowded and its members chattered
with anticipation. The stage was well set. David Lloyd George
had moved an amendment highly critical of British policy
in the Boer War. Even the more venerable members returned
from dining well for the evening session, to see, as William
Harcourt put it, the cockfight between Lloyd George and a
new Conservative member scheduled to give his maiden
speech that evening. The Conservative combatant was not
Andrew Bonar Law, another new Conservative member who
also gave his maiden speech that evening and who eventually became leader of the Conservative party and prime
minister. Bonar Law was to develop an enduring antipathy
for his early Conservative rival, who upstaged him on what
should have been his first big night, as well as on many
later nights. That rival returned the favor in surprisingly
harsh tones.[1]

Before Lloyd George rose to speak, the House rapidly
filled up and, given the paucity of seats, over.[2] The first

sight of the speaker was impressive. Lloyd George could fairly be described as good-looking, and he was, as always, well dressed, neatly and in impeccably good taste. A well-preserved thirty-eight-year-old, he looked younger than his age. He was only five feet six and a half inches tall, but with a powerful frame and deep chest.[3] He wore a magnificent mustache and long, carefully tended locks. Like some other war protestors, Lloyd George wore his hair longer than custom sanctioned. His distinctive head was surprisingly large, which Lord Beaverbrook, for one, thought gave Lloyd George an appearance of importance. Lloyd George agreed.[4] Perhaps not surprisingly, he was an enthusiastic phrenologist. His most striking physical characteristic was, however, his grayish blue eyes. They sparkled with humor one moment and flashed sparks of anger the next. At both moments, they were piercing, looking right through others. They had a hypnotic quality.[5]

The speaker's voice was, if anything, even more hypnotic. That voice was a pleasant light tenor, which possessed a silver magic. Lloyd George spoke in caressing cadences of natural music. It was probably no accident that Handel's "Largo" was among his favorite music.[6] His voice was naturally sweet and musical but not overly powerful. Although he seldom shouted, Lloyd George had mastered projecting his voice effectively into the largest audience. That voice soared out over a densely packed hall like an organ. Even in old age his voice could drown out the rest of a large congregation while singing a hymn. In the age before broadcasting such projection was necessary, and he never fully mastered speaking on the radio.[7]

Lloyd George and his audiences needed each other's physical presence, including eye contact, for maximum interaction. His audiences absorbed his presence, but he also absorbed the audience's presence. His voice was an incomparable vehicle of passion and power, and will and force emanated from him while speaking, but his audience was a crucial part of any Lloyd George performance. He spoke with, not to, an audience. He adapted his speech to the mood of the audience. He was not a virtuoso soloist but a great conductor. The works he conducted were the grandest of operas.[8] Without the active participation of the audience there would have been no music. With such participation the music could be, and often was, ethereal.

On 18 February 1901, the music was particularly impressive. Lloyd George's voice was in perfect condition. The speaker was at the height of his powers. His speech that evening may have been inflammatory; it was certainly dramatic. Instead of moving adoption of the amendment he had introduced earlier, he made a blistering frontal assault on British actions in South Africa, in the midst of which he suddenly announced he would curtail his remarks so that a new member of the House could be heard. No one was more surprised by the timing of Lloyd George's welcome than that new member.[9] In so abruptly making way, Lloyd George might have intended to catch that new member off guard, as certainly happened. It is likely, however, that Lloyd George was genuinely eager to hear that new member. Lloyd George surely recalled the first House of Commons debate he had heard, as a twenty-one-year-old visitor to London, which featured the new member's father, whose incisive speech on that occasion Lloyd George had much admired. Later, as a Commons colleague of the new member's father for the last five years of his life, Lloyd George had had many opportunities to observe and listen to his speeches. The new member, in contrast, had never heard his father speak in the House of Commons.[10]

Most members had never seen or heard of Lord Randolph Churchill's son before this evening. The new member knew surprisingly few other members before his election, and he had taken his seat only four days before he gave his maiden speech.[11] Winston Churchill's feeling of solitude may have been eased somewhat by glancing toward the ladies' gallery where he could see his mother and four of his paternal aunts: Lady Wimborne, Lady Tweedmouth, Lady Howe, and Lady de Ramsey. None of his male relatives, and no person of his own age of either gender had come to hear him, however.

The House of Commons membership was nevertheless still numerously present when Churchill rose to speak. He was, after all, to give the initial Conservative party response to Lloyd George's speech. This was certainly unusual behavior both for a new member and for Conservative party leaders. Churchill's haste to give his maiden speech may have been unprecedented, and may still be unequaled, but it was entirely characteristic of him. The typical silence of new backbenchers was not for him. In his first year in the

House, he made nine speeches. The willingness of Conservative party leaders to use Churchill in this situation is more difficult to understand. Backbenchers were seldom asked to speak for the cabinet, and to ask a new backbencher to speak was not only unexpected but, in this case, running a substantial risk. In asking Churchill to speak for it, the Conservative leadership doubtless hoped to cash in on Churchill's recent military exploits in the Boer War, exploits much discussed in British newspaper articles, especially in those numerous articles written by the new member himself. Churchill was undoubtedly, in terms of his military and journalistic experiences in South Africa, possessed of unique firsthand knowledge of events. He was among the few members of Parliament personally to have participated in the Boer War,[12] and Conservative party leaders perhaps thought Churchill would be seen as a war hero by the British electorate.

Churchill's first appearance to the members of the House of Commons can hardly have been impressive. Churchill was five feet six and a half inches tall.[13] This was no less than Lloyd George's height, but Churchill's weight was distributed less attractively. His chest measured only thirty-one inches while he was a cadet at Sandhurst. As a new member of Parliament, Churchill was already pudgy. The adult Churchill always approached obesity, which, considering how much he ate and drank, was hardly surprising. Even in extreme old age he weighed 210 pounds. His movements were generally awkward and seldom graceful. In spite of the cost of his extensive bespoke wardrobe, his appearance was seldom well tailored. Even with the lifelong services of valets, his clothes were always baggy. While he was walking in mufti as a young officer with his mother and brother, he was mistaken for their groom. When he was a bridegroom, *Tailor and Cutter* described his appearance as that of a glorified coachman, and that garb was badly wrinkled. Such periodicals had earlier complained of his "sartorial terrifics." The most generous description of Churchill at his parliamentary debut was that he looked like a belated candidate for confirmation.[14]

As a young politician, Churchill struck those first meeting him as not only a "little . . . fellow of no very striking appearance" but also as "square-headed." His head was massive and ponderous. Lloyd George's head was also large, but in his case this seemed to add to his attractiveness. Churchill was less fortunate. His head seemed too large for his body. Like Lloyd George, Churchill believed in phrenology. He was convinced that the size and shape of his head indicated that he was intelligent.[15] That Churchill was a phrenologist before he met Lloyd George is apparent from Churchill's novel *Savrola*, written in 1897. The "high and ample forehead" of the novel's hero, its author, "might have contained the answer to every question."[16]

Churchill's appearance did not help his maiden speech. Worse was to come after he opened his mouth. His voice was harsh and unpleasing. There was nothing musical about Churchill. His accent was far from Oxford, doubtless because he had never been to university, and he was capable of dropping his aitches. His was a powerful voice, as he had previously recognized, but it was also unpleasant. He stammered over his opening remark. Churchill was understandably nervous over his maiden speech, but he was to remain nervous before every major speech he ever gave.[17]

Churchill's speaking problems were not only situational. He stammered badly, and not only at the beginning of his maiden speech. Some thought, before he entered politics, that his stammer would prevent any political career for him.[18] Churchill, however, was not only convinced that this speech impediment would not hinder his career, but had suggested, in a long-unpublished essay "The Scaffolding of Rhetoric," written in 1897, that a stammer could catch the attention of an audience.[19] This was making the best of necessity. The stammering on his maiden speech was in fact pitiful. Churchill was never able to lose his stammer. At times this problem was paralyzing, but Churchill generally was able to slow his delivery, with many pauses and much deliberate hesitation, sufficiently to reduce the impact of his stammer on his audience. Dealing with his stammer may, however, have made his voice even more raspingly incisive. Perhaps Churchill was an eloquent stammerer channeled, because of his difficulty in speaking, into violent action.[20]

Stammering was not Churchill's only, or even worst, speech impediment. He also lisped badly. Before entering the House of Commons, he had taken, on Lord Rosebery's advice, elocution lessons, and, prodded by an American masseuse, sought medical help to minimize his lisp, but worried that he would never learn to pronounce an "s" correctly.[21] This fear proved justified. The lisp characteristic of his maiden speech was widely noticed. Parallels were drawn between his lisp and his father's lisp. The lisp was to remain with Churchill as long as he lived. He tried hard to avoid sibilants as much as possible, and to reduce the force of other consonants, giving emphasis to strong vowels. These techniques reduced the effect of his lisping, but, contrary to the claim that he conquered this problem, Churchill's speech remained unattractive. The lisp certainly gave his speech distinctiveness. It made him immediately identifiable to reporters overhearing him, and gave a touch of verisimilitude to fictional characterizations of him. An actor portraying Churchill in a television melodrama wore a plastic mouth plate to produce the appropriate lisp. Churchill liked to deal with people who suffered from the same handicap. When he was a young army officer he got along especially well with his regimental commander, Colonel John Brabazon, whose lisp was even more pronounced than Churchill's. Frank Sawyer, Churchill's valet, also had a distinctive lisp.[22]

Not all the notice taken of Churchill's lisp was charitable. It was ridiculed by his fellow Conservatives while he was a Conservative, and by his fellow Liberals while he was a Liberal. Tastelessness was not partisan. Early in his parliamentary career he was hissed by his enemies, of whatever party, whenever he lisped.[23] There was no denying he whistled the letter "s". This unparliamentary treatment of him may have been the origin of his phobic aversion to other people casually whistling. His reaction to any whistling within his hearing was described by his bodyguard as irrational and almost "psychiatric."[24] It may be that Churchill assumed all whistlers were ridiculing him.

To judge Churchill's maiden speech as a triumph is unjustified. The manner was distinctly ungainly. Perhaps inevitably, his speech impediments reduced the impact of his performance. His delivery was not equal to his substance. The text of his speech still reads well, but he had not yet acquired the art of delivery.[25]

That Churchill's maiden speech was well composed had little political effect. His task in the House of Commons debate that evening was not to write an attractive essay, but to refute Lloyd George's case against the Boer War as Lloyd George made it that evening. This goal Churchill did not reach. Perhaps he was not equal to the task. Careful preparation was certainly his strong suit, and possibly his sole resource. But he had no gift for speaking *extempore*.[26] When Lloyd George did not move for approval of the amendment Churchill had expected, Churchill, who had carefully prepared a response to that amendment, was lost. He had laboriously written out, memorized, and rehearsed his speech so that the speech was in fact a recitation. He did not significantly alter his recitation to meet the new parliamentary situation. His only effective riposte to the speech Lloyd George actually made was borrowed at the last possible minute from another Conservative backbencher.[27]

Early in his political career, it has been argued, Churchill could write a compelling speech but had trouble with delivery and debate.[28] This was true of Churchill as a speaker throughout his political career. To his credit, he did write most of his own speeches, but perhaps he spoke as he wrote because what he spoke he had first written.[29] Prepared completely in advance, carefully thought out and painstakingly revised, his speeches became literary exercises. His capacity to recite from memory what he had written was substantial, but when reciting, his script was omnipresent. The speeches he had not memorized he read, word-for-word, and the effect on his audience was what such a presentation might be expected to have.[30]

Churchill understood that his gifts were more literary than oratorical, and that he did not stand out as a speaker in the House of Commons or on the platform. He knew he was not a natural speaker.[31] He was not a great orator, nor was he even in the first flight of House of Commons orators. As an impromptu debater, he was outclassed by, say, A. J. Balfour, H. H. Asquith, and even Bonar Law. The list of Churchill's superiors in parliamentary debate could probably be expanded considerably.[32] In particular, Churchill was no match for Lloyd George as a speaker, even though he tried to follow some of Lloyd George's maxims about oratory.[33] But Churchill had none of Lloyd George's quickness of wit in debate.

Lloyd George set the standard for excellence in modern

British parliamentary debate. As a platform speaker, his primacy was at least as great. Out of ministerial office, he did not lose a single auditor while speaking to twenty-five thousand people for an hour and a half in pouring rain. If the spoken word is the politician's most essential public weapon, at least in a democratic political system, Lloyd George was well armed. He was the greatest master of the spoken word in modern British politics.[34]

Because Churchill could write well, his speeches will continue to read well. Churchill may in fact have been writing speeches for later readers rather than to persuade present listeners.[35] He was seldom able to convert an initially unsympathetic audience. Sometimes his audience laughed at his rhetoric. Sometimes even his later readers found his rhetoric tiresomely windy.[36]

The most serious weakness of Churchill's speeches was that they were solely expressions of himself. In each speech, he was saying a piece. A Churchill speech was a one-way flow that owed nothing to the audience. The speaker was concerned more with the sound of his words than with their effect. Churchill understood words, but he did not understand what was going on in the emotions or the minds of his audience.[37] And he may not have cared much that he did not understand. His respect for his audiences, even in the House of Commons, was minimal. While his first speech as prime minister was being applauded, he commented, "That got the sods, didn't it?"[38] En route to his last Conservative party conference as leader of the party, he predicted, "I think I can harangue the bastards for fifty minutes."[39] He understood that the most effective speakers in British politics, like Lloyd George and Aneurin Bevan, were carried away by their emotions while speaking, but he was not.[40] This lack of emotion in presentation of a Churchill speech contrasted with the tears that flowed during the composition of a particularly felicitous phrase during the writing of a speech.[41]

The most substantial strength of Churchill's maiden speech was in neither its delivery nor its situational appropriateness. The real strength was in its content. He said what he thought. He did not know how to lie effectively on behalf of his party, nor did he want to know.

As rebuttal to Lloyd George's speech, Churchill's maiden

speech was singularly restrained, Churchill paid embarrass-
ingly explicit tribute to the courage and skill of the out-
numbered Boer troops, and added, "if I were a Boer I hope
I should be fighting in the field."[42] At this point, Joseph
Chamberlain, secretary of state for the colonies and chief
author of the Boer War, revealingly muttered, "That's the
way to throw away seats."[43] While Churchill was urging the
colonial secretary to make a speedy and generous peace with
the Boers, the Conservatives surrounding the speaker
scowled.[44]

The Conservative scowls were justified. There was no
jingoism in Churchill's maiden speech; Churchill was not a
jingoist. His sympathies were with the Boers.[45] In the autumn of 1899, Churchill's views were clear: "I thought after all that the war was unjust, that the Boers were better
men than we."[46] Already in that autumn Churchill had
praised "the stubborn unpretentious valour of the Boer."[47]
His admiration was clear. His attitude toward the Boer War
was not drastically different from Lloyd George's, and he
could hardly refute a position that was close to his own.
This did not make for effective advocacy, although it might
have made for effective public policy.[48]

In his maiden speech, Churchill's major difference with
Lloyd George's position was over the origins, not the conduct, of the war. Churchill did not then accept Lloyd
George's argument that British policy in South Africa was
motivated by greed for the gold mines of the Rand. Later
he was to reconsider whether Lloyd George might have been
right also on the origins of the war.[49] After his maiden
speech, Churchill continued to attack British policy in South
Africa and further separated himself from jingoism.[50]

Churchill was too much of a Europeanist and therefore
too much of a little Englander to be an enthusiast for the
Boer War. That war was for him unfortunate in its beginning, inglorious in its course, and cruel in its conclusion.
He saw the war as a dangerous adventure that became an
immense public disaster. He was convinced that the British government intended the Boer War to distract British
voters from that government's domestic failures, and that
the popularity of the war in Britain was thoughtless. Reconciliation with the Boers was for Churchill the only viable
policy, and this is exactly what he eventually sought and

achieved in his first ministerial office, as undersecretary of state for the colonies beginning in late 1905.[51] British reconciliation with the Boers came at the expense of the black majority of the South African population; but as a pro-Boer, Churchill was hardly a conventional imperialist.

His maiden speech revealed more of Churchill than it did of the position of the Conservative party. That fact did not bother Churchill, and it did not bother his most careful listener. After Churchill's speech ended, he was introduced to Lloyd George at the Bar of the House of Commons.[52] According to Lloyd George's later recollection, he told Churchill, "You are sinning against the light." According to Churchill's later recollection, he was told, "Judging from your sentiments, you are standing against the Light." According to Lloyd George's later recollection, Churchill responded, "You take a very detached view of the British Empire." According to Churchill's later recollection, his response was, "You take a singularly detached view of the British Empire."[53] Both sets of recollections came three decades after Lloyd George and Churchill were introduced to each other. The differences in language were perhaps revealing, but the substance of the recollections was strikingly similar. Both recalled their first meeting clearly. That was appropriate, for that meeting altered the course of their lives, and of many other lives. Lloyd George and Churchill were now together.

Chapter Four

Together

Friendship should be more than biting Time can sever.
—T. S. Eliot

David Lloyd George and Winston Churchill took an immediate fancy to each other on the evening of 18 February
1901. They were drawn irresistibly together.[1] Lloyd George
later referred to "the great admiration I have always had"
for Churchill "ever since I first met him."[2] Their friendship
lasted through many vicissitudes. It may have been, as
Lloyd George observed, the longest political friendship in the
life of Great Britain. The friendship of Lloyd George and
Churchill was, after 1901, an unbroken lifelong relationship.
Churchill loved Lloyd George and Lloyd George loved
Churchill.[3] Their relationship was interwoven with the tex-
ture of their lives. Their relationship was not only a fact of
life for each, but an essential part of the fabric of each of
their lives.

The personal lives and political careers of Lloyd George
and Churchill were inextricably intertwined. To argue that
their friendship was purely political is misleading.[4] They had
met in the House of Commons, but they delighted in each
other's company outside of that House. They played golf
together. They met frequently and convivially in each other's homes and elsewhere. Lloyd George reminded Churchill

in 1914, "For 10 years there has been hardly a day when we haven't had half an hour's talk together."[5] In spite of his preference for dining at home, Lloyd George was completely at home with the Churchills. Overcoming his distaste for stately homes, Lloyd George visited Blenheim, Churchill's family home. Life was not always stately. When Prime Minister Lloyd George joined the Churchills on their summer holiday in 1917, he and his host had the contents of children's chamber pots emptied on their unsuspecting heads.[6]

Lloyd George and Churchill frequently lunched and dined together, including on special occasions. On 1 January 1904 Churchill told a Conservative colleague that he had lunched "privately" with Lloyd George the previous day. They were together at dinner on 5 December 1916, while H. H. Asquith was visiting Buckingham Palace to resign as prime minister, to be replaced by Lloyd George. They were together at dinner at 10 Downing Street on 11 November 1918. They were together at dinner on 18 October 1922, the evening before the Conservative members of Parliament met at the Carlton Club to withdraw from Lloyd George's coalition cabinet. They were together at dinner, as Churchill put it, "*à deux*," at the beginning of the parliamentary session in early 1926. Together in France in 1938, they attended a dinner for the duke and duchess of Windsor. They were together at lunch on 4 August 1939, the twenty-fifth anniversary of the 1914 British ultimatum to Germany. On this occasion, Lloyd George advised Churchill not to join Neville Chamberlain's cabinet. Lloyd George, who often gave higher priority to romantic dinners, sometimes informed Frances Stevenson that since he was dining with Churchill, she would have to fend for herself. For Lloyd George, even speaking at a printers' pension dinner was made tolerable by discovering Churchill was also there.[7]

Dinner was not always in London, and Frances Stevenson did not always have to dine alone. Lloyd George, Stevenson, and Churchill, but not Clementine Churchill, were country houseguests together over New Year's weekend, 1921. On Boxing Day of that year, Lloyd George and Churchill, without wives, left for a holiday in the south of France. They had probably begun taking foreign holidays together as far back as 1905.[8]

Their friendship was long and comfortable. At the beginning of 1936, Lloyd George, with Frances Stevenson, stayed at the same hotel in Morocco as Churchill. After Stevenson returned alone to Britain, Margaret Lloyd George arrived. Churchill stayed throughout.[9] During this holiday, Lloyd George celebrated his seventy-third birthday. Toasting him, Churchill recalled their long friendship during which "all the time I have thanked God that he has been born to work for our country, for the masses of those poor people in times of peace, and for our strength and security in the great days of the war."[10] Since both were out of governmental office, there was time for other feasts, two of them at banquets in Marrakesh. While they were in Morocco, Lloyd George intervened more than once to smooth over a quarrel between Churchill and his son Randolph. The latter wanted to stand for election to the House of Commons as an antigovernment candidate, while his father was still hoping to be called out of the political wilderness to join that cabinet.[11] Churchill does not seem to have resented Lloyd George's serving as a family counselor. Indeed, he gave Lloyd George a painting of Marrakesh that may have been one of Churchill's finest.[12] Lloyd George and Churchill often dispensed personal advice to each other, and that advice was sometimes taken. In 1911, for instance, Churchill got Lloyd George to see a new doctor.[13]

Two particular events, widely separated in time, illustrate the significant role each played in the other's personal life. The first of these events was Churchill's marriage in 1908 to Clementine Hozier, and the second was the golden wedding anniversary celebration in 1938 of David and Margaret Lloyd George.

The stag dinner before Churchill's wedding was attended by Lloyd George and the bishop of St. Asaph. The presence of the latter, who was also to perform the marriage ceremony, suggests both the decorousness of this bachelor party and the influence of Lloyd George. St. Asaph was a bishopric of the Anglican Church of Wales, and its bishop, A. G. Edwards, was Lloyd George's longtime friend. Clementine Hozier and Winston Churchill were married in London by a Welsh divine known to them only through Lloyd George, who was seated prominently, whether in the front or second pew, at their wedding. Lloyd George signed the marriage register as a witness, the only person so to sign other than the bride's brother and the bridegroom's mother. Lloyd George was also the first person to congratulate the newly married couple. Even though the bridegroom was a cabinet member, and the wedding took place in a most fashionable London church, Lloyd George was the only minister of the Crown present as a guest. It was therefore understandable that, as another guest put it, he had to be "marched round and round like the army in the Pantomime."[14] He was equally visible at the wedding reception.[15]

Marriages, even when imperfect, can last a long time. In early 1938, Margaret and David Lloyd George celebrated the fiftieth anniversary of their wedding, at Antibes, in circumstances rather more elegant, if perhaps less wholesome, than their wedding in a Nonconformist chapel in Wales. Lloyd George had been in Antibes for some time, finishing his book, *The Truth about the Peace Treaties.*[16] Frances Stevenson left Antibes for London just as Margaret Lloyd George left London for Antibes. Margaret Lloyd George was put into a hotel room some distance away from her husband's. Shortly after she arrived, David Lloyd George's seventy-fifth birthday was celebrated at a lunch hosted by Winston Churchill.[17] A week after Lloyd George's birthday, on the date of the Lloyd Georges' marriage, Clementine and Winston Churchill hosted the honorees at lunch at the Carlton Hotel, Cannes. Winston Churchill proposed the toast, stretching it into a short speech, after which the champagne was drunk from a silver-gilt loving cup. That Churchill gave the toast was appropriate, as he was the moving spirit behind this unusual celebration. A few days later, Margaret Lloyd George returned to Britain, and Frances Stevenson rejoined David Lloyd George in France.[18]

The political careers of Lloyd George and Churchill were also intertwined. Those careers were eloquent evidence for the proposition that friends stand in a common world with a common destiny.[19] If they stood together, Lloyd George and Churchill did not stand still. They moved rapidly, climbing to high cabinet offices. Without the other, neither likely would have climbed so fast so far. Their friendship was the most important single factor in the political careers of both. It is misleading to argue, as some have done, that they were an unstable tandem, a peculiar mixture thrown together by political accident.[20] They chose freely to become and remain friends, and they were never permanently estranged from each other because neither wanted to be.

When Lenin referred to "the united forces of Lloyd George and Churchill,"[21] he recognized that each was the other's closest, and most important, political ally. Each understood that.[22] Each was psychologically buttressed by the knowledge that the other was there. Lloyd George, who understood that it was Churchill's nature to climb as high as possible, nevertheless had "not the least doubt that he would be willing enough to pick me up afterwards"[23] if Lloyd George ever fell behind.

Lloyd George picked Churchill up after the latter, unfairly blamed for the unsuccessful attempt to conquer Constantinople, which had resulted in many British and colonial deaths at Gallipoli, was sacked from the admiralty in 1915. Lloyd George helped collect evidence to present to the Dardanelles Commission in Churchill's attempt to clear himself of responsibility for the catastrophe of Gallipoli. In early 1916, Prime Minister Asquith, doubtless correctly, suspected Lloyd George of providing information for Churchill to use against the cabinet of which Lloyd George was a leading member. More importantly, Lloyd George fought for a major cabinet office for Churchill after Gallipoli. It had been Lloyd George who in 1911 got Asquith to make Churchill first lord of the admiralty in the first place. When Churchill was forced to leave that job, Lloyd George urged Asquith to give Churchill another senior ministry such as the Colonial Office. Asquith, who was constructing his first coalition cabinet including Conservatives bitterly opposed to giving Churchill anything, demoted Churchill to sinecure office, which Churchill, after being repeatedly humiliated, eventually left. Lloyd George agreed that in the circumstances his friend was right to leave office, but predicted he would soon return.[24]

After Churchill rushed off to military service in France, Lloyd George visited Clementine Churchill with stronger language, "We must get Winston back."[25] These were more than consolatory statements. Lloyd George acted to implement them. When he left, in mid-1916, the Ministry of

Munitions for the War Office, he urged Churchill, who hoped for Munitions, as his successor, again to no avail. That Churchill was out of ministerial office did not prevent contacts with Lloyd George. While Lloyd George was at the War Office, Churchill energetically encouraged Lloyd George's distrust of his military advisers.[26]

While out of office, Churchill also encouraged Lloyd George to push Asquith out of the prime ministership. At the end of 1915 he wrote; "Don't miss yr opportunity. The time has come."[27] Churchill's sense of timing was imperfect. The time had not yet come, but Lloyd George succeeded Churchill as the chief source of activist agitation within the cabinet, trying, sometimes successfully, to wake up the sleeping Asquith. When Lloyd George wanted the War Office, Churchill hoped his friend would get it, though he was powerless to aid that particular effort. Churchill encouraged Lloyd George to resign from the cabinet if a reluctant Asquith would not support conscription.[28]

Even after conscription was implemented for the first time by a British cabinet, Churchill saw Lloyd George as the only possible prime minister to replace Asquith, and hoped that a Lloyd George cabinet would include Churchill. In December 1916, Lloyd George became prime minister, but Churchill was not in the new cabinet. Lloyd George wanted to include him, but the Conservative members of his coalition cabinet firmly and explicitly refused to serve with Churchill.[29] The Conservative leaders hated Churchill, and Gallipoli had given them their weapon. Lord Derby, generally inarticulate, wrote to Lloyd George that Churchill was "absolutely untrustworthy as was his father before him, and he has got to learn that just as his father had to disappear from politics so must he, or at all events from official life."[30] In such circumstances, Lloyd George did what he could for Churchill, and that was quite a lot. As prime minister, Lloyd George did not hesitate to consult the officially excluded Churchill about government policy. Churchill's enemies suspected that Lloyd George had not given up the idea of giving Churchill a ministry.[31] Those enemies were correct. Lloyd George had no intention of forever keeping his promise to the Conservatives. He told his son, "If I can't convince them, I'll outflank them. If I can't outflank them, I'll smash them."[32] To try to convince them, the prime minister told Bonar Law, leader of the Conservative party, that Asquith, hoping to return as prime minister, had promised Churchill the admiralty.[33] Since Asquith's return was unlikely, Bonar Law's personal opposition to Churchill's rehabilitation was probably only slightly softened by this argument. Other leading Conservatives were unaffected by it. That Churchill was willing to change sides was exactly what had caused their hatred of him in the first place.

Lloyd George outflanked Churchill's enemies, and smuggled him back into office. In May 1917, Lloyd George privately assured Churchill that he would soon return to office. Two months later, Lloyd George kept his word, offering Churchill his choice of the Ministry of Munitions or the new Air Ministry. Churchill chose Munitions. The next morning Churchill's appointment was announced to the press. Lloyd George had not asked Bonar Law's consent in advance.[34] A nervous civil servant at Munitions worried, "There'll be fireworks."[35] There were. The most unpopular politician in Britain had been brought back to the cabinet. The storm of Conservative protest was enormous. Churchill's appointment to Munitions may have been the most controversial ministerial appointment in modern British politics. For some days Lloyd George's throne swayed but did not fall. If Churchill's appointment demonstrated the prime minister's personal authority over his cabinet, the outcome of that demonstration was not assured in advance. Lloyd George risked his political career for Churchill.[36] As Lloyd George observed privately at the time: "I have got back Winston. That was not easy . . . but I *have had my way.*"[37] Churchill later credited the staff gathered earlier for the Ministry of Munitions by Lloyd George with any of Churchill's successes as Minister of Munitions.[38]

Churchill never forgot that Lloyd George resurrected him politically. Only Lloyd George's persistence restored Churchill to government office. That persistence was an act of friendship.[39] Churchill's Conservative enemies understood that. The *Morning Post* wrote that by appointing Churchill, the prime minister was proved "to be a man who allows private partiality to overcome public duty."[40] Even while minister of munitions, as Churchill was aware, Churchill needed Lloyd George's protection to survive.[41] He had that protection, and he did survive.

Churchill's appreciation was fulsomely expressed. While at the War Office after January 1919, he presented Lloyd George with the 1914–1915 Star, the British War Medal, and the Victory Medal. Churchill referred to the prime minister as a wonderful man, including in the prime minister's presence. Since long afterward he still spoke with pride of having served under Prime Minister Lloyd George, there is little reason to doubt the genuineness of Churchill's praise. In the general election occasioned by Lloyd George's fall from office in October 1922, Churchill was the most conspicuous of the defeated supporters of the former prime minister.[42] For once in his life, the prospect of defeat did not frighten him. From a hospital sickbed, after an emergency appendectomy, he sent a campaign message to his constituents:

> In the political confusion that reigns, and with causes so precious to defend, I take my stand by Mr. Lloyd George. I was his friend before he was famous. I was with him when all were at his feet. And now today, when men who fawned upon him, who praised even his errors, who climbed into place in Parliament upon his shoulders, have cast him aside . . . I am still his friend and lieutenant.[43]

One of Prime Minister Lloyd George's last acts, entirely appropriately, was to name Churchill as a Companion of Honour.[44] A year later, still without a parliamentary seat, Churchill, looking forward to his next electoral campaign as a Lloyd George Liberal, told his leader, "We are in for a big fight—and I am glad to think *together*."[45] This fight, too, was unsuccessful for Churchill. His next campaign was not as a Liberal of any stripe, but as a "Constitutionalist," a way station on his return to the Conservative party. Lloyd George declined to speak on behalf of Churchill's Liberal rival.[46]

Friendship is a two-way street. Churchill, as he acknowledged late in the Second World War, was the recipient of much kindness from Lloyd George, but he also treated Lloyd George with much kindness.[47] In the Marconi affair, Churchill probably helped save his friend from falling, perhaps a considerable distance.

The origins of Lloyd George's involvement in the Marconi affair were simple, although the political course of that affair was not. In 1912, while chancellor of the exchequer, Lloyd

George uncharacteristically invested in corporate stocks. Rufus Isaacs, the attorney-general, had suggested over dinner that Lloyd George invest in newly-offered shares of the American Marconi Company, of which Godfrey Isaacs, the attorney-general's brother, was managing director. Lloyd George, along with the master of Elibank, Liberal chief whip in the House of Commons, followed his advice. The master of Elibank also invested some Liberal party funds. Lloyd George then sold some of his American Marconi shares and bought others. The net result of his own short flutter on the stock market was to lose money.[48]

Lloyd George's personal financial activities were only a small part of the Marconi affair. Postmaster General Herbert Samuel was negotiating a government contract with the English Marconi Wireless Telegraph Company, Limited, which was legally separate from the American Marconi Company. Shares in one were not shares in the other. The English Marconi Company's contract with the Post Office was to build wireless stations in various parts of the British Empire. Marconi's chief international rival in wireless communication was the German Telefunken Company, hardly likely to receive a British government contract. Samuel never held any Marconi shares, and Lloyd George had no part in drawing up the contract between the Post Office and the English Marconi Company. Lloyd George's sole involvement with any Marconi company was the purchase of American Marconi shares through Isaacs, who was personally close to him.[49] Lloyd George's involvement in the Marconi affair was certainly less than that of Isaacs, who, as Lord Reading, soon became a distinguished lord chief justice. There is no evidence of any illegal behavior by Lloyd George, but he did wait many months before publicly revealing his unprofitable investment. He did nothing dishonorable, but his investment was improvident, indiscreet, and stupid. The tribune of the people should not have had such an eager eye for the financial main chance.[50]

Prime Minister Asquith, who had been Lloyd George's immediate predecessor as chancellor of the exchequer, observed during the Marconi affair that as chancellor it had never occurred to him that he was not free to buy any particular stock.[51] This was probably an accurate statement of the understanding of most British ministers of the Crown

at the time. There were few prohibitions on ministers engaging in personal financial dealings. The possibility of
conflict of interest was seldom discussed and less often
acted upon. One of the few voices raised earlier was Lloyd
George's. In an 1896 Commons debate on proposed land tax
reductions, he had demonstrated that Conservative ministers would benefit personally by their proposed legislation.
During the Boer War, Joseph Chamberlain, the colonial
secretary, had personal financial holdings in firms with
government contracts.[52] Lloyd George had no such holdings,
even during the few months he owned shares in the American Marconi Company.

It may be that the Marconi affair was not really much of
a scandal, or even that it was a trifling matter.[53] Lloyd
George's political career almost foundered over it, nevertheless. The misdeeds of the powerful can be writ large if they
have powerful enemies. Those British politicians who hated
Lloyd George, who were mostly those who had seen no
impropriety in Joseph Chamberlain's financial dealings,
seized upon the Marconi affair as a weapon with which to
destroy Lloyd George. His involvement in Marconi matters
may have been less than Rufus Isaacs's involvement, but
Churchill was probably correct when he argued that Isaacs
was attacked primarily to get at Lloyd George.[54] Isaacs,
unlike Lloyd George, only wanted desperately to join the
British political establishment, not destroy it. He therefore
had few personal enemies in British politics.

It is also probably true that if Lloyd George had not been
at serious risk in the Marconi affair, Churchill would not
have done what he did to defend what he publicly called
Lloyd George's "unstained and stainless honour."[55] Churchill
came vigorously to Lloyd George's aid. He did everything he
could, and more than any other of Lloyd George's cabinet
colleagues, to minimize the political damage. He visited Lord
Northcliffe to request, successfully, that the affair be played
down in Northcliffe's numerous newspapers. This may not
have been much of a sacrifice for Northcliffe, who had concluded, probably correctly, that the British public was much
less interested in the affair than were British politicians.
Lloyd George nevertheless appreciated Northcliffe's action
enough to write a letter of appreciation. Northcliffe was later
pleased to hear that Lloyd George for once thought Northcliffe had acted like a gentleman.[56]

Churchill also persuaded F. E. Smith, a future Conservative solicitor-general, and Edward Carson, a former Conservative solicitor-general and future attorney-general, to represent Isaacs and Samuel in their successful libel suit against *Le Matin*, which had published a damaging account of the Marconi affair.[57] Contrary to later report, Lloyd George, whose name was not mentioned in the *Le Matin* article, was not a party to this libel suit, which was nevertheless important to him because it offered a controlled opportunity publicly to reveal his purchase of shares in the American Marconi Company. Furthermore, Smith and Carson, having served as lawyers for Isaacs and Samuel, could hardly attack their clients in the House of Commons, where their tongues were generally the sharpest among Conservative debaters. Silence from the most partisan of Conservatives and relative silence from the most unpredictable of Conservative press lords were among Churchill's contributions to the cover-up of the Marconi affair. They were substantial contributions to damage control. Churchill also repeatedly carried to Prime Minister Asquith warnings from Lloyd George about the consequences for the Liberal party if Asquith's defense of his colleagues was insufficiently warm.[58]

After Lloyd George effectively defended his conduct in the Marconi affair before a House of Commons select committee and, later, the House itself, Churchill patted him warmly on the back. These gestures were doubtless sincere. Churchill told Lord Riddell that his heart had bled for Lloyd George and that he was delighted with the favorable outcome.[59] Churchill had good reason to be delighted. His most powerful friend was still the most powerful of his friends. Lloyd George survived the Marconi affair. It did not become his Waterloo, or Watergate. If, before Marconi, the world and the kingdoms thereof seemed to be at Lloyd George's feet, that was still essentially true.[60]

Claims that Churchill rescued or saved Lloyd George are exaggerated.[61] C. P. Scott's editorial defense of Lloyd George in the *Manchester Guardian* carried enormous weight within the Liberal party, and Lloyd George's most effective defender was Lloyd George.[62] When he finally swallowed his pride and spoke in his own defense in the House of Commons, A. J. Balfour, a former Conservative prime minister, was moved to tears.[63]

Even a wounded chancellor of the Exchequer has resources. Lloyd George could have found someone else to carry his messages to Northcliffe, Smith, Carson, and Asquith. It was, nevertheless, Churchill who took the initiative to save his friend's career, demonstrating his personal loyalty. He had taken risks for someone he loved.[64]

Of his general loyalty to his friends there could be no doubt.[65] The hero of *Savrola*, the young Churchill in disguise, had revealingly meditated, "a man loves his friend; he has stood by him perhaps at doubtful moments."[66] To argue that Churchill never learned the meaning of personal loyalty is to misread him badly.[67] He was uncritical of his friends, and, in contrast to Lloyd George, he viewed friendship and disagreement as incompatible. Many people were, in fact, bothered by his conception of total personal and political friendship. His friends could be moved by the intensity of his loyalty while they agreed with him.[68] When they disagreed, however, they could be in trouble.

To Lloyd George, the Marconi affair suggested that one could distinguish one's friends from one's foes only in the hours of darkness. He knew he had many enemies, but he did not blame them for his Marconi difficulties. He blamed only himself. When Leo Maxse, one of his most virulent critics in the Marconi affair, died decades later, Lloyd George genuinely grieved over the pain of Maxse's last illness.[69] Contrary to a novelist's suggestion, Lloyd George lost little sleep over his enemies' actions in 1912–1913.[70]

Publicly, Lloyd George acknowledged his debt to his friends.[71] Privately he acknowledged Churchill's loyalty to him in the Marconi affair, and added, "I . . . shall never forget it."[72] He did not forget. When he took Churchill into his cabinet in mid-1917, he invited him to dinner at 10 Downing Street. There he pointed out a framed newspaper headline from the Marconi affair, which read, "Churchill defends Lloyd George."[73]

But even if Lloyd George had wanted to forget his debt to Churchill, there was no chance of it occurring. Among those convinced that he was indebted were Clementine and Winston Churchill. The latter continued to seek repayment long after any debt had been paid in full.[74] Loyal as Churchill was, he did not believe good works were their own reward. Because Lloyd George accepted the fact of his in-

debtedness, and because he understood that Churchill believed friendship and agreement were inseparable, there was
always the possibility that Churchill would someday attempt
to collect on the debt, or even that he would attempt to
collect more than once. Some day came, sooner than Lloyd
George, believed possible. Many others might also have paid
Lloyd George's debt. That is probably the ultimate significance of the Marconi affair. Ironically, if Lloyd George's
political career had ended in 1913, his hands would have
remained as clean of human blood as they had been in the
Boer War. Survival may not be everything, even in politics.

If Lloyd George was, after 1913, asked by a creditor
Churchill to do anything against his own inclination, he had,
nevertheless, no one else, including Churchill, to blame if
he so acted. He still had freedom, and vast power. In particular, he was still Churchill's senior as a British politician. It has been argued that one consequence of the
Marconi affair was finally to make Churchill an equal of
Lloyd George; Churchill no longer had to play second fid-
dle.[75] In the context of their personal relationship, this argument is partially incorrect. Churchill was certainly not
Lloyd George's equal before the Marconi affair, and an essential inequality continued afterward. Churchill deferred to,
venerated, and was in awe of his friend.[76] Churchill thought
Lloyd George was more prestigious than he. In private conversation Churchill was quick to defend and to praise his
friend.[77]

T. E. Lawrence saw Churchill as dominated by Lloyd
George.[78] Churchill often acted as if Lloyd George were his
guru. The personality of Lloyd George certainly attracted him
deeply. He seemed to be under Lloyd George's spell, and
this spell did not disappear even after Churchill returned
to the Conservative party in 1924.[79] They had been in different parties in the beginning of their friendship, and that
friendship survived Churchill's second shift in party. Stanley Baldwin may have hoped to separate the two friends by
naming Churchill as his chancellor of the exchequer,[80] but
this did not happen. The newly Conservative chancellor of
the exchequer, having been visited by the still-Liberal member for Carnarvon Boroughs, related to his parliamentary
private secretary what had just happened: "Within five
minutes the old relationship was completely re-established.

The relationship between Master and Servant." After a dramatic pause, the chancellor added, "I WAS THE SERVANT."[81]

Lloyd George was certainly Churchill's mentor in politics. The former was the master and the latter was the pupil, and Churchill was a faithful disciple to his teacher.[82] To suggest that Churchill was the teacher who taught a provincial Lloyd George how to behave in the big city is risible.[83] Lloyd George's manners were impeccable, and no one, not even Lloyd George, could have taught Churchill good manners. Lloyd George was never a rustic, and Churchill was never a man of the world.

Lloyd George did teach Churchill other things. The first lesson, begun shortly after their first meeting, was the new liberalism, emphasizing social justice, of which he was the most articulate advocate. He wanted to convert Churchill. Lloyd George's careful nurturing and prodding, including in Churchill's own parliamentary constituency, succeeded.[84] It may be that for Churchill, his older friend filled the void that Lord Randolph Churchill could no longer fill and had never filled. Lloyd George was entirely capable of indulgently treating Churchill like a spoiled, naughty child.[85]

In 1904 Churchill marched into the House of Commons and sat next to Lloyd George on the Liberal benches.[86] Lloyd George shook his hand, and Churchill became a Liberal.[87] More precisely, he was a Lloyd George Liberal. He soon made his commitment clear in a speech in Lloyd George's own parliamentary constituency: "Mr. Lloyd George is the best fighting general in the Liberal army."[88] In December 1916, when Lloyd George abandoned the leader of the Liberal party, H. H. Asquith, to become prime minister himself, Churchill followed Lloyd George, not Asquith.[89] At the time Churchill first made clear his allegiance, however, Lloyd George had never held ministerial office, and was still intensely disliked by most Liberal imperialists because of his opposition to the Boer War. Furthermore, the Liberals were in opposition when Churchill first sat next to Lloyd George. The great Liberal electoral victory of 1906 remained in the future. Churchill's original declaration of fidelity to Lloyd George was therefore not without political risks.

Churchill became a Liberal to serve the best fighting general in the Liberal army. In his eulogy of Lloyd George in the House of Commons, Churchill was to say, simply, "I was his lieutenant."[90] That was his self-perceived role, and his language reveals his conception of the chain of command. Before switching parties in 1904, he had been Lloyd George's "young acolyte."[91] Now he was at least an officer, junior but legitimately commissioned. Lloyd George was still his inspiration and he was still Lloyd George's ardent follower, including on major policy matters.[92] Churchill was, however, not the least of Lloyd George's followers; he could fairly claim primacy among them. He became Lloyd George's right-hand man. Those who disliked both often referred to Churchill as Lloyd George's henchman.[93] Sometimes, the servant's diction sounded painfully like that of the master. In 1910, as home secretary, for electoral campaign purposes, Churchill promised the Cabinet's intention "to free Wales from its alien Church."[94]

Even a servant, especially if loyal, has prerogatives. Churchill did not hesitate to use his. In 1919, trying to persuade a reluctant Lloyd George to undo the Russian Revolution, he expressed the hope that "you will not brush away lightly the convictions of one who wishes to remain your faithful lieutenant." Masters also may know a thing or two. Lloyd George, who firmly intended to brush away Churchill's convictions about Bolshevism, responded, also in writing, reminding Churchill that "I have given you tangible proof that I wish you well."[95] This exchange suggests that the lieutenant did not always want to obey his general. This further suggests the possibility that the lieutenant wanted to become not only a general, but the commanding general.

Churchill certainly saw himself as Lloyd George's faithful lieutenant. This self-perception was essentially justified. If he followed, he followed a person, not the holder of a particular office. He was never anyone else's lieutenant. Throughout his two decades as a Liberal, he followed only Lloyd George, who was never during those decades leader of the Liberal party. Before becoming a Liberal, Churchill had been disobedient to the leader and the leaders of the Conservative party. After he returned to the Conservative party, he did not obey Stanley Baldwin or Neville Chamberlain, or any other Conservative. Long afterwards, when he was no longer leader of the Conservative party, Churchill paid no attention to Anthony Eden or Harold Macmillan, or any other Conservative. Lloyd George was by then long dead, but not forgotten.

Friendship can continue to exist after the death of one of the friends. Even across that divide, friendship can remain an echo in the heart.[96] His friend's death in 1945 did not end their relationship for Churchill. If, in 1951, he could not appoint David Lloyd George to ministerial office, he could appoint Gwilym Lloyd George.[97] When his ability to remember started failing, conversational mention of Lloyd George would prod his ability to recollect.[98]

Lloyd George remained always vibrant, but Churchill faded. Churchill forgot his friend's last illness.[99] After Lloyd George's death, there were no members of the House of Commons who could remember the young Winston Churchill. To his much younger parliamentary colleagues, Churchill was an institution, not a person.[100] They did not understand him as Lloyd George had understood him.[101] Now there was no one to be understood by, or even to follow, faithfully or not.

Leadership is the exercise of power over followers. Leaders get followers to do what they want them to do. That Churchill saw himself, as did many others, as Lloyd George's faithful follower may be striking. Even more striking is the apparent absence of any perception by Lloyd George as Churchill's leader. He appears not to have described Churchill as his follower. He would quite probably not have characterized his friend as his lieutenant. That description was Churchill's. The analogy between military and political life was also Churchill's. Lloyd George was a fighter, but not a general, combatant or otherwise. The distinctive feature of power within a military structure is the omnipresence of coercive power. Lloyd George even as prime minister gave orders only to military and civilian servants of the state. His fellow politicians he tried his best to persuade. If he did not take orders from them, he also did not try to give them orders. Even if consensual, not coercive, power had not been his preference, he was far too psychologically sensitive to attempt to coerce Churchill. He had no inner need to coerce others, let alone his best friend.

Whether Lloyd George always succeeded in persuading Churchill, or whether Churchill sometimes succeeded in persuading Lloyd George, remains an open question. Only empirical behavioral evidence can answer that question. Three particular sequences of events may be especially instructive in this respect. The first is the destruction of the legislative power of the House of Lords with the Parliament Act of 1911. The second is British intervention in the emerging Great War in 1914. The third is Winston Churchill's succession to the prime ministership in May 1940. Since the personal relationship of Lloyd George and Churchill may have had more significant political consequences than any other personal relationship in the British experience, the evidence from these three cases may have more than biographical interest.[102] Since the assumption that the friendship of Lloyd George and Churchill dominated British politics only for the first two decades of its existence, until Lloyd George left the prime ministership in 1922, is probably widely shared, evidence from the third case may be additionally instructive.[103]

Chapter Five

Renamed Roses

Names make so much difference.
. . . Some people are ill done by.
—Ivy Compton-Burnett

On Budget Day 1909, the chancellor of the exchequer walked to the House of Commons with the president of the Board of Trade, who had recently succeeded him in that office.[1] The chancellor was observed to walk "lightly and with twinkling eyes," while his friend was "grave with the weight of his colleague's responsibility."[2] The night before that friend had written, "Tomorrow is the day of wrath!"[3]

The chancellor's mood soon changed. Fully conscious of the significance for his political career of the presentation of his first budget, he had prepared a typewritten script that, uncharacteristically, he proceeded to read word for word. This script was one of the longest British parliamentary statements on record, running to about four and one-half hours.[4] The burden proved too much for even the chancellor. Halfway through, his face turned pale, his voice broke, and he started repeating sentences. The president of the Board of Trade took him out for a break, after which the chancellor resumed his speech. When he finally finished speaking, the chancellor judged his performance a "thorough flop."[5] Many of his listeners agreed; this speech may well have been the worst he ever gave. It was certainly poorly delivered.[6]

The chancellor need not have worried about the quality of his speaking. One bad speech would not affect his primacy as a parliamentary speaker. In any event, for the chancellor, speech was always less important than action.[7] Policy mattered more to him than phrasing. Even in a speech, the message was more important than the medium. Words were for him only an instrument of power. The budget speech of 1909 became not only the most important of British budget speeches, but one of the landmarks of modern Western politics because of its creative content, and also because that content was eventually implemented after unprecedentedly bitter and prolonged conflict.[8] The budget speech of 1909 mattered because the budget it presented was the most important and controversial in the British experience.[9] The chancellor wanted to alter the purposes of British government, and he did so. His was the first British budget intended to redistribute the national wealth of Britain.[10] This was no accident. Like Léon Blum, he had long viewed budgets as the central part of the national political process.[11] He had chosen Budget Day 1890 to take his seat in the House of Commons.[12] Budgets were important because they expressed national priorities. The Chancellor's priorities had already been clear in 1906: "There is plenty of wealth in this country to provide for all and to spare. What is wanted is a fairer distribution."[13] If the essence of the "new" Liberalism in Britain early in the twentieth century was that the State budget should be used as an instrument of equalitarian social policy, the chancellor and the president were new Liberals. Indeed, as the most powerful new Liberals, their policy priorities were the essence of the new Liberalism.[14] For the chancellor, he had in 1909 created a "War Budget" designed to raise money "to wage implacable warfare against poverty."[15] Unlike most chancellors, he used his budget to spend, not to save, money.[16] He proposed taxing the wealthy, especially aristocratic landowners, to pay for social welfare programs, in particular, old age pensions.

The chancellor got his way, with the crucial help at every stage of the president of the Board of Trade. They may even have drafted the budget together.[17] With his enormous persuasive gifts, David Lloyd George had made Winston Churchill, in British terminology, a Radical.[18] Together they were determined to create a British welfare state. They did so, and in the process they also reformed the way legislative decisions were made in Britain. The struggle over the budget of 1909 revealed many aspects of power in British society, but none of those aspects was revealed with greater clarity than the personal and political identities of Lloyd George and Churchill. They were again revealed as fighters, and the conflict of 1909–1911 helped reveal what they were willing to fight for, and what they were willing to fight against. They were also revealed as successful fighters, which might not have been evident in 1909. They were the only two cabinet members totally committed to the budget. The cabinet was distinctly unenthusiastic. Only the chancellor's threat to resign got cabinet to accept his budget, which had been discussed at fourteen cabinet meetings before its approval.[19]

Even in the House of Commons, with their fellow Liberals still in solid control after the overwhelming Liberal party victory in the 1906 general election, the task of Lloyd George and Churchill was not easy. There was strong opposition to the budget on the Liberal back benches. Six Liberal members of Parliament left the party with the introduction of that budget.[20] The Gladstonian tradition of "retrenchment" was still strong in the Liberal party. Putting it bluntly but accurately, this tradition meant cutting, not raising, taxes, let alone raising taxes for social justice programs. Traditional Liberals denied that "the State has anything to do with Old Age Pensions or Housing the people."[21] Lord Rosebery, the only living former Liberal prime minister, spoke for these traditionalists when he attacked the 1909 budget as "the end of all, the negation of faith, of family, of property, of Monarchy, of Empire."[22] Gladstone's State had been essentially a night watchman, governing best, in Liberal judgment, because it governed least. Gladstone's Liberalism meant freedom from governmental power.[23] Liberalism in Britain still had the individualistic, rather than social, emphasis it had in the United States before 1933. But governing least was not what Lloyd George and Churchill were in the government to do. Lloyd George put it succinctly, "The duty of a Government is to govern."[24] For him,

"Gladstone was no Liberal," because he had not really cared about the poor.[25] The 1909 budget would certainly have shocked Gladstone. The last Liberal budget that was Gladstonian was Asquith's, in 1908. That had been introduced by the new prime minister, not the new chancellor, under the argument that the former had largely prepared it while still chancellor, probably in the hope of delaying the day of wrath. All six of Lloyd George's budgets as chancellor prior to August 1914 were of a piece.[26]

If Lloyd George's budget speech had been long, the House of Commons debate it initiated was even longer. No other chancellor has had such an endurance test. For seventy parliamentary days and nights the House of Commons argued, taking 554 divisions on specific aspects of the budget. Lloyd George and Churchill would spend their mornings together, planning parliamentary strategy. Churchill was frequently absent from Commons, especially in the evenings, to preside over mass meetings of the Budget League, a single-purpose pressure group created to mobilize public opinion behind Lloyd George's budget. The chancellor had conjured up money to finance this group from rich Liberals.[27]

The House of Commons finally accepted the budget, 379 to 149. Without appropriate modern precedent, the House of Lords rejected it by 350 votes to 75.[28] Prime Minister Asquith dissolved the House of Commons, forcing a general election on the issue called "The Peers versus the People." The ensuing intense struggle over the institutional structure of British government resulted eventually in the Parliament Act of 1911, which effectively destroyed the legislative power of the House of Lords. The major opponents of the legislative power of the House of Lords were Lloyd George and Churchill.[29] The general election of early 1910 kept the Liberals in governmental office. Churchill's prediction that "the people will restore" the budget proved accurate. After the new House of Commons approved Lloyd George's budget, as had its predecessor, the House of Lords accepted it without a division.[30]

Since Lloyd George and Churchill continued unabated their attack upon the House of Lords after it had surrendered on the *casus belli*, the question arises: was the 1909 budget intended to arouse the opposition of the House of

Lords so that its legislative power could be destroyed? That question has been answered negatively, affirmatively, and even with a question mark.[31] Having won the battle with the House of Lords, Lloyd George and Churchill did not later say much about whether they had been eager for combat. In the 1930s, Lloyd George did tell Churchill's son that, as chancellor, he deliberately included land taxes in his 1909 budget to provoke the House of Lords, but such an *ex post* statement by itself proves little about 1909–1911.[32]

Lloyd George and Churchill certainly pursued the House of Lords from 1909 to 1911 with vigor and glee. Even before the Lords rejected his budget, and probably to encourage that rejection, Lloyd George made his memorable speech, arranged by Churchill's Budget League, entitled "The Land and the People" at Limehouse, in which he proclaimed, "Oh, these dukes, how they harass us!"[33] Harassment is, of course, a crime. Shortly after the rejection, Lloyd George told the National Liberal Club, "We have to arrest the animal. We have to see that he perpetrates no further crime." Vengeance was in the air as Lloyd George reported that "we have got them at last. And we do not mean to let them go until all the accounts in the ledger have been settled."[34] To his constituents in North Wales, he confessed that he could not pretend to regret the conflict with the House of Lords. To his brother, he expressed the hope the Lords would reject his budget. To his cabinet colleagues, he made it clear he would resign if this conflict were not settled to his satisfaction.[35]

When the moment of decision came in 1911, the cabinet did in fact accept "the LG-Winston view of tactics—the wisest and the boldest."[36] Those tactics were, as Churchill told Asquith, to "clink the coronets in their scabbards."[37] The new king, George V (Edward VII had died in 1910) was forced to promise that the prime minister could, if necessary, name enough new peers to assure passage by the House of Lords of the Parliament Bill. Churchill wanted to see five hundred new peers created, and informed his acquaintances that they could expect such appointment.[38] The rest of the cabinet was not willing to abolish the House of Lords. Since the cabinet included one baron, one viscount, three earls, and one marquess, this was hardly surprising.[39] Churchill got nowhere with his 1910 suggestion to Prime

Minister Asquith, "The time has come for the total aboli-
tion of the House of Lords."[40] Asquith did, however, entrust
to Churchill much of the strategic burden of guiding the
Parliament Bill through the House of Commons. Lloyd
George, who was also "a single chamber man," was spend-
ing much of his time preparing what would become the
complex National Insurance Act of 1911, the most important structural element of the British welfare state until after
the Second World War. Asquith, especially in the evenings
after dining well, was too drunk to make decisions, as
Churchill lamented. Churchill managed the strategy in
Commons well, and the House of Lords was soon presented
with the Parliament Bill. Mass creation of new peers proved
unnecessary. The House of Lords approved the bill by 131
to 114, with most Lords, as usual, neither present nor
voting.[41]

The continued existence of the House of Lords was
enough for 131 peers. They would not have legislative power, but they would continue to be members of an institution that was the focus of a value system that gave them
social prestige, if it no longer gave them political power.
Until 1911, the House of Lords had been the last institutional weapon of the power of the landed aristocracy, which
had for so many centuries governed Britain. Since the
Reform Act of 1832, when the urban middle class got the
suffrage, the power of the landed aristocrats had gradually
disintegrated. Now that power was gone.[42] Even though the
House of Lords was powerless after 1911, it still had a
function to play in the British political system, as a retirement home for aging members of the political elite. At least
two-fifths of those who held cabinet rank between 1918 and
1959 eventually accepted a peerage.[43]

That Lloyd George and Churchill would be in the van-
guard of the struggle against the House of Lords in 1909–
1911 was predictable on the basis of their earlier words and
deeds. Churchill, at the holiest temple of British Liberalism, the Free Trade Hall in Manchester, had, in 1907, attacked the House of Lords as "the fortress of negation and
reaction." He confidently expected that fortress would fall
and the House of Commons "will be master." He continued
his argument in 1907 by explicitly suggesting that the Liberal cabinet should use a budget to defeat the House of

Lords.[44] This is exactly what happened in 1909–1911. In late 1908, Churchill was saying privately of the House of Lords, "We shall send them up such a Budget . . . as shall terrify them, they have started the class war, they had better be careful."[45] In early 1909, publicly in Birmingham, he envisioned a conflict "upon the plain simple issue of aristocratic rule against representative government."[46] In autumn 1909, he was hoping that the House of Lords would reject the budget.[47] Budget Day 1909 was the first chance either Lloyd George or Churchill had to present a budget, and no other leading Liberals had their devotion either to social justice or to destroying the power of the House of Lords, let alone to both goals.

If there was prior intention to use the 1909 budget against the House of Lords, it was shared by Lloyd George and Churchill, and probably, at least fully, by no other major Liberal leader. Churchill was the only Liberal minister (and not yet at cabinet level) to support Lloyd George's eagerness for action against the House of Lords in 1907.[48] Lloyd George did not give up. The next year he attacked "the malignant destructiveness" of "the charnel house across the road."[49] His persistence was not surprising, since already in 1893 he had urged "the pursuit and lynching" of the House of Lords, and at the turn of the century he wanted to geld the House of Lords.[50] On the evening after the 1909 budget was approved by the House of Commons, Lloyd George entertained at a celebratory dinner where there was only one toast: "May the Lords reject the Budget!"[51] When, in late 1909, Churchill published a book-length personal campaign manifesto attacking the House of Lords in some of his most elegant, polished prose, it was hardly likely that such prose was born in the heat of a general election campaign whose timing appeared entirely situationally determined.[52] Churchill, like Lloyd George, had been waiting for the opportunity to speak his piece, and, like Lloyd George, he had his words ready.

When Lloyd George and Churchill walked to the House of Commons on Budget Day 1909, they knew what they were doing, and the importance of what they were doing. They understood that the budget would be a bitter pill not only to Edward VII but to all the remaining elements of the oldest order in British society.[53] When Edward VII wrote to the

Prince of Wales that Winston Churchill's initials made him "well named," the king, for once, knew what he was doing.[54] When Queen Alexandra tried to prevent Churchill from being invited to a Court function with other ministers of the Crown, she knew what she was doing. When Edward VII refused to have Lloyd George as the minister in attendance at Windsor Castle, he knew what he was doing. When their son, George V, disliked Lloyd George and Churchill, he knew what he was doing. To the royal entourage, Lloyd George and Churchill were ignorant and irresponsible. When the occupants of the aristocratic stands at the coronation of George V booed Lloyd George, they knew what they were doing. The duke of Beaufort had spoken for an entire social class when he yearned to get Lloyd George and Churchill in the midst of his large pack of hounds.[55] The hostility was mutual, and the hunters had become the hunted.

British political metaphors were still close to the earth. During the conflict over the House of Lords, Lloyd George described the eldest sons of peers as "the first of the litter."[56] His closest friend may have winced slightly at the language. Churchill was the son of Lord Randolph Churchill, who was, in turn, a younger son of the seventh duke of Marlborough. Winston Churchill's paternal grandfather was tenth in seniority among the twenty nonroyal dukes of the United Kingdom when his grandson was born in 1874. The Marlboroughs were not, as Benjamin Disraeli correctly told Queen Victoria, especially rich for dukes. Winston Churchill was nevertheless born in what came at least close to being the biggest private house in England, Blenheim Palace.[57] Whether or not Blenheim was correctly named, it was undeniably a palace. As a small boy, Churchill received a gift from the Prince of Wales, who was dining at the home of Lord and Lady Randolph Churchill. As a teenager, Winston Churchill sailed with the future George V.[58]

For a time in the 1890s, after the death of Lord Randolph Churchill and before his cousin, the ninth duke of Marlborough, had a son, Winston Churchill was the heir presumptive to the dukedom of Marlborough. While some persons seem to have assumed that he was a nobleman, Winston Churchill was born, lived, and died a commoner. His father was also a commoner, contrary to the beliefs of some. Lord Randolph Churchill had a title by courtesy only. Younger sons of dukes are entitled, in the United Kingdom, by courtesy only, to be called "Lord." Holders of courtesy titles are not peers.[59] Since he was not an eldest son, Lord Randolph Churchill got no more than courtesy. If he had been a Peer of the Realm, he would have been called "Randolph, Lord Churchill" and his brilliant if abbreviated career in the House of Commons would have been impossible.

Winston Churchill's social origins were in fact upper middle class. He was a child of privilege, but two privileges commonly associated with his social class were denied him. He did not receive a university education, and he did not inherit wealth. He was shipped off by his parents to Sandhurst, not Oxford nor Cambridge. He did not inherit wealth from his parents because they had almost nothing to leave him or his brother. At his death, Lord Randolph Churchill's debts to a Rothschild bank almost exceeded his assets. His widow, therefore, received less than £10,000. She had no other source of income.[60] Her older son complained to her that "we are damned poor."[61] Poverty was in this case relative, but the claim by Joseph Goebbels that Churchill was "a British plutocrat" was a substantial exaggeration.[62] The net value of Lady Randolph Churchill's estate was only £2,480.[63] Her son lived well indeed as an adult, as did Lloyd George, but he earned himself what he so readily spent, as did Lloyd George.

Not only could Winston Churchill not inherit a real title from his father, he could not inherit even a courtesy title. He was simply "Mr. Winston Churchill." That was not originally his name; he was christened Winston Leonard Spencer-Churchill. When he entered Harrow, he signed his name Winston Spencer-Churchill. Throughout his adult life, he was identified as Spencer-Churchill in the Court Circular whenever he had an audience with the monarch. The Spencers had entered the picture when Anne, daughter of John Churchill, first duke of Marlborough, married Charles Spencer, earl of Sunderland, making, under special dispensation, their progeny the line of the dukes of Marlborough.[64]

While at Harrow, Winston Spencer-Churchill simplified his name, probably because he disliked being near the end of the line whenever school boys were arranged alphabetically.[65] The simplified name had its own disadvantage, how-

ever. The initials it gave Winston Churchill might not always arouse respect. Lesser personages than Edward VII
made fun of them.[66] In consequence, as a young man he
settled gradually upon Winston Spencer Churchill, which
was dignified but not stuffy, a commoner's name but still
distinctive. Churchill would have agreed with Lord Northcliffe, who thought an appropriate name was helpful in a
political career, and with Rufus Isaacs's son, who thought
a politician's name should be a proclamation of personal
identity.[67] Churchill's new name also helped, especially when
he was trying as a young politician to support himself by
journalism and authorship, to avoid his being confused with
an American novelist also named Winston Churchill. It is
possible that some readers of the British Churchill's only,
and early, novel *Savrola* nevertheless thought they were
reading a book by the American Churchill.[68] Being confused
with someone else appealed to Winston Spencer Churchill
as little as standing near the ends of lines had earlier.

Churchill's chosen name satisfied him until almost the
end of his long life. He declined more than one opportunity
to acquire a new, noble, name. During the Second World
War, some of his followers hoped to make their leader a
duke, but nothing came of this hope. After his forced retirement from the prime ministership when the Conservative party lost the general election of 1945, Churchill was
offered, by George VI, a dukedom. He would apparently have
become duke of Dover. This was the first offer of a dukedom to a non-royal Britisher in the twentieth century. But
Churchill refused a dukedom, as he also refused George VI's
offer of a consolation prize, which would have made him a
Knight of the Garter. In the Honors List published at the
beginning of 1946, Churchill's name appeared as a recipient of the Order of Merit, the highest honor in the gift of
the Crown that does not confer any title upon the recipient. Later that year, Clementine Churchill accepted the
Grand Cross of the Order of the British Empire. Contrary
to conventional usage, she refused to be called "Dame Clementine," preferring to remain plain Mrs. Winston Churchill.
In May 1965, a few months after her husband's death,
Clementine Churchill accepted a life peerage, becoming
Baroness Spencer-Churchill of Chartwell.[69]

Winston Churchill resolutely refused to accept a peerage.

He would not listen to suggestions from his Conservative party subordinates during his second prime ministership, after 1951, that he go to the House of Lords, which would have made his continued exercise of power difficult even if he had remained prime minister.[70] Those Conservatives who wanted to ship him off to the House of Lords probably thought it would be a polite way to enable themselves to exercise governmental power, but Churchill may not have considered such suggestions even to be polite. In 1907, he had spoken with contempt of a fellow politician who "luckily escaped from the rage of his constituents into an asylum in the House of Lords."[71] Churchill's lieutenant, Brendan Bracken, was probably expressing his master's view when he referred to the House of Lords as "the Morgue."[72] For Churchill, the House of Lords was at best a place of rest for defeated politicians, and Churchill did not view himself as defeated, not yet anyway. In 1953 he had a nightmare in which he found himself speaking in the House of Lords.[73]

Also in 1953, Churchill did accept, from a young Elizabeth II, who had not been around for any of the struggles Churchill had had with or over several of her predecessors, the Order of the Garter, becoming Sir Winston Churchill, K.G.[74] He may have forgotten his earlier acceptance of the view that there was "no damned merit" about the Garter.[75] In 1955, finally defeated by old age, Churchill retired from the prime ministership and toyed with the idea of becoming duke of London before deciding against it.[76] He preferred to stay in the House of Commons. He would speak there no more, but at least he would be where the interesting speeches and the action were. Furthermore, the company was more congenial to him, and he was still Father of the House. He retired from the House of Commons only a few months before his death in 1965. He never sat, and he never wanted to sit, in the House of Lords. His doctor was correct in perceiving, "The House of Lords means nothing to him."[77]

Lloyd George's nomenclature is equally revealing. As Lloyd George realized, Churchill was the only British politician ever to address the adult Lloyd George as "David."[78] That was Churchill's customary usage, except when he addressed Lloyd George, even in public, as simply "My dear."[79] The rest of the world, not being permitted, or in some cases not wanting, this degree of familiarity, was less certain of how to address, or refer to, Lloyd George.[80] Some called him "Lloyd George" and others called him "George." The latter usage angered him, for he considered it an insult. His enemies therefore took pains to address him as "My Dear George."[81] Which surname was (or is), used helps to sort out, at least among the knowledgeable, those who admired (or admire), Lloyd George from those who did (or do), not.

Lloyd George's father's name was William George. Before her marriage, Lloyd George's mother was Elizabeth Lloyd. Their older son was born in 1863 in Manchester.[82] When her husband died, Elizabeth Lloyd George, pregnant with another son, moved back to North Wales, to live with her unmarried brother Richard Lloyd. Her sons, and an older daughter, addressed the head of their childhood household as "Uncle Lloyd."[83] Lloyd George was baptized into the Disciples of Christ tradition at the age of twelve. The baptismal record, in Richard Lloyd's hand, gives the new disciple's name as "David Lloyd-George."[84] Throughout his childhood he had been called, and had called himself, "David Lloyd."[85] When he was nineteen, the *Carnarvon Herald* referred to him as "Mr. George." When he was first in Parliament in 1890, he was already identified in Hansard as "David Lloyd George." His signature was unhyphenated.[86]

Lloyd George liked to recall that he was "one of the children of the people" who had become "a man of the people."[87] He claimed to have been raised "in a workman's home."[88] These appealing assertions were taken at face value by many, who accepted the picture of a cottage-bred boy who was "at heart, a peasant." The gullible saw Lloyd George as a "plebeian" who "had earlier tasted poverty." Whether he had been "poor" or "penniless" in childhood, his working-class origins were seen as "very humble."[89] Long after his death it was reported that Lloyd George had been born in a small Welsh cottage.[90]

Although no British prime minister before Lloyd George had come from humbler origins, Lloyd George was not in his social origins the British Lincoln.[91] Britishers of working-class background had no chance to climb to the top of the greasy pole in Lloyd George's generation. His social origins were in fact petty bourgeois or lower middle class.[92] His childhood was not spent in poverty. His family was

probably the best off in the village of Llanystumdwy. Richard Lloyd's shoemaking business employed five persons. The
Lloyd and George home was comfortable. It still stands, solid
as the Welsh rock from which it is made. Everyone in that
home understood that William George's children would never
work at manual labor.[93]

Lloyd George and his brother were both trained as solicitors. Shortly after his sixteenth birthday, the older brother
was articled to a firm of solicitors, specializing in agricultural interests, in a nearby market town. The additional
training needed to become a barrister might have been impossible for Lloyd George's family at the time, but later,
when he could well afford that additional training, Lloyd
George declined to qualify as a barrister. While he was a
young practicing solicitor, requirements for qualifying as a
barrister were reduced, but he did not take advantage.[94] For
him, the practice of law at any level had no inherent value,
only instrumental value, as a gateway to politics. His first
legal cases, especially those defending Nonconformists
against religious discrimination, made Lloyd George's name
known throughout North Wales. All of his legal cases helped
support him and his growing family while members of Parliament were still unsalaried, which they were until 1911.
To gain the support of reluctant Labor members of Parliament for his National Insurance Bill, Chancellor Lloyd
George decided that members of Parliament should receive
a salary. Lloyd George did not regret not becoming a barrister. He suggested, probably correctly, that being a solicitor was better preparation than was being a barrister for
making practical political decisions. He saw, and practiced,
the legal profession as a means of resolving, not creating,
human conflict. He was the first solicitor to serve as chancellor of the exchequer, and of this he was proud. He was
also the first,[95] and so far the only,[96] solicitor to become
prime minister.

As a solicitor he was a member of the professional middle class. When he died one of his properties was a farm
with seven hundred acres of productive land, employing
eighty persons. He left an estate of approximately
£140,000.[97] That was quite a tidy sum in 1945. What was
surprising was not that Lloyd George had acquired so much,
but, considering the luxurious scale on which he lived, there

was anything left. He was never thrifty. Even as a teenager he was a generous tipper.[98] Lenin was not far wrong when he described Lloyd George as "that big, not petty, bourgeois."[99]

Lenin was, however, entirely off the mark when he described Lloyd George as "the leader of the British bourgeoisie."[100] To see Lloyd George as "essentially a middle-class statesman" is mistaken.[101] He was from, but not of, the British middle class. His political values were those of a radical reformer of society. He was not a man of the people, but he was on the side of the people. More precisely, he was not a peasant, but he spoke for the peasants. He was a rural radical, whom Trotsky, much more wisely than Lenin, saw as an agrarian reformer, and whom his British enemies correctly saw as an agrarian agitator.[102] The North Wales in which Lloyd George grew up was still essentially agricultural, and characterized by great inequalities in economic, political, and social aspects of rural life. For him, one of Gladstone's many sins was being a landlord in North Wales.

Lloyd George's earliest political memory was of newly enfranchised Liberal voters being evicted from their land by Conservative landlords after the 1868 general election, before the secret ballot was adopted in Britain.[103] He never forgot such injustices, and to remove them became his cause. That cause became a, perhaps the, major unifying theme in his political life. Throughout his career, he never deviated from hostility to the rural landlords of Britain. He fought constantly for land reform, by urging measures ranging from heavy taxes on wealthy landowners, as in the 1909 budget, to nationalization of the land. Accepting the labor theory of value, he saw hardworking peasants oppressed by idle landowners.[104] The "land of England" therefore properly belonged, not to landed aristocrats, but to "the peasants of England."[105] Lloyd George's position on land reform was always the most advanced among major British politicians, although Churchill went some of the way with him. He was often more advanced than many of his rural followers. In early 1914, for instance, he favored more sweeping land reform than did the National Farmers Union. As prime minister, he pushed through Parliament the Agriculture Act (1920), which secured tenancy. Under him, cabinet policy favored farm workers and small farmers at the expense of large aristocratic landowners.[106] This preference reflected his conviction that "the land and the agricultural laborer are at the root of the whole social evil." Because "the land question" was "the real issue," it was necessary to "break down the remnants of the feudal system."[107]

That he always tried to improve the lives of those who worked the land, generally without owning much of it, was one of Lloyd George's strengths, but it has also been seen as a possible weakness. There were certainly remnants of feudalism in twentieth-century Britain. The North Wales where he grew up probably had more such remnants than most of the rest of Britain. That rest, however, was already urbanized and industrialized when Lloyd George began his political career, during which agriculture became increasingly less typical of Britishers' lives. It has been argued that Lloyd George saw, and continued to see, social conflict in rural rather than urban terms.[108] His continuing devotion to land reform is therefore seen as having been increasingly irrelevant to urbanized Britishers. Among those were industrial workers, of whose problems Lloyd George seemed to some critics to have had insufficient understanding. He seemed to lack cultural identity with the working class.[109] This divergence received its classic expression at Christmas 1915, when David Kirkwood, a toolfitter at a Clydeside factory, introduced the minister of munitions as "the enemy of the workers."[110]

Enemy Lloyd George never was. He was not born into, nor did he live in, the working class, and there were relatively few factory workers in his parliamentary constituency. Thus, he may have lacked substantial direct personal experience of the lives of urban industrial workers.[111] To assume, however, that he was the enemy of the workers because he was not one of them is to make a serious intellectual error, compounded in this case due to Lloyd George's distinctive characteristics. Far more than most politicians, he understood other people's problems without needing to have been, or be, in their shoes. His unquestioned devotion to land reform did not rest on his having been, or being, a tenant farmer or farm laborer. He fought other people's battles for them, whether he knew them personally or not. He had never met a Boer farmer before he began his fight against the Boer War. It is probably true that Lloyd George's concern was greater for British workers who were in weak unions or who had no union to fight for them, just as his concern for British farmers was greater for the landless than for the landed.[112] Since he was no respecter of institutions, his concern was for industrial workers as persons more than for their institutions, trade unions, and the Labor party. His preference among British social classes was clearly for the working class.[113] Lloyd George's budget of 1909 was in their interest. Lloyd George's National Insurance Bill of 1911, so bold as to have made Beatrice Webb "aghast," was in their interest.[114] British workers knew who was on their side. For many decades, health and old age benefit payments under the National Insurance Act were popularly known as "the Lloyd George benefit," or simply "the Lloyd George."[115] Some recipients of those benefits might have said, with Flora Thompson's grateful old age pensioners, "God bless that Lord George!"[116] Some recipients might even have agreed with the author of the National Insurance Act when he proclaimed that the act was "doing the work of the Man of Nazareth."[117]

Churchill was correct in arguing that no British politician had done more for the working class than Lloyd George as chancellor of the exchequer.[118] Lloyd George was the leading Liberal most sympathetic to the Labor party. He was therefore the most popular Liberal politician among working-class Britishers. Early in the twentieth century, Keir Hardie, who counted him among the socialists, urged Lloyd George to become the leader of the Labor party. Early in 1931 George Lansbury made the same appeal.[119]

Lloyd George was surely tempted by such offers. His instincts, as he recognized, were on the left, and there he stayed until the end. He may well have been anticapitalist.[120] He saw "something fundamentally wrong with our economic system. It is based upon injustice and it cannot last."[121] He did not respect the wealthy any more than he despised the poor. He criticized his own party for being excessively plutocratic.[122] He nevertheless stayed in that party while the British working class was creating and sustaining its own party. What separated Lloyd George from British workers was not Lloyd George, but the Liberal party.

Chasing landed aristocrats, and catching them, undeniably gave special pleasure to Lloyd George, and for many decades he did nothing to conceal his contempt for them. As the victorious prime minister at the end of the First World War, he accepted the Order of Merit and refused, from a repentant George V, any honor that carried a knighthood with it. Although his wife became "Dame Margaret," Lloyd George had determined to remain a commoner. Since he detested titles this was appropriate. At heart he was a republican, not a monarchist. After a royal visit to Wales in 1937, Lloyd George laughed at the thought of a knighthood. A few months later, on his seventy-fifth birthday, playing golf at Antibes, he enjoyed hearing that entirely false rumors were spreading back in Britain that he was going to the House of Lords. The closest he came in the next several years to a seat in the House of Lords was in 1942 to preside, presumably in his capacity as Father of the House of Commons, at an unusual joint gathering of the two Houses to hear Jan Smuts speak.[123]

The time came when Lloyd George's life and political career both took a decisive, and dramatic, turn. In late 1944, ill with carcinoma of the liver and arteriosclerosis, he became preoccupied with the physical demands presented by campaigning for reelection to his House of Commons seat in the next general election, whose date would presumably be determined by the end of the Second World War. He recognized that wartime geographical mobility had changed the social composition of the Carnarvon Boroughs electorate. He was not confident that any Liberal candidate, even the most famous, could carry the constituency if there were other candidates. Other parties were not willing to commit themselves in advance not to contest the seat, and he did not feel physically able to make the several speeches a contest would surely require.[124] He desperately wanted to have an official platform from which to speak on the forthcoming peace settlement.[125] As the only surviving author of the Treaty of Versailles, perhaps he was not only entitled but obligated to speak. After the request was indirectly passed along to him, Prime Minister Churchill offered his oldest friend an earldom, and Lloyd George accepted, apparently with pleasure.[126] If it is difficult to imagine Lloyd George seeking membership in the House of Lords, it is even more difficult to imagine him seeking such membership from any prime minister other than Churchill. The officials of the Order of the Garter, whose life experiences had perhaps not been extensive, refused the request of the new earl to bear the title "Earl Lloyd George of Dwyfor" because, they argued, his name was George, not Lloyd George. Upon production of Lloyd George's baptismal certificate, Letters Patent were issued for Earl Lloyd-George of Dwyfor.[127] Lloyd George chose for his new name the River Dwyfor, which falls from the North Welsh mountains into the sea at Cardigan Bay. On the banks of the Dwyfor, David Lloyd had grown into David Lloyd George.

Churchill had once shed a hyphenated name, and now, a half-century later, he gave Lloyd George a spare hyphen. Earls in the United Kingdom wear coronets, and are officially styled cousins of the monarch.[128] The great commoner of British politics became an honorary cousin of George VI. The new earl's loyal followers were much saddened, and Richard Lloyd would have been. Lord Beaverbrook, of all people, gently told Lloyd George as much.[129] From this perspective, Beaverbrook was right. Lloyd George's renunciation of himself seems not only sad but pointless. Not many paid much attention to his new name. Richard Lloyd George, who had been cut out of his father's will, inherited his father's title if not his money. Questions from the curious about the title aggravated the son, who was slow to call himself "Earl Lloyd-George."[130] In registering her husband's death, the Countess Lloyd-George of Dwyfor gave the name of the deceased as "David Lloyd-George."[131] His great tomb, where he lies alone, overlooking the wildest rapids of the River Dwyfor and covered by an enormous rock from that river, bears only the legend: David Lloyd George.[132] At Chequers, the country home of British prime ministers, acquired as a gift to the nation by Prime Minister Lloyd George, windows are decorated with coats of arms of individual prime ministers, including Churchill. There is no Lloyd George window. However, the first Earl Lloyd-George of Dwyfor did construct his own noble coat of arms. He chose as his motto these words, in Welsh: "Truth against the World."[133] These words are also the motto of the Eisteddfod.[134] Lloyd George's fear in late 1944 that he would lose his seat at the next election may have been overly pessimistic. An obscure Liberal candidate won the contested by-election occasioned by Lloyd George's resignation from the House of Commons, although the seat was later narrowly won by the Conservative party in the general election of 1945.[135] Lloyd George died before he could sit in the House of Lords, and he had been dead many months before the general election of 1945 took place.[136] Even if he had lived, he would never have been able to speak on the peace settlement ending the Second World War, for there was no peace settlement. Only the last of these developments would have saddened David Lloyd George. That was why, long before 1945, he was one of the lords of the earth.

On 28 March 1955, the prime minister rose to speak one last time as prime minister, and one last time in the House of Commons, to move approval of a statue of the late member for Carnarvon Boroughs. The prime minister's motion was approved. A statue of Lloyd George now flanks the Churchill Arch leading into the chamber of the House of Commons.[137] There is no memorial to Lloyd George and Churchill in the House of Lords except for the idle chatter of the powerless.

Chapter Six

Scorched Flesh

The very core of friendship, then,
is the ability to make demands.
     —Andrew M. Greeley

Largely because of his determined opposition to the Boer
War, David Lloyd George was widely regarded as having been
a pacifist before the First World War. Some thought he was
that unappealing creature, a known pacifist, and others
thought he represented militant pacifism. It has been assumed that his opposition to the Boer War was a demonstration of his pacifism and that at particular times after
the Boer War but before 1914, Lloyd George was still a
pacifist. A more inclusive judgment is that for the first
twenty or twenty-four years of his parliamentary career, he
was a pacifist. A variation of the latter judgment is that
before 1914, Lloyd George was a pacifist.[1] That at some
point in his life he became a former pacifist is often assumed.[2] For those who do not approve of pacifism, 1914
brought "a change in convictions and the finest opportunity of his life" to Lloyd George, who "had always been a
pronounced pacifist."[3] A less partisan judgment is that in
1914, the prospects of action dissolved his pacifism.[4] The
implication that only lack of ministerial office prevented his
support of the Boer War is surely unjustified, as is the

assumption that before 1914, Lloyd George's life lacked action. Others have argued with equal certainty and simplicity that Lloyd George was never a pacifist, not even in the Boer War.[5] That he was not a pacifist is as common a conclusion as that he was a pacifist.[6]

Both conclusions often flow from conceptual confusion about the nature of pacifism. Such confusion is not confined to those trying to understand David Lloyd George.[7] Whatever pacifism is, it involves a conviction that since no war is just, no war should be waged. For a pacifist, peace is not only a value, but the highest value, in politics. Politics is about priorities, and for a pacifist, peace is the highest priority. There is no evidence that a pacifist position was ever articulated in public by Lloyd George. Even if he had made such a statement, his convictions should be ascertained by deeds, not words. He was, after all, a man of political action, not a philosopher. His actions might reveal something hidden by, or from, his words. This possibility is suggested by the argument that Lloyd George was before 1914 a *de facto* pacifist.[8] Enough refusals to concede the justice of particular wars might be evidence of an unexamined pacifist consciousness. Opposition to one war, however dramatically expressed, hardly suffices as proof of pacifism.

Politicians who hold more advanced views than their followers might well decline to express their convictions in public. Timidity in public expression of his views was hardly typical of Lloyd George, however. There is no evidence that he ever expressed pacifist conviction in private conversation or correspondence. Considering the general candor of his conversation and correspondence, it is unlikely that he was holding something significant back from his followers. Indeed, it may be that at least some of those followers were more advanced in their views on peace than was their leader. During the Boer War, Lloyd George surely led pacifists, although his own opposition to that war may have been because it did not meet his criteria for a just war.[9] Lloyd George may have been "next door to a pacifist," but pacifism is an either-or proposition.[10] Next door is another household, not the indivisibility of peace. During the Boer War, Lloyd George may have only been visiting his pacifist neighbors, perhaps for the purpose of leading them, without being or becoming one of them.[11]

Lloyd George suggested as much, in speaking to a Nonconformist audience in November 1914. Recognizing those who maintain that war "is not justifiable under any conditions," Lloyd George described himself as unable "to attain in this world quite that altitude of idealism."[12] Much later, during the Second World War, Lloyd George refused to meet with "one of the Pacifist types that I have never been, nor am likely to become, until I reach the infinite tranquillity of the Elysian Fields."[13] Those fields may have never been reached. Lloyd George confessed he found it very hard to be a Christian, for he could not bring himself to turn the other cheek.[14] Very hard does not mean impossible, and Lloyd George may have been unduly hard on himself there. If he found turning the other cheek difficult, he was hardly alone among Christians. He was far from a violent person. He never killed another human being, and he had nothing but contempt for those who hunted animals to kill them. He never, so far as is known, committed any act of physical violence on another person. He was never fascinated by weapons. In this he was unlike Winston Churchill, who even as a civilian not only frequently carried a gun but knew how to use it and was warmly praised by his bodyguard for understanding guns.[15]

Intellectually, Lloyd George accepted the legitimacy and efficacy of some violent acts in politics. Before he was elected to Parliament, he wrote approvingly in his diary of assassinations of British landlords, including Lord Limerick in Ireland. Political murder could be "an act of political justice and expediency of the highest order," dangerous primarily because it could be construed "by both fanatics and villains as a justification and incitement for all murder."[16] Political violence could therefore be licit. This situation did not involve that form of political violence called war, but Lloyd George acknowledged, for instance, the right of the Boers to defend themselves against British soldiers.[17] If defensive violence, including war, was legitimate, Lloyd George's residence was not in the house of the pacifists.

There is no doubt, however, that Lloyd George detested war. As he assumed the prime ministership in December 1916, he stated: "I hate war; I abominate it."[18] Even his most severe critics within the Liberal party conceded that his hatred of war and his love of peace were real. He had, after all, been nurtured in a Nonconformist community that hated war. War was to him a calamity, and he was never a warmonger. Before 1914 Lloyd George was persistently peace minded.[19] Peace was certainly a value for him, but it may have been at least partly an instrumental rather than an inherent value. He saw peace as the prerequisite for social justice, which was undoubtedly his highest political value. War was the negation of everything for which he stood because it prevented—as one of many obstacles—real political achievement.[20] This good shepherd was willing, if necessary, to defend his flock from the wolves.

It has been argued that before 1914, war and its problems had never crossed Lloyd George's horizon.[21] This argument is unkind and, worse, untrue. Lloyd George had certainly taken due note of the Boer War, and much of his criticism of British policy in that war was aimed precisely at what he viewed as the unnecessary cruelty of that policy. It is nevertheless true that Lloyd George seldom thought about the horrors of war in the abstract. He was horrified, however, as a new member of Parliament, by the indifference with which advocates of new weapons spoke of their superior destructiveness "as if it were a matter of destroying vermin."[22] Armaments were for him "the mechanism of butchery."[23] As chancellor of the exchequer, he nevertheless consented, if reluctantly, to substantial expenditures for new armaments. He could have refused and meant it. He was, after all, the leader of the British left.

Lloyd George did not expect these British armaments to be used in a major war. He paid little attention to the possibility of a general European war because, like many other European liberals before 1914, he thought such a war was too irrational to be a serious possibility. He was at heart a peacemaker who believed in the rationality of all human beings.[24] He was, as he acknowledged in 1903, a hopeful man, who believed that "the time will come when, in spite of the armaments . . . there will be no more war."[25] That time would come soon, he was confident. He argued in 1911 that war is not a permanent institution, for it was already receding along the same dark road as the duel.[26] That communities of human beings could be even more bloodthirsty than individual human beings did not strike him. In this he was a liberal to the core.

Because war was for him an avoidable, indeed eradicable, human problem, Lloyd George along with so many others did not foresee the First World War. At the beginning of 1914, the Liberal *Daily Chronicle* published an interview in which the chancellor of the exchequer opposed further increases in British armaments precisely because there was no threat of war.[27] Even this modest embrace of limitations on the arms race was later judged to be "as provocative of war as any public utterance recorded by history."[28] On 17 July 1914, the chancellor told an audience of City bankers that in foreign affairs, "the sky has never been more perfectly blue."[29] Six days later, on the day of the Austro-Hungarian ultimatum to Serbia, he told the House of Commons that, since British-German relations had improved, his future budgets could reduce expenditures on armaments. On the evening of 26 July 1914, Lloyd George was convinced that, though the European situation was serious, there would be no war.[30] Two days later, he wrote to Margaret Lloyd George, "I still believe peace will be preserved."[31] He certainly did not expect Britain to become a belligerent.[32]

The argument that at the turn of July-August 1914 it was reasonable to assume that Lloyd George would come out forcefully for British intervention in the emerging European war is without foundation.[33] So is the assertion that Lloyd George's instincts were for war.[34] Those instincts were surely against war. Many noninterventionists, including pacifists, expected him to oppose British entry into the war.[35] That was an entirely reasonable expectation. Although he was not a pacifist, Lloyd George was hardly likely to be among the enthusiasts for any war, let alone one so utterly lacking in justification as the emerging European war.

There were in early August 1914 many Britishers who wanted Britain to remain neutral. Some, but not all, of those who opposed British entry into the war were pacifists, mostly Nonconformist pacifists. The political situation required only a decision concerning British involvement in a particular war, not proclamation of a universally binding ethical norm. All pacifists would oppose this war, as they would oppose all wars. Many, perhaps most, Britishers who were not pacifists initially favored neutrality in this particular war. The British debate over intervention was therefore not simply a case of pacifists *versus* nonpacifists.

The social forces supporting British neutrality were substantial. A novelist's claim that a majority of Britishers
favored neutrality may well be correct. On 1 August 1914,
George V wrote in his diary that public opinion in Britain
was "dead against our joining in the war."[36] A single-purpose pressure group, the Neutrality League, had been created on 28 July 1914 by Norman Angell, supported
financially by, among others, C. P. Scott, editor of the
Manchester Guardian, to argue that the power that Britain
could exercise as a neutral would be lost to a belligerent
Britain. Not only the *Manchester Guardian*, the keeper of the
Liberal conscience, but almost all Liberal newspapers and
journals of opinion, from the mass-circulation *Daily Chronicle* to the intellectuals' *Nation*, supported neutrality. Robert Donald, editor of the *Daily Chronicle*, spoke with Lloyd
George, who was his suburban neighbor, before coming out
for neutrality.[37]

Capital and labor were agreed on the necessity of British neutrality. The bankers and financiers of the City of
London visited the chancellor of the exchequer to urge
neutrality. Prime Minister H. H. Asquith accepted that the
City opposed war.[38] The bankers and financiers feared that
if Britain entered the war, it would cease to be the wealth-
iest of nations and London would cease to be the financial
capital of the world. By 1918 both of these fears had been
realized. On 30 July 1914, the Parliamentary Labor party
unanimously approved a resolution opposing British intervention. This resolution reflected the feelings of many British workers. Two days later the British Section of the
Socialist International issued a manifesto—signed by its
chairman, Keir Hardie, and its secretary, Arthur Henderson—against the war. Hardie and Henderson feared that if
there were a general European war, the international socialist movement would disintegrate. This fear was also
realized.[39] National consciousness eventually triumphed in
1914–1918 over class consciousness for European workers.

The Liberal party, not the Labor party, was of course
governing Britain. The claim that before 1914, the bulk of
the Liberal party was pacifist at heart is exaggerated, but
many Liberals were pacifist, and most British pacifists,
including the Nonconformist contingent, were still in the
Liberal party.[40] Rank and file members of the Liberal party

were in 1914 certainly dismayed at the prospect of war. Many party organizations approved resolutions favoring British neutrality. On 30 July 1914, Arthur Ponsonby wrote to Prime Minister Asquith that nine-tenths of the Liberal party was opposed to any Cabinet decision for war. On 1 August, the *Daily Chronicle* argued that "the vast majority" of Liberals favored neutrality. Asquith accepted this argument.[41]

Within the House of Commons, the opposition to war of many Liberal members of Parliament was clearly and vigorously articulated. On 2 August, Asquith estimated that at least three-fourths of the Liberal members of Parliament were for "absolute non-interference at any price."[42] In such circumstances, with any cabinet dependent for continuance in office upon the consent of the House of Commons, many Liberals did not expect a Liberal cabinet to declare war. This expectation was not confined to Liberal backbenchers. Among Nonconformists, in particular, hope for British neutrality was not extinguished until 11 P.M. on 4 August 1914, when British intervention came.[43] The lamps had gone out all over Europe, as Foreign Secretary Edward Grey had foreseen the previous evening.

One of the lamps permanently dimmed, if not extinguished, on those lovely summer evenings of 1914 was that of the British Liberal party. Even Gladstonian Liberalism had placed peace at least as high as retrenchment. War, as Winston Churchill had argued in 1906, turned out to be fatal to Liberalism as an ideology.[44] British participation in the First World War was for the Liberal party the negation of its earlier values.[45] A state at war could be neither merely a nightwatchman nor a good shepherd for the poor. War cost money that could neither be left in private hands nor redistributed by government to the needy. Both Liberalisms, old and new, Gladstone's and Lloyd George's, were in mortal danger. An early casualty, already in 1914, was the imposing organization of the Liberal party. Worse soon followed. In the stress of more than four years of war, which gradually became total war, the Liberal party was fragmented. War broke it. It perished between 1914 and 1918. As more thoughtful Liberals realized relatively soon, the unity of their party would become a casualty of total war. In the 1918 general election, the first after 1914, Liberal pacifists were obliterated. By 1939, there were no prominent Liberal pacifists left to oppose British entry into the Second World War, and precious few prominent Liberals of any stripe. The Liberal party was never to recover from its wounds of 1914–1918.[46]

Many of these wounds were self-inflicted, and flowed directly from the military intervention by the Liberal cabinet, in the absence of British treaty obligations, in the European war in August 1914.[47] By committing the British Empire to that war, the Liberal cabinet made that war the First World War. In the process of lacerating itself, the Liberal cabinet took along many innocent victims. Every British village, even the smallest, and every British colony, no matter how distant from Europe, got its roll of honor and its line of war memorial crosses. No Liberal prophet ever proved more mistaken than Grey, who proudly assured the House of Commons on 3 August 1914: "For us, with a powerful fleet, which we believe able to protect our commerce, to protect our shores, and to protect our interests, if we are engaged in war, we shall suffer but little more than we shall suffer even if we stand aside."[48]

Grey in 1916 finally lost governmental office and was shunted off to the House of Lords. The suffering of 9 percent of Britain's adult males under forty-five years of age was terminal.[49] Grey's private assurances in August 1914 that the war could not last more than three months before Germany collapsed were as valid prophecy as his public statement.[50] That he was so mistaken is perhaps not surprising. Like many other imperialists, Grey was astonishingly ignorant of Europe. He had never travelled there, except for two days in Paris, and he spoke no French. Indeed, as foreign secretary, he tried to minimize his personal contact with foreigners.[51] Since the empire was the responsibility of the colonial secretary, Europe was before and in 1914 the focus of the responsibility of the foreign secretary. Robert Boothby's argument that if Lloyd George, not Grey, had been foreign secretary in 1914, there would have been no world war is exaggerated, but surely British policy decisions would have been far more informed and British peace-seeking diplomacy more active.[52] In 1914, Lloyd George already knew personally many of the leading

European politicians, and his natural instinct was for face-to-face summit diplomacy.

It is doubtless true that executive power was greatly increased within Britain, as well as elsewhere, during the First World War. Cabinet power expanded at the expense of parliamentary power. That expansion was not only the result of responses to wartime events. The British military intervention against Germany in 1914 was itself the result of discussions and decisions within the cabinet, whose discussions and decisions often seemed to be taking place within a vacuum. Relatively, and perhaps surprisingly, little attention was paid by the cabinet to all those social forces within Britain that favored neutrality, which were probably substantial enough, given sufficiently dynamic leadership, to make any British war effort impossible.[53] The cabinet's actions were in fact molded by the personal preferences and relationships of its more powerful members, especially those who had reached, or could reasonably hope to reach, the prime ministership. The cabinet never voted for, or against, an explicit declaration of war, or even for, or against, the fatal ultimatum to Germany, and its deliberations were far from any model of collective responsibility.[54] No minutes were kept of meetings, and no staff was employed to implement decisions. Its members took actions collectively and individually, and some of the few explicit decisions it made were either ignored or disobeyed by individual members.

Some of those members were far more equal than the others. The key actors were Prime Minister Asquith, Foreign Secretary Grey, Chancellor of the Exchequer Lloyd George, and the first lord of the admiralty, Churchill. The War Office was vacant in July 1914, and had been so for several months. Asquith was also acting as secretary of state for war, but paid little attention to those additional responsibilities. Only after war had been declared did he fill that office, disastrously, with Lord Kitchener.

British intervention in the European war may have been an exercise of executive power, but it was not yet an exercise of independent prime ministerial power. The great expansion of independent decision making by a prime minister, at the expense of the power of his or her cabinet colleagues, was not to come until Lloyd George became prime minster in late 1916. By creating a cabinet office to serve his personal exercise of power,[55] Prime Minister Lloyd George attempted to institutionalize his charisma. The cabinet office survived Lloyd George's fall from office in 1922, but the gift of grace went with Lloyd George.

In July 1914, even the personal policy preference of the prime minister was uncertain. Asquith had earlier, including in the Boer War, been an enthusiastic Liberal imperialist. In 1914, however, his foreign policy preference was significantly less clear. Europe was hardly part of the empire. Britain's last European war before 1914, the Crimean War, remained "indefensible" to him.[56] Asquith's mind, often difficult to read, became particularly opaque as another European war approached.[57] His initial reaction, on 24 July, to the possibility of such a war was to report "happily" that there was no reason for the British to be "anything more than spectators."[58] Two days later, ever the barrister, he concluded that Austria may have had a better case than Serbia. His chief goal in 1914 appears to have been keeping the Liberal cabinet as united as possible behind whatever policy was implemented. His greatest fear was that "we shall have a split in the Cabinet."[59] Any serious cabinet split, of course, might well result in a new prime minister.

Given his goal, Asquith's tergiversation was understandable. The cabinet was deeply divided over the appropriate British response to the possibility of a general European war. The cabinet as a whole neither wanted nor expected war. During the last week of July 1914, at least one-half to three-fourths of its members were determined not to be drawn into a European war unless Britain were attacked.[60] On 30 July, Edmund Harvey, a Liberal member of Parliament who was a Quaker, expressed his confidence that the cabinet would not declare war. At the next day's cabinet meeting, Lewis Harcourt passed a note to J. A. Pease precisely to that effect. At the end of 31 July, it appeared that at least seven or eight ministers of the nineteen in the cabinet were so strongly opposed to a declaration of war that they would resign upon such a declaration.[61] On 1 August, the split within the cabinet widened, making it a black day for those Britishers who wanted war. The cabinet decided that if war came to Europe, Britain would not send an expeditionary army to the Continent, but would confine its response, at most, to Royal Naval involvement. The cabinet discussions of 2 and 3 August proceeded on that assumption. On 2 August, it appeared that the majority of the cabinet would resign if Britain declared war. On that day, Asquith expected the cabinet to disintegrate.[62]

When Britain went to war late on 4 August, only John Morley, lord president of the council, and John Burns, president of the Board of Trade, resigned from the cabinet.[63] A major change had clearly taken place within the cabinet. That change centered on Lloyd George. According to Asquith, on the morning of 2 August, Lloyd George was still against any kind of British intervention in any event.[64] On his way to lunch that day, Lloyd George spoke freely of his determination to resign from the cabinet in the event of British intervention. Shortly before the cabinet meeting that evening, John Simon, a neutralist, whispered to Morley, "I think I've got Lloyd George, he is with us!"[65] That appeared to be the case, for minutes later Lloyd George informed the cabinet of his determination to resign if Britain intervened. Throughout that long Sunday he had contemplated retiring to North Wales if Britain went to war. It appears that until 3 August he intended to resign from the cabinet upon any British declaration of war.[66]

Such a decision was entirely consistent with Lloyd George's arguments within the relevant cabinet meetings prior to 3 August.[67] Since he did not resign when war was declared, it is understandable that many observers concluded that his response to the European war was doubtful, halfhearted, hesitant, or uncertain, or even that he abstained from a cabinet vote that was never taken.[68]

The first days of August 1914 were certainly emotionally agonizing for Lloyd George.[69] But to assume that he had no policy at the most critical moment of his political career is nevertheless mistaken. In fact, Lloyd George was first firmly against war, and then equally firmly for war. He changed his mind shortly before Britain declared war. That his change of mind was not without its inner pain was evident from his anguished reaction to the cheers of a London crowd on 3 August, "This is not my crowd. I never want to be cheered by a war crowd."[70] On the same day, he wrote to Margaret Lloyd George, "I am filled with horror at the prospect. I am even more horrified that I should ever appear to have a share in it but I must bear my share of the ghastly burden through it scorches my flesh to do so."[71] It was not, of course, Lloyd George's flesh that was scorched as a result of his decision.

Lloyd George's private and public explanations of his change of mind similarly centered on German violation of Belgian neutrality.[72] This explanation has been accepted by some and rejected by other observers.[73] The evidence suggests doubt is in order. On 27 July, in conversation with C. P. Scott, Lloyd George assumed that any German war effort would violate Belgian neutrality, yet he continued for a full week to oppose British intervention. During that week, he argued that German troops marching into France through the southernmost tip of Belgium would not justify British intervention.[74] Respecting the neutrality of other states was not one of his sacrosanct totems. In October 1915, he was eager to have British troops advance through neutral Greece into the Balkans.[75] This hardly suggests that German violation of Belgian neutrality was decisive for Lloyd George, any more than for Grey and Churchill, the cabinet's leading enthusiasts for British intervention. Grey favored war before he learned of the impending German entry into Belgium. Churchill, as first lord of the admiralty, had, in 1913, ordered contingency planning for British seizure of Dutch and Scandinavian naval bases. On 3 August 1914, the first lord urged Asquith and Grey to push Belgium, the Netherlands, and Norway into alliance with Britain. In December 1914, Churchill argued for violation of Dutch air space by British planes.[76] In any event, Belgium was not much loved within Britain prior to 1914. Its foreign policy had been consistently pro-German. The most recent occasion on which Britishers had noticed Belgium was in 1908, with the Belgian annexation of the Congo, which was widely unpopular in Britain.[77]

Belgium was, for Lloyd George, a convenient excuse, not the reason, for his change of mind. That change was caused by events in Britain, not Belgium. More precisely, events at cabinet meetings caused his change of mind. Beside Grey, who as a veteran Liberal imperialist had never been close to Lloyd George, only one other senior member of the cabinet strongly favored British military and naval intervention from the beginning of the European crisis. Churchill wanted war, and he got it. The first lord of the admiralty mobilized, early on 2 August, the Royal Navy. Churchill and his apologists conceded that this mobilization was not only without legal sanction, but contrary to a cabinet decision.[78] Within the cabinet Churchill was the most enthusiastic and articulate advocate of war.[79] Cabinet advocates of British neutrality saw him as reckless and irresponsible, eager to use the Royal Navy, which he came perilously close to regarding as his navy, as an instrument of destruction.[80] Even Asquith, on the fence, described Churchill as "very bellicose."[81] Lord Hugh Cecil, who had been Churchill's best man at his wedding, and who was a Conservative opponent of war in 1914, heatedly blamed Churchill for the prospect of war.[82]

Churchill seemed in highest spirits precisely while Lloyd George was most emotionally agonized by the prospect of war.[83] Churchill admitted, on 28 July, to his wife that he was "geared up & happy" making preparations, which "have a hideous fascination for me," for "catastrophe."[84] Unlike Grey, Churchill had long understood that British military involvement in a general European war would mean total war.[85] He knew that such a war would be "vile and wicked folly and barbarism," yet he willed it anyway, while emitting a cry of inner pain, "Is it not horrible to be built like that?"[86] When war came, he was, as Lloyd George described him, a really happy man.[87] While it continued to be his war, Churchill continued to be happy. In January 1915, he told Margot Asquith, "Why I would not be out of this glorious delicious war for anything the world could give me."[88]

Several years before 1914, Churchill had talked to Lloyd George about how Churchill would command the decisive army in the next war. Lloyd George had quickly asked, "And where do I come in?"[89] There appears to have been no answer from Churchill. Also before 1914, John Morley had predicted that if there were a war, Churchill would "beat L.G. hollow."[90] The expectation that war would elevate Churchill to supreme leadership appeared in 1914 to be entirely sensible. No one could foresee that Lloyd George and Churchill would have one war apiece.[91]

First, however, there had to be one war, and without Lloyd George there would probably be no war for Britain. The decision would revolve around him. Only Lloyd George could keep a majority of the cabinet behind neutrality. Only Lloyd George, as Lord Beaverbrook put it, could play Charles James Fox. If there was to be a peace party, Lloyd George would be necessary. Those favoring peace banked on him. Without Lloyd George as their leader, the neutralists' position within the cabinet was politically hopeless. The die would be cast.[92] With Lloyd George as their leader, the neutralists could, realistically enough, hope.

Alternatively, only with Lloyd George's active consent could the Liberal cabinet declare and wage war without fragmenting fatally. Churchill and Grey understood the possibility of such a fatal cabinet fragmentation. So did Asquith, who also understood that only Lloyd George's continued presence could assure continuation in office of Asquith's cabinet.[93] Outside the cabinet, only Lloyd George could persuade the Nonconformist conscience to support war. If Lloyd George came down on the side of war, Nonconformity would support the war, and there would be national unity.[94] For Asquith, therefore, the paramount question was: "What is Lloyd George going to do?"[95]

That question was on many other minds in the cabinet. One of those minds was supremely active and determined. The first lord of the admiralty understood that Lloyd George, for whom tribal unity meant little, would need somehow to be persuaded. On 1 August, Churchill therefore instructed Major A. H. Ollivant, a general staff officer seconded to the admiralty, "to lecture Lloyd George on the European military situation." The audience of this lecture was unimpressed by Ollivant's analysis, which was far from masterful.[96] Clearly Churchill's own words would be needed. The argument that Churchill's eloquence was unnecessary to convert Lloyd George to war is the reverse of the truth. John Morley had it right when he attributed Lloyd George's change of mind to Churchill's words, although Morley never saw the decisive written words. Morley certainly heard, at cabinet meetings, enough of Churchill's spoken words. So did Lloyd George, to whom they were primarily addressed.[97]

Churchill's principal contribution to the British declaration of war in 1914 was, in fact, to put pressure upon Lloyd George.[98] This pressure was unrelenting. Churchill's monologues in cabinet meetings were lengthy and urgent in tone precisely because he was trying to persuade an unwilling listener. Enormous as was the matter at issue, more was at stake for Churchill than war or peace. When the power of his speech proved inadequate, he put his case in writing, in a series of private notes to Lloyd George.[99] In these notes Churchill pushed even his expansive conception of the privileges and obligations of friendship to its outermost limit. In his novel *Savrola*, Churchill had been able intellectually to distinguish between personal and political friendship.[100] In his own life that distinction collapsed. For him friendship was all-inclusive. It was all or nothing. In his hastily scrawled cabinet notes to Lloyd George, Churchill used the ultimate weapon of friendship: threatening to end friendship. That weapon was available to him alone among the cabinet advocates of war. Used by anyone else in the cabinet, Lloyd George would have laughed. That which has never existed cannot be ended. It is difficult, however, to imagine any other cabinet member using such a weapon even if it had been available. It is also difficult to imagine Lloyd George choosing to use such a weapon. There is no evidence that he ever did so, against Churchill or anyone else. Perhaps Churchill did not so choose. Perhaps, given his personality, the importance for him of the decision on war or peace, and the importance of Lloyd George's friendship for him, he had no choice, but was compelled to act as he did.

In his notes to Lloyd George, Churchill observed, entirely accurately, "I am most profoundly anxious that our long cooperation may not be severed."[101] That such severance would not be temporary was clear: "All the rest of our lives we shall be opposed. I am deeply attached to you and have followed your instinct and guidance for nearly 10 years."[102] The second sentence of that note was undeniably true. Churchill had renounced a great deal, including the party to which his father had belonged and to which most of his living relatives adhered as well as the interests of his own social class, to follow Lloyd George, even in the Marconi affair. Churchill had been loyal to Lloyd George as he had been or was to be to no other leader. He had given much to, and asked relatively little of, Lloyd George in the past. Now, however, he was asking everything. He was asking Lloyd George to renounce his own past, for the sake of an uncertain future together: "Please God—it is our whole future—comrades—or opponents."[103] This plea hit home. Lloyd George caved in.[104]

In pulling out all the stops, Churchill revealed himself. He loved war more than he loved Lloyd George. In surrendering his will to Churchill's for the first and last time, Lloyd George also revealed himself. He loved Churchill more than he loved peace. That this self-revelation may not have wholly pleased Lloyd George is suggested by the fact that he soon uncharacteristically tore up and discarded Churchill's cabinet notes to him. These notes were carefully retrieved and pieced together by Frances Stevenson, doubtless as one of many quiet acts of love for Lloyd George.[105] Whether this particular act of love served its intended purpose is uncertain at best. Without the evidence of Churchill's notes, Lloyd George's later excuse, Belgium, might be more acceptable as the reason for his decision. He was prudent to try to destroy the evidence.

After doing as Churchill wanted, Lloyd George also uncharacteristically fell silent in public. He did not address his followers for the first six weeks of the war. Quite probably he did not know what to say. Eventually he decided to speak at a public rally in support of Kitchener's military recruitment campaign. Before this rally, he said he felt as if he were about to be executed. If execution was in the air, it was not Lloyd George's execution. One of his lines at the Queen's Hall was probably the most astonishing of his political career: "I envy you young people your opportunity." That opportunity, it was revealed a few sentences later, was to die "consecrated deaths." This imagery was consciously, and ominously, borrowed from the Gettysburg Address. At the end, evoking as only he could do the overwhelmingly beautiful mountains of North Wales, Lloyd George saw among them "clad in glittering white, the great pinnacle of Sacrifice pointing like a rugged finger to Heaven."[106] The speaker's vision was clouded. Sacrifice would not come clad in white, but in red, "as the stained stones kissed by the English dead." The faithful Nonconformist had become Abraham, who "slew his son, And half the seed of Europe, one by one,"[107] except that Gwilym Lloyd George would not become Isaac. The chancellor had already privately assured Margaret Lloyd George that "I am not going to sacrifice my nice boy."[108] The courageous opponent of

Kitchener's policies in the Boer War now saw Kitchener's finger pointing the way to Heaven.

Two decades after 1914, Lloyd George's imagery had changed. It was the God of War who had sent Europe "reeling through the gates of hell" in 1914.[109] This imagery was more accurate, but it still left something to be desired. The God of War had not acted alone. He had had help. In 1914 the gates of Hell had been pushed open for Britain by the Heavenly Twins, working together. Alone, Churchill could not have pushed them open. Alone, Lloyd George would not have.

Lloyd George and Churchill were not separated in 1914. For a brief time even after the British declaration of war it appeared they might be. For the first three weeks of the First World War, Lloyd George and Churchill did not speak privately.[110] This lack of personal contact while they were both in London was unprecedented in their relationship. Since their offices were across the street from each other, and both regularly attended cabinet meetings, there had been some chill in the air. Perhaps Lloyd George resented becoming the follower. Churchill, who in his own words "felt intensely the need of contact with him," eventually sought out Lloyd George, and "was relieved and overjoyed at his response."[111] If Lloyd George resented briefly Churchill's unprecedented mastery over him, that resentment did not last. If he had not blamed his enemies for the Marconi affair, he did not blame his friend for his own actions in August 1914. He had only himself to blame, but this he did not do. The bitter critic of armaments as the mechanism of butchery became in 1915 the first, and enormously successful minister of munitions. The bitter critic of the pointless loss of British as well as Boer lives in South Africa presided, as the successor to Kitchener at the War Office when the latter drowned at sea in 1916, over the almost endless Battle of the Somme in which British casualties were almost beyond comprehension. The peacemaker who believed in the rationality of all human beings stubbornly refused, as prime minister for the last two years of the war, to make or even seriously consider making peace with Germany until the latter had been crushed. The man from Nazareth was shelved for the duration.

Lloyd George had been changed by his friendship with

Churchill. This is not uncommon in friendship. The friendship in this case survived August 1914, contradicting an
intellectual's claim that the "true domain" of friendship is
"peace, only peace," and sustaining the worldly wisdom that
friendships made in peace survive into war.[112] The truth of
the latter would be demonstrated not only by the events of
1914–1918, but also by those centering on May 1940.

Chapter Seven

The Last
Twenty Minutes

Winston is the new Lloyd George.
—John Colville

On 7–8 May 1940, the House of Commons engaged in what might well have been the most important debate in the history of that institution.[1] David Lloyd George's proposition that in the twentieth century "parliament has no control over the Executive" is doubtless generally true.[2] This debate was to demonstrate, nevertheless, that at least occasionally Winston Churchill's counterproposition, that "the Cabinet is the creature of the House of Commons," can be a valid description of British political reality, not merely an outdated myth.[3] This debate forced Neville Chamberlain, one of the most skillful party leaders in modern British politics, to resign as prime minister even though he had received a vote of confidence, to be replaced by Churchill as the head of a coalition cabinet.

The mood of the House of Commons members as they began their agonizing reappraisal of the Conservative cabinet was angry and frustrated. So many things were uncertain.[4] The British declaration of war against Germany that had been made so easily in September 1939 was finally being implemented at enormous cost and with even more

substantial risks. The cabinet's chickens were coming home
to roost. The British pledge to Poland in 1939 had, as only
Lloyd George among senior British politicians predicted at
the time, proved meaningless without Soviet support.[5] Not
only had the British halfhearted approach to the Soviet
Union in the summer of 1939 failed to produce results, the
British cabinet later came perilously close to war with the
Soviet Union over Finland. British resistance to Germany
in Norway was both provocative and ineffective. The expected
German invasion of Belgium and the Netherlands would
finally occur on 10 May. The phony war was becoming ter-
ribly real. *Sitzkrieg* was being replaced by *blitzkrieg.*

Chamberlain was to die of cancer six months later. The
tenacity with which he clung to the leadership of the Conservative party until the end, even after his resignation as
prime minister, suggests that but for the debate of 7–8 May,
he might have clung to the prime ministership even after
he became seriously ill a month after that debate.[6] Chamberlain would leave the most powerful office only if he were
pushed out. The last six months of Chamberlain's life were
to be no ordinary period. Those months were to include the
Battle of Britain. It is difficult to imagine Germany failing
to win that battle if even a healthy Chamberlain had remained as prime minister.[7]

That Chamberlain would fall became increasingly clear
during the extended parliamentary debate of 7–8 May. Who
would succeed Chamberlain was far from certain. To conclude that Churchill was the only possible choice is mistaken.[8] There were other possibilities. Churchill's succession
was in fact a touch-and-go matter.[9] If public opinion polls,
then in their British infancy, meant anything, Anthony Eden,
who had resigned as foreign secretary two years earlier in
opposition to appeasement of Germany and Italy, probably
would have been the most popular choice to succeed Chamberlain.[10] The choice was not left to the British electorate.
There was no general election between 1935 and 1945.

The British political establishment decided on Chamberlain's successor. Within that establishment there was a clear
favorite: Edward Wood, Lord Halifax, who had replaced Eden
as foreign secretary. Those favoring Halifax included George
VI, the Conservative party whips, Neville Chamberlain, and
most of the most powerful leaders of the Labor party.[11]

Halifax could certainly have formed a cabinet supported by a majority of the House of Commons. Although most British political leaders favored Halifax, the argument that all those leaders would have at least accepted Halifax as prime minister neglects to consider Lloyd George, who had no use for Halifax.[12] While showing his prized orchard to a visitor, Lloyd George had pointed to a particular tree, like its namesake tall and thin: "Observe its rich foliage. See how magnificently it casts its shadow. But it bears no fruit. I call this tree—Halifax."[13] Lloyd George's judgment may not have been unfair. Halifax was, after all, foreign secretary at the time of the Munich agreement in 1938. His choice as Chamberlain's successor would have meant no real break in administrations. That he was not chosen was a painfully close call.[14]

If Halifax had not been born into the British ruling class, he would have remained unknown.[15] His gifts were minimal. A novelist saw him correctly as "a mediocre fellow."[16] He and Churchill had little in common beyond their speech defects. When Halifax was appointed undersecretary of state for the colonies on 1 April 1921, the prime minister, Lloyd George, perhaps feeling the date was too appropriate, did not bother to inform his new minister, who learned of his appointment from the newspapers. The secretary of state for the colonies, Churchill, refused to see his new deputy. Later Halifax was viceroy of India while Churchill was making his frontal assault on British policy there. Churchill was no more eager in 1940 for Halifax than was Lloyd George. Halifax fully understood that, and after Churchill became prime minister, Halifax lost no opportunity to belittle his successful rival.[17] Halifax may have felt about Churchill as had his father in 1906: "I could have strangled him with my own hands."[18]

Not many of those who attacked Chamberlain expected or wished Churchill to succeed him. During the late 1930s, Churchill's name did not surface when Conservatives speculated privately about Chamberlain's eventual successor. This was not surprising, since he had only three or four followers in the House of Commons.[19] In 1938, Lord Beaverbrook dismissed Churchill as "not an important factor" in British government.[20] Churchill would have agreed. In that same year, he described himself to Léon Blum as "a very old minister now in retirement(!)."[21] A feeling of distrust approaching hatred of Churchill was still prevalent in the Conservative party. Three months before the outbreak of the Second World War, *The Times* refused to publish a letter from Violet Bonham Carter, high priestess of the Liberal party, urging Churchill's inclusion in Chamberlain's cabinet. Only the arrival of that war had brought back Churchill, a quarter century after Gallipoli, as first lord of the admiralty. Even then, Clement Attlee, an expert observer of British political careers, thought Churchill would never become prime minister. Several years earlier a sympathetic biographer had argued that Churchill still had one good job left in him: ambassador to the United States. As it turned out, Churchill was able to exile Halifax to Washington for most of the Second World War since, as Churchill put it, he had no future in Britain.[22]

On the whole, the House of Commons debate of 7–8 May did not do much to advance Churchill's cause, let alone his name.[23] Given the circumstances of the debate, this was not surprising. The debate had been scheduled because of widespread distress over British military and naval failures in Norway, including the precarious situation of those British troops still ashore in Norway.[24] Among the British public, Chamberlain probably commanded majority support until the Norwegian campaign. The failure of that campaign led many Conservative members to revolt against their own prime minister, and led to his fall from office. Since the operations in Norway had primacy in British war strategy, judging the cabinet on Norway was fair.[25]

It might have been less fair to judge only the prime minister by those operations, whose chief architect had been the first lord of the admiralty. Churchill was much more responsible for both the existence and the flaws of British operations in Norway than was Chamberlain. It was Churchill, not Chamberlain, let alone Halifax, who inspired and directed the British campaign on Norway.[26] It was on Churchill's orders that an inadequate and ill-armed British expeditionary force was sent to Norway. The fatal choice of Narvik, rather than Trondheim, as the target of that British force was Churchill's. It was Churchill who urged and got the cabinet to violate Norwegian neutrality before Germany did so.[27] Indeed, the eventual German invasion of

Norway, to which Churchill had looked forward eagerly, and which he welcomed, may have been in response to those British initiatives.[28] Some of the first lord's decisions concerning Norway were made before the cabinet could even discuss the matter. Having made the Norwegian expedition his own, Churchill kept his admirals waiting while he worked on a book for which he had a lucrative publisher's contract. His admirers, with only one apparent exception, conceded that he had bungled the Norwegian campaign, and that it was he who let the Germans into Norway.[29] Clementine Churchill later wrote that Norway might well have ruined her husband, who acknowledged privately at the time having been completely outwitted there by the Germans.[30] In a House of Commons debate on Norway 11 April 1940, Churchill had come close to being outwitted also by his parliamentary critics.[31]

The clouds of Gallipoli in 1915 hung over the snows of Narvik in 1940. So that those clouds would remain visible, Admiral of the Fleet Sir Roger Keyes lobbied his fellow members of Parliament almost incessantly.[32] Chamberlain's loyalists were equally energetic in privately trying to pin all the blame for Norway on Churchill. The latter's few parliamentary supporters were worried that such efforts would succeed. At least one of those supporters voted to express confidence in Chamberlain's cabinet lest he be understood to vote against Churchill.[33] This was a reasonable action, since the final speech in defense of the cabinet was given by the first lord of the admiralty, wearing white tie and full evening dress. Churchill's eloquence on this occasion did not match the intended elegance of his appearance.[34] His heart was perhaps not in it, but Chamberlain had surely been judicious in insisting on deferring to him as the final government speaker. The prime minister had already said too much, not too little, in his own defense. The formal result of the debate on 7–8 May was a vote of confidence,[35] by a much reduced margin, for Chamberlain; but the direct political consequence of the debate was that the first lord of the admiralty, who had been unjustly sacked from that office over Gallipoli, was rewarded with the ultimate promotion in British politics as a result of his failure in Norway.[36] At the age of sixty-five, Churchill had finally climbed to the top of the greasy pole.

That he survived his self-admitted Norwegian fiasco may
have surprised Churchill.[37] It did not surprise Lloyd George,
who had been initially reluctant to speak at length in the
Commons debate precisely because he understood the difficulty of saving Churchill while sinking Chamberlain.[38]
Privately Lloyd George held Churchill responsible for the
Royal Navy's share in the Norwegian catastrophe.[39] If anyone other than Churchill had been responsible, there is little
doubt Lloyd George would have gone for the jugular in
public. Since Churchill was involved, he did not. Instead,
in a newspaper article he wrote for publication 5 May 1940,
he stressed that Norway was only one of a series of blun-
ders by "the Cabinet."[40] By lengthening the list of errors
and broadening the responsibility for them, Lloyd George
substantially weakened the case against Churchill. Lloyd
George had not been trained as a solicitor for nothing.

Lloyd George's contribution to the first day of the House
of Commons debate on Norway was essentially confined to
eliciting, apparently without even rising from his seat, from
the first lord of the admiralty the statement that Churchill
had no official responsibility for coordinating all British
operations in Norway.[41] This hinted at the need, already
urged by Churchill, for a coordinating minister of defense.
If cabinet structure had been inadequate, one minister could
hardly be held solely responsible. The system was at fault,
not Churchill. Here Lloyd George was offering his audience
of past and prospective ministers an argument that many
of them had used, or could use, to justify their own errors.
This argument had the further merit of broadening the
debate still more. If Churchill did not become prime minister, at least he might become the first British minister of
defense.

Lloyd George still needed, however, an effective opening
wedge before he could extricate Churchill from sharing in
Chamberlain's fall, if that fall occurred. Such an opening
came when Chamberlain, ever the party leader, appealed for
support from his "friends" in the House of Commons.[42] This
explicit appeal for party loyalty weakened Chamberlain's
chances to become prime minister in any forthcoming coalition cabinet, and also angered those Conservatives convinced that a world war was a national, not a party,
emergency. The claim that Lloyd George spoke in the sec-

ond day of the debate on Norway only because he was "provoked" by Chamberlain's appeal[43] is exaggerated. The prime minister's language did give Lloyd George his opportunity, which he used with enormous effectiveness, demonstrating that it was better to have a friend in the House, especially if it was Lloyd George, than to claim to have many friends in the House. Churchill later characterized Chamberlain's language as "a wonderful opportunity" for himself: "the stars in their courses" had fought at his side.[44] It was, in fact, Lloyd George who seized the opportunity, leaving Churchill free to play the loyal subordinate of a wounded prime minister. This Churchill did well. Playing this role cannot have been easy. In addition to his own career aspirations, he was fully aware of what Chamberlain and his followers thought of him. One of those followers, R. A. Butler, a junior minister, had claimed in an interview with a foreign newspaper that Churchill still did not count in the British government, even now that he was first lord of the admiralty.[45] There was also the fact that Churchill had no use for his prime minister. Privately, Churchill considered Chamberlain "the narrowest, most ignorant, most ungenerous of men."[46]

Given those circumstances, Lloyd George's role in this debate was also not easy. Fortunately for his performance level, the Father of the House of Commons remained physically and intellectually full of vigor.[47] He had much preparation for this role. In twenty minutes of speaking on 8 May 1940, Lloyd George drew upon two decades of hostility to Neville Chamberlain, four decades of love for Winston Churchill, and five decades, recently celebrated, of experience in the House of Commons.[48] Those twenty minutes may have been, as Churchill put it, his last decisive intervention in the House of Commons, or as others put it, his last decisive action in that institution, or even his last decisive intervention in British politics.[49] Those twenty minutes were, by any interpretation, decisive.

Lloyd George's last great speech was far from his least.[50] It was certainly his deadliest speech. He spoke with undeniably great effect, plunging his knife into the prime minister. His slashing attack was, in Churchill's judgment, absolutely devastating, deeply wounding Chamberlain. Lloyd George gave the *coup de grâce* to Chamberlain's prime min-

istership. Chamberlain's wound was more than political,
however. Lloyd George literally stabbed Chamberlain to
death in the open forum.[51] Not only had he held the House
spellbound, his speech had changed the content and
strength of opinions held by his audience.[52] When he urged
Chamberlain to resign, the House of Commons responded
with loud cries of "Hear, hear!"[53] The triumphant Lloyd
George perhaps should have heard other voices, now si-
lenced. It was, after all, Joseph Chamberlain's son and
Austen Chamberlain's half brother whom he had just destroyed. He had venerated as well as opposed the father and
respected as well as been followed by the half-brother. Lloyd
George's victim did hear a voice from the past. One of
Chamberlain's last visitors at 10 Downing Street was Margot Asquith, ever convinced that her husband had been
stabbed in the back by Lloyd George in 1916. Chamberlain
sought consolation for both by reminding her of Asquith's
wound, which she had made her own, at the hands of a
fraud. When Churchill had returned to the admiralty, she
had accurately predicted that he would "*oust* the P.M. from
10 Downing St. just as Ll.G. ousted us."[54]

Lloyd George would not have minded this mutual sympathy. He had gotten what he wanted in 1940 as in 1916.
He had no objection to being the agent of Neville Chamberlain's destruction, but he was, as always, more interested
in the future than in the past. He had, to apply Max Weber's
phrase, again turned the wheel of history. He had advanced
the cause of his oldest friend as the most appropriate candidate to succeed Chamberlain. As the most vehement British critic of appeasement after 1936, having voted against
the Munich agreement while Churchill abstained, Lloyd
George could hardly be expected to favor anyone, including
Halifax, in Chamberlain's entourage.[55] This was recognized
by a sympathetic biographer of Halifax, who was to see Lloyd
George's speech of 8 May 1940 as "a last flicker of destructive genius."[56] That speech was destructive not only of
Chamberlain's power but of Halifax's succession.

Lloyd George had a candidate other than Halifax. Though
some would have welcomed and others would have tolerated his return to the most powerful office, Lloyd George's
candidate was not himself.[57] There is no evidence that he
took seriously talk about his own candidacy, although there

is also no evidence that he tried to prevent such talk. Certainly he made no move to return in 1940 as prime minister. If in 1940 Lloyd George had the chance for a comeback, he did not take advantage of it.[58] It is quite likely he was not looking for a comeback. He had no inner need to prove himself in ministerial office. If he had ever had such a need, it had been fully satisfied. He had already served almost seventeen years uninterruptedly in cabinet-level office. When he finally fell from the highest office in 1922, he had done so with grace and remarkably little bitterness. He had now been out of ministerial office for an equally long period. Even in the political wilderness he had been a happy man. He had already had his chance, and certainly made the most of it. Now it was his friend's turn. That friend needed power, and, in Lloyd George's estimation, deserved it. Envy, even of Churchill, was foreign to Lloyd George; admiration, at least of Churchill, was not.

That his friend should become prime minister was Lloyd George's determination in May 1940. This did not mean that Lloyd George was looking for cabinet office under Churchill. Alone of the major speakers in the debate of 7–8 May, Lloyd George neither held ministerial office in Chamberlain's cabinet nor accepted such office in Churchill's cabinet. Beginning on 13 May 1940, he repeatedly refused offers of membership in Churchill's cabinet.[59] This did not mean that he was no longer Churchill's friend, but the contrary. He understood how completely Churchill identified friendship and political agreement. Churchill's pressure in 1914 had, after all, been applied on him. Lloyd George did not become Churchill's cabinet colleague in 1940 because he did not want to lose Churchill's friendship. He knew Churchill, and he also knew himself.

If the prestige of ministerial office meant little to Lloyd George, what ministers did mattered much. If he were in ministerial office, there would inevitably be occasions for disagreement on policy decisions, whether within cabinet meetings or within the official prime minister-minister relationship. For Lloyd George, friendship did not necessitate agreement, and lack of agreement did not necessitate lack of friendship. Lloyd George suspected that Churchill would expect agreement from his ministers. That suspicion proved correct. Most of Churchill's ministers lived in fear of being sacked.[60] By October 1940, Lloyd George observed that "Winston now feels that he is God & the only God."[61] Since Lloyd George worshipped no human being, sparks would have flown if he had joined Churchill's cabinet. If the prime minister expected agreement from ministers he barely knew, his expectation of agreement from someone so close to him personally as Lloyd George would have been far higher.

Lloyd George was not afraid of losing cabinet office. He was afraid of losing his oldest friendship, so important a part of his life. By 1940, he seldom saw Margaret Lloyd George, and was, partly in consequence, in various degrees of estrangement from his children. Few of his political contemporaries survived. Most of his close personal relationships had been with other politicians. Now there was only Churchill left among them. At seventy-seven, losing his best friend did not appeal to Lloyd George. He did not want to become the only cabinet member "to argue with Winston," which would be "no good" for either friend.[62] He did not want to lose Churchill's friendship, but he also did not want Churchill to lose his friendship. He understood that Churchill needed not only power but to be loved, especially by those who knew him best. If in 1914 Lloyd George had loved Churchill more than he loved peace, in 1940 he loved Churchill more than he loved power. His excuses for declining Churchill's repeated offers of cabinet power were many, but his reason was: "I don't want to quarrel with Winston, I am fond of him."[63]

That fondness was accompanied by expert political judgment. Lloyd George understood that the most important issue in the Commons debate of 7–8 May was: could Churchill be saved from the collapse of Chamberlain's cabinet?[64] When he rose to speak, he rose to defend Churchill. To use Harold Macmillan's term, Lloyd George tried in his speech to rescue Churchill. To use Churchill's term, Lloyd George tried to exculpate his friend.[65] In his attempt to distinguish between Churchill and the rest of the Conservative front bench, Lloyd George was successful.[66] No other speaker in the debate of 7–8 May was as explicit, or as daring, in making this distinction. Other speakers, such as Herbert Morrison and Duff Cooper, tried to avoid blaming Churchill for the errors of the Chamberlain cabinet,[67] but this was passive resistance. Lloyd George went on the offensive, probably without consulting anyone else, including Churchill, as to his strategy. His self-confidence was justified. He understood the political situation, his audience, and Churchill.

In his speech, Lloyd George casually stated, "I do not think that the First Lord was entirely responsible for all the things which happened in Norway." Churchill immediately interrupted, as Lloyd George doubtless expected, saying, "I take complete responsibility for everything that has been done by the Admiralty, and I take my full share of the burden."[68] The first half of Churchill's statement was precisely what any responsible minister who spoke would have had to say in such a situation, but no more. The second half of the statement was double-edged. It could be interpreted by the Conservative front bench as loyalty to Chamberlain, but it could be interpreted by others as a hint that others, too, should take their full shares of the burden. Churchill did not mean to become the only sacrificial lamb. Churchill's interruption was perfect from the perspective of Lloyd George, who could now get to the heart of the matter: "The Right Honourable Gentleman must not allow himself to be converted into an air-raid shelter to keep the splinters from hitting his colleagues."[69] The House erupted in laughter.[70] The speaker could rest content. There was no need for overkill. He had made his point, and given his grateful colleagues release from the tension which had pervaded the chamber throughout the extended debate. Churchill, wisely, did not again interrupt the speaker.

Less directly, but even more importantly, Lloyd George shifted the focus of the debate from the specific errors of the Chamberlain cabinet to the need for effective future leadership in a total war. Only Lloyd George, with his enormous prestige as the victorious prime minister of 1918, could have accomplished this shift. That the British political system was in peril was his deepest message in his speech. Crisis situations demanded unconventional leadership. That was surely Lloyd George's belief. His most significant achievement in his speech was to persuade much of his audience that the chips were now down for Britain. He thereby paved the way for parliamentary acceptance of the necessity of a national leader as unconventional in his own way as Lloyd George had been in the First World War.

The more thoughtful members of the British political establishment accepted the case Lloyd George had made with so
much passion. The less thoughtful members did not know
how to refute Lloyd George's case. Perhaps it was, in the
circumstances, beyond refutation. There were many of the
less thoughtful, most of them Conservative members of the
British political establishment.[71] One of the self-proclaimed
members of that establishment, R. A. Butler, saw his new
prime minister as a "half-breed American whose main support was that of inefficient but talkative people of a similar
type, American dissidents like Lady Astor and Ronnie
Tree."[72] This reaction suggests the establishment did not
know what had hit it. Nancy Astor had favored Lloyd George,
not Churchill, as prime minister, and Ronald Tree was a
follower of Eden, not Churchill.[73] The latter's main support
in May 1940, as so often before, was in fact a native British oak.

When Churchill first entered the House of Commons as
prime minister, to make his "blood, toil, tears and sweat"
speech, he was cheered much less warmly than was Chamberlain. Lloyd George, however, welcomed the new prime
minister affectionately.[74] Since it was Lloyd George who had
paved the way for Churchill, in 1940 as so often before, it
was appropriate that he now made a short speech, as one
listener put it, "telling Winston how fond he is of him."[75]
While Lloyd George spoke the prime minister buried his face
in his left hand after his eyes had filled with tears.[76] The
invocation by the member for Carnarvon Boroughs was simple and direct:

> May I, as one of the oldest friends of the Prime Minister in this
> House—I think on the whole that we have the longest friendship
> in politics in spite of a great many differences of opinion—con-
> gratulate him personally upon his succession to the Premiership?
> But that is a small matter. I congratulate the country upon his
> elevation to the Premiership at this very, very critical and ter-
> rible moment. . . . We know the right hon. Gentleman's glitter-
> ing intellectual gifts, his dauntless courage, his profound study
> of war, and his experience in its operation and direction. They
> will all be needed now. I think it is fortunate that he should
> have been put in a position of supreme authority.[77]

Chapter Eight

Alone

I am a solitary creature in the midst of crowds.
                                    —Winston Churchill

When Winston Churchill wept while being welcomed to the prime ministership by Lloyd George, he was engaging in behavior uncommon within the British political elite. It is not a career advantage for a British politician to weep in public.[1] Not even the uninhibited Lloyd George did so. Since he wept in private, and inconsolably so when grieving for the death of someone he loved, Lloyd George was clearly capable of tears. The closest he came to political tears, however, was probably in an angry private confrontation with H. H. Asquith in 1915 over which was more loyal to the other, when both apparently wept.[2] Sometimes Lloyd George could speak with "a tear in his throat," as one auditor of his 1936 conversation with Adolf Hitler put it.[3] This was not quite the same thing as actually weeping, and probably was one of the devices Lloyd George used when in his judgment his audience would appreciate feeling some heart-felt emotion. He liked to make his audiences weep, and often did so, but he did not want to weep himself. Coming close was enough for a master thespian. Lloyd George was, for all his emotional dynamism, much less addicted in public to the melting mood than was Churchill.[4]

When the new prime minister wept in the House of Commons, he was behaving like himself. When, and perhaps whenever, someone actually said something kind about him there, Churchill wept. One of the hallmarks of his life, including his political career, was the frequency of his tears. The Churchill who wept was the essential Churchill. To make his Churchill recognizable, a dramatist had his character weep.[5] In childhood and in oldest age and in between, at happy occasions and at sad occasions, in relative privacy and in public, before the powerful and before the powerless, Churchill wept. The ease with which his tears flowed was noteworthy.[6]

That ease raised some sophisticated eyebrows. If Churchill's tears came easily, they could also end easily. It was difficult for some in Churchill's audience to believe his tears were genuine. In view of the indiscriminateness of his weeping, this skepticism is understandable. That he could honestly weep at Neville Chamberlain's funeral does seem doubtful. That the same person could honestly weep for both a departing Edward VIII and an arriving George VI does seem unlikely. That a prime minister could honestly weep while casually butchering three of his ministers does seem to stretch credulity.[7] It is not surprising that some persons suspected that Churchill willed his tears into being. As Charles de Gaulle, in admiration, put, "How he cried, but what a great artist!"[8] That Churchill's were an actor's tears is possible. There appears to have been no physiological cause for them, with the likely exception that in old age, after his strokes, they came with even greater ease. Much earlier, on first witnessing them, his doctor had been "surprised."[9]

If Churchill's tears were planned, they were often well-planned. If he was using what Alfred Adler called "water power" to get his way, he often succeeded.[10] In 1912, his tears prevented mutiny against the first lord of the admiralty by his subordinates. In July 1940, they produced a great ovation from the House of Commons for his defense of his controversial decision that the British navy should try to sink the French navy. Throughout the Second World War they helped the prime minister stifle disagreement from his cabinet colleagues.[11]

The effect of his tears was certainly to convince many of Churchill's sincerity. Most of his audiences were probably less dubious of that sincerity than was de Gaulle. They were moved by Churchill's show of emotion.[12] When the prime minister visited the bomb-damaged East End of London, an elderly woman spoke for these believers: "You see, he really cares, he's crying."[13] Even his doctor, originally uncertain, eventually concluded that Churchill's tears were never manufactured.[14] Probably most of them came honestly. That his tears were generally real, not manufactured, does not in itself mean that Churchill's East End believer was correct. Actions, not tears, are the real test of a politician's sincerity. Sometimes Churchill's tears blinded his audience to the fact that he was not doing much about their problems beside weeping. Nancy Astor grasped this when she told Churchill on a visit to bomb-damaged Plymouth, "It's all very well to cry, Winston, but you got to do somethin'."[15]

That he often could not prevent them does not explain the cause of Churchill's tears. If he genuinely cared, it may not have been about the problems of other people, but about his own problems. He may have been weeping less for other people than for himself. Certainly many of his tears were in contexts where the sadness of the human condition was not immediately relevant, but where the only constant element was himself. Words could move him to tears, and they were often his own words. He wept while composing a speech. He wept while rehearsing a speech. He wept when his books were being praised. He wept while himself reading those books.[16]

Churchill loved his own words, because they were so important a part of himself, and he loved himself, although he was not quite sure he was worthy of love, even self-love. He needed constant affirmation from others of his worthiness for, and by, being loved. If his tears were to any degree, to use Adler's terms, offensive weapons, they demonstrated his inner weakness, his need for help from others.[17] At the same time, he also needed to have other people do what he wanted them to do. The need for love and the need for power were the two driving forces of Churchill's life. The intersection of these two forces was where he lived. That is why he could be, as in 1914 with Lloyd George, such a demanding friend. Churchill could not separate the love of power from the power of love. To understand him, psychological perspectives are necessary. They may also be sufficient.

Traditional hagiographical studies of Churchill have generally avoided emphasizing psychological perspectives, sometimes quite intentionally. Esmé Wingfield-Stratford remarked, "Indeed, if the modern fashion in biography should persist, one does not envy the unhappy practitioner who at some future date is turned on to Churchill the man, with instructions to get as great a kick as possible out of this side of his life."[18]

Churchill, who dismissed psychology as irrelevant and ignored Sigmund Freud and Lytton Strachey, and whose distaste for psychology was known to novelists as well as expressed to his doctor, probably would have agreed with the hagiographers.[19] The claim that he was intensely interested in psychological analysis is without foundation.[20] Even if he had been interested, he was, as Lloyd George understood, without the ability to read other people, especially where their reactions to him were concerned. In fact, he was not interested. The inner lives of his fellow politicians did not interest him. The biographies he published are free of any attempt at psychological insight into their subjects.[21] His two-volume account of his father's life, for instance, is a great formal epic, dutiful and therefore not probing into his father's personal life. Churchill used his father's public record to explain his father's life, rather than using that life to explain the public record. The level of analysis of that father was, appropriately, appreciated by a fictional adolescent public-school student.[22] More sophisticated readers will be disappointed by *Lord Randolph Churchill*, which seems almost intended to be the pompous chronicle Samuel Johnson warned biographers against.[23] To expect Churchill to understand other people might be unfair, for he did not understand himself. The author of a biography authorized by the Winston Churchill Foundation concluded that Churchill did not know himself.[24] Unable to analyze personalities, including his own, he could only dramatize them, including his own.[25] That he certainly did.

The hagiographer's, and possibly Churchill's own, fears have now been realized. Psychological analyses of Churchill's life have explicitly addressed "Churchill the Man," motivated, as the most penetrating of those analyses puts it, by recognition that "the personal and emotional relationships of those who pursue power are often sadly inadequate."[26] Biographers rejecting psychological insights tend to assume that any attempt at psychological understanding inevitably denigrates a biographical subject. Why they have such pessimistic expectations of the personalities of their subjects and/or of the intentions of psychobiographers is not clear. Seeing into a human being is not the same as seeing through a human being. Seeing into a human being might cause a biographer to admire the capacity of his or her subject to surmount the psychological problems that every human being faces, and to identify those problems unique to that subject. Where there is much light there is also much shadow.[27] All those who exercise power are human beings, sometimes all too human. Because they choose to exercise power over other human beings, their psychological strengths and weaknesses are not only legitimate but necessary questions of inquiry. By seeking power, they have proclaimed their fitness to exercise power, and by exercising it they have affected the lives of other (sometimes, as in Churchill's case, many other) human beings (sometimes, as in Churchill's case, decisively). Whoever goes into the political kitchen might, and perhaps should, end up on the psychiatric couch.

Winston Churchill loved power. Few human beings have pursued power so fervently for so long. Few human beings have been so triumphant in the possession of power, and fewer yet have been so broken by its loss. Seeking and exercising power were at the core of Churchill's personality, and losing power revealed that personality with tragic clarity. Politics was Churchill's life, and without power that life had no meaning in his eyes. Power was his supreme passion, his fickle mistress. Power delighted him and he rejoiced in it.[28] Even at his wedding Churchill talked politics with Lloyd George. His bride had important family connections in his new parliamentary constituency.[29] Entirely aptly, his doctor called the period of his final retirement from governmental office "When Life was Over."[30] Churchill loved power so much because he needed power so much. The need to dominate other human beings was his most evident personality trait.[31]

Churchill's first, unsuccessful, candidacy for election to

the House of Commons came when he was twenty-four years old. A year later, consumed by personal ambition, he was first elected to the House, from which he did not finally retire until a few months before his death at the age of ninety.[32] On his last visits to the House he was, for all practical purposes, carried in, and visits is what they were. He retired from elective office as Father of the House of Commons, even though his membership after his first election had been repeatedly interrupted by election defeats. Those defeats were noteworthy, but his parliamentary career was nevertheless memorable in its length.[33] It was also memorable for Churchill's refusal to consider repeated electoral defeats to mean that voters did not want him to represent them. Whenever he was not in the House of Commons, he was seeking entry.

For some British politicians, membership, especially lengthy, in the House of Commons is sufficient success. Churchill was fond of proclaiming that he was first of all a "House of Commons man," and his admirers praised him as the great backbencher.[34] This was not, however, Churchill's preferred role. He sat on the back benches when he could not sit on the front benches. The House of Commons was not the center of his world. While he was prime minister, the British practice of the prime minister serving also as the leader of the House of Commons did not appeal to him. In early 1942, the prime minister, therefore, abandoned the leadership of the House of Commons to someone else.[35]

Churchill had ambitions beyond the House, in Whitehall. He was not content to remain a spectator, even of a great drama. He wanted governmental office, especially at the cabinet level. When out of the cabinet, he was ravenous for a taste of office.[36] His ultimate aim was to climb to the prime ministership. As he put it, "What is the use of racing all your life if you never win the Derby?"[37] In the context of the British political system, Churchill's will to power translated into his will to govern. The real rulers of Britain, as Churchill understood, are ministers of the Crown. Successful British politicians have much prestige in British society, but Churchill was not satisfied to receive deference. He wanted governmental office so he could do things, not merely occupy the office.[38] He no more wanted sinecure governmental office than he wanted to become even the most venerable backbencher. That he sought power rather than prestige was apparent when he repeatedly declined to enter the still prestigious but now powerless House of Lords.

Churchill's ministerial career was certainly externally successful. He first became a minister of the Crown, as undersecretary of state for the colonies, at the tender age of thirty-one. When he was promoted to cabinet level, as president of the Board of Trade, at thirty-three, he became the youngest cabinet member in more than four decades. He later became the youngest home secretary since Sir Robert Peel.[39] Churchill eventually held every major cabinet office but one: the foreign secretaryship.[40] He did not reach the prime ministership until he was sixty-five years old, and without Adolf Hitler, he would never have done so, but when he did, he justified for one brief but glorious moment in 1940 his lifelong confidence in his own capacity to govern.

The external success of his ministerial career was not enough for Churchill's happiness, however. Throughout his adult life, which was coextensive with his political career, he suffered repeatedly from extended periods of severe depression.[41] This depression Churchill called his "black dog."[42] He used this term often enough as an adult for it to be picked up by Lloyd George to describe his own, much less frequent and severe, periods of depression. Churchill had learned this distinctive term in his childhood from his nanny, Elizabeth Everest. In British folklore, on whose vocabulary Everest probably drew, a black dog is one of the guises of the Devil.[43]

Like many other depressive personalities, Churchill was preoccupied with death, which he viewed as "the greatest gift God has made to us."[44] Long before his death he thought he had not long to live. In old age he prayed daily for death.[45] Since by then he lacked a religious consciousness, this may have been his only prayer.

The argument that Churchill was a practicing Christian is unjustified, and even the claim that he was a traditional Anglican is strained.[46] As a young soldier he appears to have prayed, but return to civilian life seems to have suspended his prayers for many decades.[47] Already in his twenties he described himself as "a rationalist."[48] He did not attend church services except for special family or state occasions. On such occasions, too much Christianity in the service did not please him. That state occasions should be religious in form did not in itself offend him. There was none of the Nonconformist in Churchill. His understanding of religion was communal, not personal. To him, every nation creates God in its own image, and nations that think much about the next world rarely prosper in this.[49] Probably he made the latter assumption also about individual persons. The Christian faith in another life was meaningless to him. He did not believe in personal survival after death. He did not seek personal consolation in religion any more than in psychiatry. On their honeymoon, he declined to join his wife at a church service after a joint visit to the grave of his father. Whatever religious feelings he had rested on him comfortably and unconstrictingly. He detested, to use his own term, goody-goodies.[50] He explicitly rejected the Christian ethic as the appropriate norm for political action.[51]

Churchill's preoccupation with death was, of course, with his own death. The deaths of others, even significant others, were of less interest to him. In his triumphant moments in early spring 1945, Churchill did not attend the funerals of David Lloyd George or of Franklin Roosevelt. The argument that there is no obligation to attend a friend's funeral is surely false. There might be valid reasons for not meeting that obligation. Neither the time required nor dangers involved in traveling to Roosevelt's funeral are valid reasons for Churchill's absence. He traveled endlessly before and after that funeral. A few weeks earlier he had found time for, and faced the dangers of, a tour of the battlefront in Germany. The reasonable inference about Roosevelt's funeral is that Churchill did not want to attend.[52] Roosevelt was an ally, not a friend.

Churchill's absence from Lloyd George's funeral in Wales is a more complex matter. His initial intention was probably not only to attend, but to be active at, his friend's funeral. Soon after Lloyd George's death, Churchill called Gwilym Lloyd George with the message, "Of course he will be buried in the Abbey."[53] When informed that Lloyd George's careful planning of his own funeral ruled out such pomp, Churchill did not travel to Wales. The crowd gathered for the funeral there clearly expected the prime minister to attend. He did attend the memorial service held later in Westminster Abbey, but this service was inevitably anticlimactic.[54] Lloyd George was not present. In view of the magnificent eulogy that Churchill gave in the House of Commons before Lloyd George's funeral, disinterest hardly explains Churchill's absence from the main event.[55] That eulogy would have sounded just as impressive at a funeral in the abbey. Churchill may have discerned that at a simple Nonconformist funeral in Wales, he would not have the central role he would, as prime minister, have at a funeral in Westminster Abbey. He was still offended, years later, by the simplicity of the funeral he did not attend, so different from the ostentation he equally carefully planned for his own funeral.[56] Perhaps also Churchill did not want to risk seeing Lloyd George again. He may have understood that with the death of a friend, we die a little ourselves.[57] This last possibility is consistent with Churchill's preoccupation with his own death.

It is also consistent with the connection made explicitly by Churchill between his father's death and his own impending death. Lord Randolph Churchill had died peacefully in his sleep at 6:15 on the morning of 24 January 1895. The son did not forget that date, even in 1945. In the early 1950s, he told one of his joint principal private secretaries about his father's death, and added, "It is the day that I shall die, too."[58] It was. Winston Churchill died peacefully in his sleep at 8:00 on the morning of 24 January 1965. Clinging unexpectedly to life through his last days until that morning may have been the last of the son's many acts of will.[59]

Churchill's depression was not confined to his old age, after he was pushed out, at the age of eighty, of his second prime ministership, as he fully understood, by other Conservative cabinet members eager to make room closer to, or at, the top for themselves.[60] When he was out of governmental office he was never happy, but miserable and lost. For Churchill, powerlessness was unhappiness, and power was the only real solace. Already during the First World War "whenever he was excluded from active official participation" he became depressed.[61]

Indeed, one of the two deepest and longest periods of depression Churchill experienced began in May 1915 when he was, to use his own later term, "sacked" as first lord of the admiralty.[62] The happiest period of his life may have been the four years he spent at the admiralty before that sacking. Not only was Churchill happy at the admiralty, he was supremely competent. He nevertheless became the scapegoat for the British military defeat at Gallipoli, a fact that depressed him deeply.[63] He fell from his proud position as first lord to the powerless sinecure of the chancellorship of the duchy of Lancaster, a post from which he eventually resigned.[64]

Churchill's treatment by the British political elite at the time of Gallipoli almost destroyed not only his political career but his will to live. He sat silent for hours with his head in his hands. Half a century later, Clementine Churchill recalled, "I thought he would die of grief." This recollection was justified. After he lost the admiralty, Churchill wept, repeatedly saying "I'm finished."[65] Many others agreed. Gallipoli was the nadir of Churchill's political career. It was the sharpest and deepest wound he suffered in that career, and it haunted him to the end of his life.[66] As he later recalled, "my veins threatened to burst from the fall in pressure."[67] More than a year after Gallipoli Churchill was still severely depressed. During this depression he first took up painting, which proved to be effective therapy. He confided, "If it weren't for painting, I couldn't live; I couldn't bear the strain of things."[68] He nevertheless told a visitor who found him painting, "There is more blood than paint upon these hands."[69]

The second long period of severe depression came for Churchill when the Conservative party, led by him, was, unexpectedly to him, decisively defeated in the general election of 1945.[70] The voters had been asked to choose for or against him, and they chose against. This defeat burned deep into Churchill's soul.[71] He moved from 10 Downing Street into an upper floor of a hotel, where he worried openly about the balcony: "I don't like sleeping near a precipice like that. I've no desire to quit the world, but thoughts, desperate thoughts, come into the head."[72] This worry was similar to those he expressed about standing on a railway platform or on the side of a ship. He felt that suicide was permissible in cases of incurable disease or disgrace.[73]

Churchill's level of depression in 1945 was indicated by his comment to his doctor, "It would have been better to have been killed in an aeroplane, or to have died like Roosevelt. . . . I think I'll go to the Riviera. I don't mind if I never see England again."[74]

Lake Como, not the Riviera, saw Churchill then, and he did see Britain again. Remaining as leader of His Majesty's opposition, in itself, held no attraction for him, and he was not much good at the job, but the only way he could return to the prime ministership, which he was determined to do, was to hold on.[75] That he did. Even though his attendance in the House of Commons was still sporadic, he reacted violently to suggestions from fellow Conservatives that he retire as party leader. Such suggestions were only the tip of an iceberg.[76] When Lord Halifax, who had been his chief rival for the prime ministership in 1940, urged him to resign as leader of the opposition, Churchill responded acidly, "My dear Edward, you can tell our colleagues that one of the unalterable rules of my life is never to leave the pub until closing time."[77] Since his second prime ministership was essentially a failure, Churchill, whose hearing was deteriorating, missed the publican's last call, and found himself alone.[78] The decade of his final retirement from power was immeasurably sad.

Churchill was undeniably reluctant to abandon power, or the search for power, after the Second World War.[79] In this reluctance he was hardly alone among politicians. He was also hardly alone in becoming depressed by the loss of power.[80] The duration and intensity of both his love of power and his depression when denied power suggest, however, that, even among politicians, psychological factors were especially significant in his choice of career and his conduct therein. Churchill tried to solve, or at least to submerge, his personal problems in a public context. He needed to politicize everything. Everything included, of course, friendship. Everything became a political question, but every political question became for him a personal question.[81] H. H. Asquith described Churchill as so wrapped up in himself that he fed upon his own vitals.[82] During the Second World War, Churchill became convinced that his own military commanders were "framing up" with American military commanders against him.[83] His political career was an attempt, mostly successful so long as he had power, to compensate against a particular personal deprivation.

All power seekers may be attempting to compensate against some personal deprivation, but the particular deprivation may not be the same for all power seekers.[84] At some point in his life Churchill was deprived of something he needed, causing him to feel so inadequate that he may well be a classic case of what Alfred Adler termed a compensatory striving for power, which can become so exaggerated and intensified that it must be called pathological.[85] Churchill's particular personal deprivation, however, still needs to be identified.

Political ambition and depression were connected in Churchill's life, and they probably both originated in his childhood. His political career was an attempt to overcome the disadvantages of his earliest life.[86] Depressive personalities, convinced they are unloved by those close to them, may seek acclaim from a larger public.[87] As a soldier in India, Churchill wrote, fittingly to his mother, "I play for high stakes and given an audience there is no act too daring or too noble. Without the gallery things are different."[88] Brendan Bracken, who was close enough to Churchill to be regarded, incorrectly, by some as his illegitimate son, had it correctly when he observed that "to understand Winston you must go back to his childhood."[89] That childhood was profoundly unhappy.[90] Love was sadly missing. Because the power of love was insufficiently demonstrated in Churchill's childhood, the adult Churchill loved, and needed, power.

Churchill's childhood was almost pathetically lonely.[91] That world was almost entirely one of adults. Other children, outside his family, were strikingly absent. Churchill's only sibling, John Strange Churchill, was born when Churchill was five years old, and Churchill had little opportunity to know him before he was himself sent away to school at seven years of age. Such separation, typical of Churchill's social class, may be one explanation for the hypothesis that fraternal love is rare in Britain.[92] Churchill and his brother spent only one term together at school, at Harrow, during Churchill's last, and his brother's first, term there.

Geographical distance and the age difference combined

to make his brother not much consolation to Churchill, at least during his childhood. John Strange Churchill was as amiable a child as he was an adult, which might have been one reason Lord and Lady Randolph favored him over his older brother.[93] As an unexceptional child, John Strange Churchill demanded little attention from Lord and Lady Randolph, for which they were duly appreciative. Lord Randolph was especially fond of pointing out to Churchill that in "never doing stupid things Jack is vastly your superior."[94] Constant criticism from his parents, perhaps predictably, made Churchill "feel quite dull."[95] In any event, Lord Randolph probably loved one the less rather than another the more.

Lord Randolph's preference was only one sign of the overwhelming fact of Churchill's childhood, that the most important adults in his world, his parents, were cold and uncaring toward him. They denied him their love. Even by the low standards of upper-middle-class late Victorians, they were neglectful, unloving parents. Considering the parental love he received in childhood, Churchill might as well have been an orphan. His parents paid him little attention. He did not often see them, even before his school years.[96] They did not bother to make the customary daily inspection of their infant son. "Mamma had no time," and neither did Lord Randolph, who did not know how old his son was or which public school he attended.[97] Churchill, in turn, knew little about his parents, who told their son almost nothing about themselves. His first newspaper reading was to search for reports of his father's activities. His first biographical book was, appropriately, an attempt to get to know the father who had always repelled his efforts at closeness. In his old age the son wrote a short story, "The Dream," in which he finally had a conversation with the ghost of his father.[98]

At the age of twelve the son asked his father the innocent question, "Did you go to Harrow or Eton?" There appears to have been no answer.[99] Lord Randolph's silence was typical. For the most part he ignored his son. When he did notice him, it was to express uniformly and strongly negative judgments. Churchill's father certainly disliked and possibly hated his son.[100] As the son grew older, Lord Randolph's criticisms became ever more sweeping. When Churchill, on his third try, passed the examination for entrance into Sandhurst, the British military academy, Lord Randolph wrote that he no longer attached "the slightest weight to anything you may say about your own acquirements & exploits."[101]

Lord Randolph's last letter to his son was an entirely typical tirade against the expense of his son's desire to become a cavalry, not infantry, officer. Lord Randolph earlier decided, in spite of the reservations of his son who preferred the Church, that Churchill was unfit for any but a military career.[102] Even when he did what he was told to do, Churchill was not praised by his parents. Parental pride was absent. When Lady Randolph published her memoirs, they made no mention of the birth of Winston Churchill, who had just reached cabinet rank. Those memoirs included seventy illustrations, but her older son appeared in none, although in one photograph John Strange Churchill appeared, with his mother. Since she had forgotten his birth, it is no surprise she also forgot her older son's birthday.[103]

Much of what communication there was within the Churchill family was by letter. Not only were the sons away at school, but Lord and Lady Randolph were frequently apart. When her older son was eight years old, Lady Randolph wrote, with satisfaction, to her husband, "It appears that he is afraid of me."[104] Distaste for their son was one of the few things that she shared with her husband. Their marriage was a token partnership. They led separate lives, and did not understand each other or love each other.[105] Lord Randolph was frequently ill until he died, when Churchill was twenty, of general paralysis of the insane induced by syphilis.[106] Until Lord Randolph's last months, Churchill had no idea his father was seriously ill.[107] Lady Randolph, who did know the nature of her husband's illness, chose, not surprisingly, not to cohabit with him. The vigor of her search, after her older son's birth, for substitute partners was, nevertheless, surprisingly great.[108]

In spite of almost literally endless petitions from their son, and prodding from headmasters, neither parent visited Churchill while he was away at his first school. Each visited him only once, separately, at Harrow. At his second, intermediate school, at Brighton, Churchill was not visited by his father when Lord Randolph had an appointment across the street. Churchill's reaction to this snub by his father was anguished, but Lord Randolph did the same thing later.[109]

In view of Churchill's school experiences, rather more parental visits would have been in order. Later, Churchill recalled that he had hated his school years, including at Brighton, which he regarded as penal servitude, and at Harrow, which he saw as the unhappiest period of his life.[110] His adult contacts with his former public school were hardly those of an enthusiastic old boy. In 1940, he declined, as prime minister, to visit Harrow until it was bombed, and he lamented it had produced so few Royal Air Force pilots.[111]

While Churchill was a student at Harrow, the headmaster birched students, and Churchill was frequently beaten.[112] His academic progress at Harrow was uninspiring. At least once he was in danger of academic expulsion, and he never emerged from the indignity of the Junior School. His academic inadequacy occasioned ridicule among his fellow students.[113] He lisped and he stammered.[114] There appears to have been only one friendly face among his classmates, a face Lady Randolph predictably found "rather dull and stupid."[115] When Churchill left Harrow, there was no traditional "leaving breakfast" for him. He left his last school, alone, in a cab.[116]

This solitary departure was appropriate, since Churchill had also started his school years alone. When he was seven years old, his mother left him at Paddington Station, London, to make the train trip to Ascot alone. For many British children, the only explanation for their being sent away to school is that they are not loved at home. In Churchill's case, this was precisely the reason. London, where his parents mostly lived, had many excellent day schools. Churchill, whose school holidays were generally spent with aunts and uncles, understood that his parents had sent him away to school to get rid of him.[117] At the age of ten, he wrote to his mother, "You must be happy without me, no screams from Jack or complaints. It must be heaven upon earth."[118] Later he wrote, also to his mother, "Let me at least think that you love me."[119] No illusions were permitted, however, and Churchill's judgment of his mother was severe: "Your unkindness has relieved me

however from all feelings of duty. I too can forget."[120] Try
as he might, he could, of course, never forget.

It is unlikely that even in Churchill's absence his parents' home was Heaven upon earth, but his first school, St.
George's School at Ascot, certainly was not such.[121] There
Churchill was literally bullied and bruised. Although
Churchill got little sympathy from his peers, the bully was
not a fellow student, but the headmaster, the Reverend H.
S. Sneyd-Kynnersley, who was fond of birching the bare
bottoms of young boys up to twenty times a session. Even
among British headmasters Sneyd-Kynnersley's enjoyment
of this practice appears to have been of legendary propor-
tions. Churchill was repeatedly birched. While he was visiting his parents, his nanny, Elizabeth Everest, noticed the
scars, and her insistence led to Churchill being withdrawn
from St. George's School.[122]

Everest's concern was entirely typical. Churchill's greatest good fortune in childhood was that the nurse hired by
his parents when he was one month old was Everest, an
experienced nanny then in her early forties. She alone of
the adults in his childhood world loved him.[123] She may have
been the only responsible adult in the Churchill household.
She did not hesitate to tell Winston when his behavior was
wrong, but she made even her criticisms gently, adding to
them the reminder that "although you are not perfect I do
love you so much."[124] Churchill knew that was true. He knew
that to his parents he was an object, not a person. To
Everest, he was always, from his earliest years, a person.
She was the only real friend of his childhood.[125]

Lonely upper-middle-class British children frequently not
only are loved by, but also love, their nannies. Churchill
loved Everest, whom he called "Woom," after his first, unsuccessful, attempts to say "woman."[126] This nickname was
surely appropriate. It may be that Churchill loved Everest
"like a mother," but it is more likely that, as he later told
his nephew, he loved Everest more than he loved his mother.[127] Perhaps he loved Everest as he would have loved his
mother if she had loved him.

Churchill certainly had reason to love Everest. She had
time for him and visited him at school frequently. She was
rewarded, in what may have been the bravest act of
Churchill's long life, by a kiss in full view of his Harrow

schoolmates.[128] Churchill's attachment to Everest is eloquent evidence for the observation by Alfred Adler: "Sometimes a single person in the environment offers an opportunity of concord; when this happens the child joins himself to his friend in a very deep relation."[129]

When Everest died, Churchill pointedly wrote to his mother: "I shall never know such a friend again."[130] He owed a great deal to Everest, and he paid that debt with more than a kiss. When she was dying, Churchill, who was twenty years old, arranged for a doctor and a nurse. When the end came for Everest, Winston Churchill was with her, holding her hand.[131] He organized her funeral, where he wept as he had not wept for his father a few months earlier. His tears were fitting, for Everest's death was a greater emotional loss for him than was his father's. Only two Churchills were at Everest's funeral. Winston Churchill had arranged for his younger brother to attend. Even if Lord Randolph had still been alive, he would hardly have attended a servant's funeral. Lady Randolph was the notable absence. She was represented only by a wreath, and that symbol had been, without her consent, arranged in her name by her older son.[132] He paid for the headstone on Everest's grave, and for many years he paid a florist for upkeep of that grave. To the end of his life, Everest's picture was displayed prominently in his home.[133]

Most of these expressions of Churchill's love for Everest were private. Other expressions were as public as his kiss at Harrow had been. The moving description of the nanny in his novel, *Savrola*, is clearly of Everest, and the hero "did not forget her."[134] Winston Churchill had been shocked when the aging Everest was fired, without a pension, by his parents when she was no longer needed by them. Short of money himself, he sent her some.[135] Churchill remembered Everest, and he eventually learned, from Lloyd George, that there were many other Everests in British society. His enthusiasm in creating, with Lloyd George, old age pensions while they were in the cabinet before the First World War was partly at least a memorial to Everest.[136]

Elizabeth Everest's most direct monument, however, was Winston Churchill. That the adult Churchill was able to function was probably the result of Everest's love for him, which showed to Churchill that he was worthy of being loved, and of his love for Everest, which showed to Churchill that he could love. While his principal love-object remained himself, his love for Everest demonstrates the inaccuracy of the assumption that he was incapable of loving another person.[137] Churchill's childhood created much psychological damage, and Everest's love minimized but did not save him from damage. Churchill was in fact sustained in childhood by Everest's love, and that sustenance did not end with his childhood.[138]

That sustenance inevitably weakened, however, with the passage of time. If, as has been argued, Churchill's adult friends were successors to Elizabeth Everest, David Lloyd George was the most important of these successors.[139] He alone was the political mentor, and he alone was full witness to, and object of, Churchill's greatest tantrum, in August 1914. Like Everest, Lloyd George forgave the tantrum, because he loved Churchill. That last condition prevented Lloyd George from fully playing the role of Lord Randolph Churchill in the adult life of Winston Churchill, even if the latter were looking for his father. Lord Randolph never forgave or loved his son, but Lloyd George did both.

Adolf Hitler saw Churchill as mentally ill, and others judged Churchill to be a megalomaniac.[140] Andrew Bonar Law was convinced that Churchill had an entirely unbalanced mind, and one of Churchill's senior naval aides at the admiralty considered his first lord to be lunatic.[141] Churchill's admirers, on the other hand, were impressed by his "profound sanity."[142] All of these generalizations are simplistic. If Churchill was sane and capable of moral choice, if he was neither mad nor bad, much, perhaps most, of the credit is rightfully Everest's.[143] One of her greatest gifts to Churchill was rigorous moral guidance. Churchill was raised in a home that was otherwise far from morally strict.[144] Whatever voice of rectitude there was in the adult Churchill's life did not speak in the cultivated accents of the highest social circles. When he had wanted to be confirmed, his mother ridiculed him, but Everest understood.[145] Only she had taught him to pray.

Many great personages, including royalty, dined in his parents' home during Churchill's childhood. Few of these visitors, however eminent, shone as brightly as their glittering host and hostess, the politically gifted younger son of the duke of Marlborough and the legendary American beauty who was his wife. No one except a lonely child noticed the plain, unfashionably dressed, middle-aged woman quietly making her way downstairs to have her supper with the other servants.[146] In her journey Elizabeth Everest nevertheless illuminated the power of love and thereby the possibilities of the human condition.

Notes

Preface

1. Sarah Grand, *The Heavenly Twins* (London: William Heinemann, 1894).

2. John Colville, *The Fringes of Power: 10 Downing Street Diaries 1939–1955* (New York: W. W. Norton, 1986), p. 420.

3. Elie Halevy, *The Rule of Democracy 1905–1914 (Book II)*, 2nd ed., trans. E. I. Watkin (New York: Peter Smith, 1952), p. 506; Margaret Crosland, *Beyond the Lighthouse: English Women Novelists in the Twentieth Century* (New York: Taplinger, 1981), p. 4.

4. D. H. Lawrence, *The Complete Short Stories*, vol. I (New York: Penguin Books, 1981), p. 3; Bruce Chatwin, *On the Black Hill* (New York: Viking Press, 1983), pp. 135, 184.

5. Sarah Grand, *The Beth Book: Being a Study of the Life of Elizabeth Caldwell Maclure A Woman of Genius* (New York: Dial Press, 1981), pp. 350, 407.

6. Grand, *The Heavenly Twins*, p. 42.

7. Ibid., pp. 126, 132, 142.

8. The Earl of Swinton, *Sixty Years of Power: Some Memories of the Men Who Wielded It* (London: Hutchinson, 1966), p. 40.

9. John Ehrman, "Lloyd George and Churchill as War Ministers," *Transactions of the Royal Historical Society*, 5th series, vol. XI, p. 101; Sir Dingle Foot, *British Political Crises* (London: William Kimber, 1976), p. 84; Michael Foot, *Aneurin Bevan: A Biography*, vol. II (New York: Atheneum, 1974), pp. 273–74; Thomas Jones, *A Diary with Letters: 1931–1950* (London: Oxford University Press, 1954), p. 379; Harold Macmillan, *The Past Masters: Politics and Politicians 1906–1939* (London: Macmillan, 1975), pp. 162–63; Harold Macmillan, *Winds of Change 1914–1939* New York: Harper & Row, 1966), p. 292; Henry Pelling, *Winston Churchill* (London: Macmillan, 1974), p. 632; Sir Geoffrey Shakespeare, *Let Candles Be Brought In* (London: Macdonald, 1949), p. 64.

10. Randolph S. Churchill, *Winston S. Churchill*, companion vol. II, part 2 (London: Heinemann, 1969), p. 774.

11. Mary Soames, *Clementine Churchill: The Biography of a Marriage* (Boston: Houghton Mifflin, 1979), p. 110.

12. Violet Bonham Carter, "Winston Churchill—As I Know Him," in Sir James Marchant, ed., *Winston Spencer Churchill: Servant of Crown and Commonwealth* (London: Cassell, 1954), p. 149.

13. Stuart Hodgson, *Portraits and Reflections* (New York: E. P. Dutton, 1929), p. 31.

14. Myron Brenton, *Friendship* (New York: Stein and Day, 1974), p. 170.

15. C. S. Lewis, *The Four Loves* (New York: Harcourt Brace Jovanovich, 1960), p. 124.

16. *The Boston Globe*, April 10, 1982, p. 9.

17. Lord Boothby, "Founder of the Welfare State," *Books and Bookmen*, 17 (September, 1972): 17; Olivia Coolidge, *Winston Churchill and the Story of Two World Wars* (Boston: Houghton Mifflin, 1960), p. 111; William Manchester, *The Last Lion: Winston Spencer Churchill: Visions of Glory 1874–1932* (Boston: Little Brown, 1983), p. 5; Kenneth O. Morgan, *Consensus and Disunity: The Lloyd George Coalition Government 1918–1922* (Oxford: Clarendon Press, 1986), p. 350; Patrick Renshaw, *Nine Days That Shook Britain: The 1926 General Strike* (Garden City, N.Y.: Anchor Books, 1976), p. 94.

18. Jones, *A Diary with Letters*, p. 145; John Evelyn Wrench, *Geoffrey Dawson and Our Times* (London: Hutchinson, 1955), p. 322; Robert Rhodes James, *Memoirs of a Conservative: J. C. C. Davidson's Memoirs and Papers, 1910–37* (New York: Macmillan, 1970), p. 410; John Campbell, *Lloyd George: The Goat in the Wilderness 1922–1931* (London: Jonathan Cape, 1977), p. 46; Sir Dingle Foot, *British Political Crises*, p. 114; Jones, *A Diary with Letters*, p. xxxii.

19. Kenneth O. Morgan, *Labour People: Leaders and Lieutenants, Hardie to Kinnock* (Oxford: Oxford University Press, 1987), p. 47; Robert Blake, *The Conservative Party from Peel to Churchill* (New York: St. Martin's Press, 1970), p. 236; Kenneth O. Morgan, *Consensus and Disunity*, p. 364; R. W. Thompson, *Generalissimo Churchill* (London: Hodder and Stoughton, 1973), p. 42.

20. Earl Lloyd George, *My Father, Lloyd George* (New York: Crown Publishers, 1961), p. 181; C. P. Snow, *Variety of Men* (London: Macmillan, 1967), p. 123.

21. Colin Cross, ed., *Life with Lloyd George: The Diary of A. J. Sylvester 1931–45* (New York: Barnes & Noble, 1975), p. 16.

22. Eugen Spier, *Focus: A Footnote to the History of the Thirties* (London: Oswald Wolff, 1963), p. 50.

23. Grand, *The Heavenly Twins*, p. 61.

Introduction

1. Carolyn G. Heilbrun, Introduction to Vera Brittain, *Testament of Friendship: The Story of Winifred Holtby* (New York: Wideview Books, 1981), p. xv; William A. Sadler, Jr., "The Experience of Friendship," *Humanities* 6 (Fall 1970): 177.

2. Myron Brenton, *Friendship* (New York: Stein and Day, 1974), pp. 13, 42, 152.

3. See James Drever, *The Penguin Dictionary of Psychology*, rev. Harvey Wallerstein (Harmondsworth: Penguin Books, 1982), p. 103; and Odd Ramsoy, "Friendship," *International Encyclopedia of the Social Sciences*, vol. 6, p. 13.

4. Joel D. Block, *Friendship* (New York: Collier Books, 1981), pp. 3, 10, 206; also, Judith M. Hughes, *Emotion and High Politics: Personal Relations at the Summit in Late Nineteenth-Century Britain and Germany* (Berkeley: University of California Press, 1983).

5. Carl Schmitt, *The Concept of the Political*, trans. George Schwab (New Brunswick, N.J.: Rutgers University Press, 1976), pp. 26, 67; Jürgen Fijalkowski, "Carl Schmitt," *International Encyclopedia of the Social Sciences*, vol. 14, p. 58. *Foe* is probably a better translation of Schmitt's meaning in using *Feind* than is *enemy* (George Schwab, *The Challenge of the Exception: An Introduction to the Political Ideas of Carl Schmitt between 1921 and 1936* [Berlin: Duncker & Humblot, 1970], pp. 51–55).

6. Henry David Thoreau, *Walden and Civil Disobedience*, ed. Owen Thomas (New York: W.W. Norton, 1966), p. 236.

7. Otto Buniz, *Modern German Political Theory* (Garden City, N.Y.: Doubleday, 1955), p. 44.

8. José Ortega y Gasset, *Man and People*, trans. Willard R. Trask (New York: W.W. Norton, 1963), p. 150.

9. Schmitt, *The Concept of the Political*, p. 64; Fijalkowski, "Carl Schmitt," p. 59.

10. Carl Joachim Friedrich, *Man and His Government: An Empirical Theory of Politics* (New York: McGraw-Hill, 1963), pp. 161, 412.

11. Harry Crews, *A Childhood: The Biography of a Place* (New York: Harper & Row, 1978), p. 21; Reece McGee, *Academic Janus* (San Francisco: Jossey-Bass, 1971), p. 139.

12. Andrew M. Greeley, *The Friendship Game* (Garden City, N.Y.: Image Books, 1971), p. 15.

13. David Grayson, *Adventures of David Grayson* (Garden City, N.Y.: Doubleday, Doran, 1925), p. 262. David Grayson was, ironically, a pen name of Ray Stannard Baker, close observer of one of the most important political friendships, the one analyzed by Alexander L. George and Juliette L. George in *Woodrow Wilson and Colonel House: A Personality Study* (New York: John Day, 1956). The relationship between Wilson and House hardly deserved, nevertheless, the sensationalist account by George Sylvester Viereck, *The Strangest Friendship in History* (New York: Liveright, 1932).

14. Brenton, *Friendship*, pp. 27, 29, 99; Studs Terkel, *American Dreams: Lost and Found* (New York: Pantheon Books, 1980), p. 21; David Michaelis, *The Best of Friends: Profiles of Extraordinary Friendships* (New York: William Morrow, 1983), p. 233; Anthony Powell, *The Kindly Ones* (New York: Popular Library, 1976), p. 38.

15. Ruben E. Reina, "Two Patterns of Friendship in a Guatemalan Community," *American Anthropologist* 61 (February 1959): 44–50; For a classic statement of the former kind of friendship, see Paul van Ostaijen, *Patriotism, Inc. and Other Tales*, ed. and trans. E. M. Beekman (Amherst: The University of Massachusetts Press, 1971), p. 52.

16. Willa Cather, *Obscure Destinies* (New York: Vintage Books, 1974), pp. 193–230; Theodore Zeldin, *France 1848–1945: Taste & Corruption* (Oxford: Oxford University Press, 1980), p. 307.

17. Ada W. Finifter, "The Friendship Group as Protective Environment for Political Deviants," *The American Political Science Review* 68 (June 1974): 607–8.

18. C. P. Snow, *A Coat of Varnish* (New York: Charles Scribner's Sons, 1979), p. 317.

19. René Kraus, *Young Lady Randolph: The Life and Times of Jennie Jerome* (New York: G.P. Putnam's Sons, 1943), p. 257.

20. *Cicero on Friendship and on Old Age*, trans. Cyrus R. Edmonds (London: George Bell & Sons, 1889), pp. 18, 29.

21. *The Education of Henry Adams: An Autobiography* (Boston: Houghton Mifflin, 1918), pp. 108, 418; Sakari Virkkunen, *Ståhlberg: Suomen ensimmäinen presidentti* (Helsinki: Otava, 1978), p. 112; the passage from *Prometheus Unbound* is

found in Carlos Baker (editor), *The Selected Poetry and Prose of Percy Bysshe Shelley* (New York: The Modern Library, 1951), p. 91.

22. Kevin B. Harrington, quoted in *Boston Evening Globe*, February 13, 1975, p. 3. See also James A. Burke, writing to *Boston Sunday Globe*, June 18, 1972, p. A7; John Blatnik, "With Randolph in Yugoslavia," in Kay Halle, ed., *The Grand Original: Portraits of Randolph Churchill by his Friends* (Boston: Houghton Mifflin, 1971), p. 93; Jane Byrne, quoted in *The Boston Globe*, October 9, 1979, p. 3.

23. Mike Mansfield, interviewed in *The Boston Globe*, November 23, 1975, p. B4.

24. Alden Hatch, *The de Gaulle Nobody Knows: An Intimate Biography of Charles de Gaulle* (New York: Hawthorn Books, 1960), p. 15. See also George Macaulay Trevelyan, *Grey of Fallodon: Being the Life of Sir Edward Grey afterwards Viscount Grey of Fallodon* (London: Longmans, Green, 1937), p. 175.

25. Stephen Roskill, *Churchill and the Admirals* (New York: William Morrow, 1978), p. 176.

26. *The Art of the Possible: The Memoirs of Lord Butler* (London: Hamish Hamilton, 1971), p. 165.

27. *Churchill: Taken from the Diaries of Lord Moran: The Struggle for Survival, 1940–1965* (Boston: Houghton-Mifflin, 1966), p. 684; *The Memoirs of the Rt. Hon. The Earl of Woolton* (London: Cassell, 1959), p. 349; Kenneth Young, *Churchill and Beaverbrook: A Study in Friendship and Politics* (New York: James H. Heineman, 1966), p. 240. Surprisingly, it has been claimed that "Churchill never grasped" this theme (A. J. P. Taylor, "More Snakes Than Ladders," *The Observer*, October 24, 1976, p. 31).

28. Maurice Ashley, *Churchill as Historian* (New York: Charles Scribner's Sons, 1968), p. 140; Tom Clarke, *Northcliffe in History: An Intimate Study of Press Power* (London: Hutchinson, 1950), p. 119; Cameron Hazlehurst, *Politicians at War: July 1914 to May 1915: A Prologue to the Triumph of Lloyd George* (London: Jonathan Cape, 1971), pp. 205–6; Thomas Jones, *A Diary with Letters: 1931–1950* (London: Oxford University Press, 1954), p. 52; Lord Riddell, *More Pages from My Diary: 1908–1914* (London: Country Life, 1934), p. 121; John Grigg, *The Young Lloyd George* (London: Eyre Methuen, 1973), p. 140.

29. Irwin Edman, ed., *The Works of Plato* (New York: The Modern Library, 1938), p. 323.

30. Iris Murdoch, *The Sacred and Profane Love Machine* (New York: Warner Books, 1974), p. 359; Irish Murdoch, *The Philosopher's Pupip* (New York: The Viking Press, 1983), p. 74; *The Works of Robert Browning*, vol. 10 (London: Smith, Elder, 1912), pp. 360–67; John Crowe Ransom, ed., *Selected Poems of Thomas Hardy* (New York: Collier Books, 1966), p. xxiii; W. E. Williams, ed., *Browning* (Harmondsworth: Penguin Books, 1981), pp. 143, 191, 260; Vera Brittain, *England's Hour* (London: Futura Books, 1982), p. 223.

31. Paul Tillich, *Love, Power and Justice: Ontological Analyses and Ethical Applications* (London: Oxford University Press, 1974), pp. 11, 49.

32. Richard McKeon, ed., *Introduction to Aristotle* (New York: The Modern Library, 1947), p. 471.

33. Harold D. Lasswell, *Psychopathology and Politics*, new ed. (New York: The Viking Press, 1960), p. 193.

34. Arnold Bennett, *Lord Raingo* (New York: George H. Doran, 1926), p. 147.

35. Arthur C. Murray, *Master and Brother: Murrays of Elibank* (London: John Murray, 1945), p. 3.

36. Herbert du Parcq, *Life of David Lloyd George*, vol. 4 (London: Caxton, 1913), p. 645.

37. Harold D. Lasswell and Abraham Kaplan, "Appendix: On Power and Influ-

ence," in Lasswell, *Power and Personality* (New York: W.W. Norton, 1976), pp. 225, 228.

38. J. H. Grainger, *Character and Style in English Politics* (Cambridge: Cambridge University Press, 1969), p. 237; see also Grigg, *The Young Lloyd George*, p. 14.

39. Block, *Friendship*, p. 5; Gilbert Meilaender, *Friendship: A Study in Theological Ethics* (Notre Dame, Ind.: University of Notre Dame Press, 1981), p. 3; Ramsoy, "Friendship," p. 12; Michael Gelven, *Winter, Friendship, and Guilt: The Sources of Self-Inquiry* (New York: Harper & Row, 1972), p. 5; J. Glenn Gray, *The Warriors: Reflections on Men in Battle* (New York: Harper & Row, 1967), p. 90; Greeley, *The Friendship Game*, pp. 39, 109; Eugene Kennedy, *On Being a Friend* (New York: Continuum, 1982), p. 112; Kaspar D. Naegele, "Friendship and Acquaintances: An Exploration of Some Social Distinctions," *Harvard Educational Review* 28 (Summer 1958): 243.

40. Kennedy, *On Being a Friend*, pp. 51, 81; C. S. Lewis, *The Four Loves* (New York: Harcourt Brace Jovanovich, 1960), p. 190.

41. Marcel Proust, *Within a Budding Grove*, trans. C. K. Scott Moncrieff (New York: Vintage Books, 1970), p. 351.

42. *The Complete Essays of Montaigne*, trans. Donald M. Frame (Stanford, Calif.: Stanford University Press, 1958), p. 139.

43. Grayson, *Adventures*, p. 262; E. M. Forster, *The Longest Journey* (New York: Vintage Books, 1962), p. 69.

44. Naegele, "Friendship and Acquaintances," p. 236.

45. Lord Beaverbrook, *Politicians and the War, 1914–1916* (London: Oldbourne, 1960), p. 353.

46. Ramsoy, "Friendship," p. 16.

47. J. Davidson Ketchum, *Ruhleben: A Prison Camp Society* (Toronto: University of Toronto Press, 1965), p. 138; Gray, *The Warriors*, p. 89; Lewis, *The Four Loves*, p. 99; W. H. Lewis, ed., *Letters of C. S. Lewis* (New York: Harcourt Brace Jovanovich, 1975), p. 245; Meilaender, *Friendship*, p. 77; Sadler, "The Experience of Friendship," pp. 178, 183; *Cicero on Friendship*, p. 15; Heilbrun, Introduction to Brittain, *Testament of Friendship*, p. xvi.

48. Robert Brain, *Friends and Lovers* (New York: Basic Books, 1976), p. 14; Greeley, *The Friendship Game*, p. 33; also José Ortega y Gasset, *On Love: Aspects of a Single Theme*, trans. Tony Talbot (New York: Meridian Books, 1971), pp. 175–76; Proust, *Within a Budding Grove*, p. 261.

49. C. S. Lewis, *The Four Loves*, p. 87.

50. Gelven, *Winter, Friendship, and Guilt*, pp. 28, 121; Francis Bacon, *The Essayes or Counsels Civil & Morall* (New York: The Heritage Press, 1944), p. 84; Lasswell and Kaplan, "Appendix," p. 225.

51. Brain, *Friends and Lovers*, p. 206; Meilaender, *Friendship*, p. 46; William A. Sadler, Jr., *Existence and Love: A New Approach in Existential Phenomenology* (New York: Charles Scribner's Sons, 1969), pp. 334–35; Jeffrey L. Sammons, *Heinrich Heine: A Modern Biography* (Princeton, N.J.: Princeton University Press, 1979), p. 170.

52. William Rounseville Alger, *The Friendships of Women* (Boston: Roberts Brothers, 1868), p. 416.

53. Max Weber, *The Theory of Social and Economic Organization*, trans. A. M. Henderson and Talcott Parsons (New York: The Free Press of Glencoe, 1964), p. 119.

54. Nicholas Berdyaev, *Slavery and Freedom*, trans. R. M. French (New York: Charles Scribner's Sons, 1960), pp. 56–57.

55. Kenneth Rose, *The Later Cecils* (New York: Harper & Row, 1975), pp. 2, 71;

John Colville, *Winston Churchill and His Inner Circle* (New York: Wyndham Books, 1981), p. 210; Mary Soames, *Clementine Churchill: The Biography of a Marriage* (Boston: Houghton Mifflin, 1979), pp. 569–70.

56. Block, *Friendship*, p. 224; Vilhelm Moberg, *Unto a Good Land*, trans. Gustaf Lannestock (New York: Popular Library, 1971), p. 79.

57. Greeley, *The Friendship Game*, pp. 34–35; Gray, *The Warriors*, p. 94; Tillich, *Love, Power and Justice*, p. 33; C. S. Lewis, *The Four Loves*, p. 90.

58. Donald McCormick, *The Mask of Merlin: A Critical Study of David Lloyd George* (London: Macdonald, 1963), p. 32; Ashley, *Churchill as Historian*, p. 229; J. B. Priestley, *The Edwardians* (New York: Harper & Row, 1970), p. 114; Leo Abse, *Private Member* (London: Macdonald, 1973), p. 263.

59. Colin Cross, ed., *Life with Lloyd George: The Diary of A. J. Sylvester, 1931–45* (New York: Barnes & Noble, 1975), p. 281.

60. W. R. P. George, *The Making of Lloyd George* (London: Faber & Faber, 1976), p. 98.

61. Peter Rowland, *Lloyd George* (London: Barrie & Jenkins, 1975), p. 314; Stephen Koss, *Nonconformity in Modern British Politics* (London: B.T. Batsford, 1975), p. 189.

62. John Grigg, *Lloyd George: The People's Champion, 1902–1911* (Berkeley: University of California Press, 1978), pp. 181–82; Rowland, *Lloyd George*, pp. 205–215.

63. Bennett, *Lord Raingo*, pp. 33–34, 234; Joyce Cary, *Prisoner of Grace* (New York: Harper & Brothers, 1952), p. 276.

64. Reginald Pound, *Arnold Bennett: A Biography* (New York: Harcourt, Brace, 1953), pp. 11, 276; *The Journal of Arnold Bennett* (New York: The Literary Guild, 1933), p. 899.

65. Richard Hughes, *The Fox in the Attic* (Frogmore: Triad Panther Books, 1979), p. 72; John Masters, *Now, God Be Thanked* (New York: McGraw-Hill, 1979), p. 170; Phillip Rock, *The Passing Bells* (New York: Dell, 1978), p. 74.

66. Chris Cook, *The Age of Alignment: Electoral Politics in Britain, 1922–1929* (Toronto: University of Toronto Press, 1975), p. 256; Giovanni Costigan, *Makers of Modern England: The Force of Individual Genius in History* (London: Macmillan, 1969), p. 226; Paul Johnson, ed., *The Oxford Book of British Political Anecdotes* (New York: Oxford University Press, 1986), p. xiii. For a memorable poetic definition of goathood, see Clive James, "Sack Artist," *London Review of Books* 7 (18 July 1985): 22.

67. The Earl of Birkenhead, *Halifax: The Life of Lord Halifax* (London: Hamish Hamilton, 1965), p. 147; John Campbell, *Lloyd George: The Goat in the Wilderness, 1922–1931* (London: Jonathan Cape, 1977), p. 242; Martin Gilbert, *Winston S. Churchill*, vol. 5 (Boston: Houghton Mifflin, 1977), p. 354; Robert Rhodes James, *Memoirs of a Conservative: J. C. C. Davidson's Memoirs and Papers, 1910–37* (New York: Macmillan, 1970), pp. 113, 117, 309, 356; Ferdinand Mount, *The Theatre of Politics* (London: Weidenfeld and Nicolson, 1972), p. 187; Frank Owen, *Tempestuous Journey: Lloyd George, His Life and Times* (London: Hutchinson, 1954), p. 671; Kenneth Young, *Stanley Baldwin* (London: Weidenfeld and Nicolson, 1976), p. 30.

68. Michael Holroyd, *Lytton Strachey: A Critical Biography*, vol. 2 (New York: Holt, Rinehart and Winston, 1968), p. 169.

69. John Maynard Keynes, *Essays in Biography* (New York: W.W. Norton, 1963), p. 35.

70. David V. Erdman, ed., *The Complete Poetry and Prose of William Blake*, rev. ed. (Berkeley: University of California Press, 1982), p. 36.

71. A. J. P. Taylor, ed., *My Darling Pussy: The Letters of Lloyd George and Frances Stevenson, 1913–42* (London: Weidenfeld and Nicholson, 1975), photogra-

phy following p. 116; Cross, ed., *Life with Lloyd George*, pp. 16–17; Rowland, *Lloyd George*, pp. 315, 532.

72. Lady Olwen Carey Evans and Mary Garner, *Lloyd George Was My Father* (Llandysul: Gomer Press, 1985), p. 68; Rowland, *Lloyd George*, p. 643.

73. Cross, ed., *Life with Lloyd George*, pp. 162, 230–31, 259; John Grigg, "Lloyd George," in *Great Britons* (London: British Broadcasting Corporation, 1978), p. 197; John Grigg, *Lloyd George: From Peace to War, 1912–1916* (Berkeley: University of California Press, 1985), p. 82; Kirsty McLeod, *The Wives of Downing Street* (London: Collins, 1976), p. 204.

74. McLeod, *The Wives of Downing Street*, p. 197; Taylor, ed., *My Darling Pussy*, pp. 109–111; Earl Lloyd George, *My Father, Lloyd George* (New York: Crown, 1961); p. 42; George Malcolm Thompson, *The Prime Ministers: From Robert Walpole to Margaret Thatcher* (London: Nationwide Book Service, 1980), p. 192. Before the birth of this daughter, Frances Stevenson apparently had at least one abortion. (Grigg, *Lloyd George: From Peace to War*, pp. 224–25).

75. Taylor, ed., *My Darling Pussy*, pp. 12–14, 53, 90–93.

76. Costigan, *Makers of Modern England*, p. 200; Lloyd George, *My Father, Lloyd George*, pp. 219, 221, 237.

77. Grigg, *Lloyd George: The People's Champion*, p. 142; W. Watkin Davies, *Lloyd George, 1863–1914* (London: Constable, 1939), p. 437; A. J. Sylvester, *The Real Lloyd George* (London: Cassell, 1947), p. 49.

78. Tallulah Bankhead, *Tallulah: My Autobiography* (New York: Harper & Brothers, 1952), p. 168; Stephen E. Koss, *Lord Haldane: Scapegoat for Liberalism* (New York: Columbia University Press, 1969), p. 235; Malcolm Thomson, *David Lloyd George: The Official Biography* (London: Hutchinson, no date), p. 100; Alan Clark, ed., *"A Good Innings": The Private Papers of Viscount Lee of Fareham* (London: John Murray, 1974), p. 319.

79. C. P. Snow, *Variety of Men* (London: Macmillan, 1967), p. 103; Cross, ed., *Life with Lloyd George*, p. 189; Grigg, *Lloyd George: The People's Champion*, p. 128.

80. Cross, ed., *Life with Lloyd George*, p. 186.

81. Lloyd George, *My Father, Lloyd George*, p. 44.

82. Hazlehurst, *Politicians at War*, p. 218; Grigg, *The Young Lloyd George*, p. 228; Owen, *Tempestuous Journey*, p. 88.

83. Grigg, *The Young Lloyd George*, p. 234; McCormick, *The Mask of Merlin*, p. 46.

84. Grigg, *The Young Lloyd George*, pp. 237–38; McLeod, *The Wives of Downing Street*, p. 190.

85. Keynes, *Essays in Biography*, pp. 34, 36, 38.

86. Thomas Jones, *Lloyd George* (London: Oxford University Press, 1951), p. 275; Cook, *The Age of Alignment*, p. 250.

87. Priestley, *The Edwardians*, p. 113. See also Emil Ludwig, *Nine Etched from Life* (New York: Robert M. McBride, 1934), p. 241; Owen, *Tempestuous Journey*, pp. 752–53.

88. Sir Oswald Mosley, *My Life* (New Rochelle, N.Y.: Arlington House, 1972), p. 277.

89. Taylor, ed., *My Darling Pussy*, pp. 112–13; Virginia Woolf, *Orlando: A Biography* (Harmondsworth: Penguin Books, 1975), p. 155. *Orlando* was first published in London by the Hogarth Press in 1928.

90. Taylor, ed., *My Darling Pussy*, p. 112n.

91. Jones, *Lloyd George*, p. 97.

92. Randolph S. Roman, *Twenty-One Years* (Boston: Houghton Mifflin, 1965), p. 36.

93. Peregrine Churchill and Julian Mitchell, *Jennie: Lady Randolph Churchill* (Glasgow: Fontana/Collins, 1976), p. 129.

94. Robert Lewis Taylor, *Winston Churchill: An Informal Study of Greatness* (Garden City, N.Y.: Doubleday, 1952), p. 416. Television makeup was not a likely problem, for Churchill never gave a television interview, and was not much interested in television. David Childs, *Britain since 1945: A Political History* (London: Methuen, 1984), p. 74).

95. Moran, *Churchill*, p. 735.

96. Violet Bonham Carter, *Winston Churchill: An Intimate Portrait* (New York: Harcourt, Brace & World, 1965), p. 173; Piers Brendon, *Winston Churchill: A Biography* (New York: Harper & Row, 1984), p. 40; John Colville, *The Fringes of Power: 10 Downing Street Diaries, 1839–1955* (New York: W.W. Norton, 1986), p. 158; Ted Morgan, *Churchill: Young Man in a Hurry, 1874–1915* (New York: Simon and Schuster, 1982), p. 239; Soames, *Clementine Churchill*, p. 69; Anthony Storr, "The Man," in A. J. P. Taylor and others, *Churchill: Four Faces and the Man* (Harmondsworth: Penguin Books, 1973), p. 211.

97. Jack Fishman, *My Darling Clementine: The Story of Lady Churchill* (New York: David McKay, 1963), p. 19; Gerald Pawle, *The War and Colonel Warden* (New York: Alfred A. Knopf, 1963), p. 282.

98. Winston S. Churchill, *The Second World War: Closing the Ring* (New York: Bantam Books, 1974), p. 290; Robert Payne, *The Great Man: A Portrait of Winston Churchill* (New York: Coward, McCann & Geoghegan, 1974), p. 303.

99. Soames, *Clementine Churchill*, p. 44; C. P. Snow, *Variety of Men* (London: Macmillan, 1967), p. 103; Robert Lewis Taylor, *Winston Churchill*, p. 95.

100. Randolph S. Churchill, *Winston Churchill*, companion vol. 2, part 2 (London: Heinemann, 1969), p. 800.

101. Moran, *Churchill*, pp. 201, 286; Robert Lewis Taylor, *Winston Churchill*, p. 95; William Manchester, *The Last Lion: Winston Spencer Churchill: Visions of Glory, 1874–1932* (Boston: Little, Brown, 1983), p. 367.

102. Moran, *Churchill*, p. 184.

103. Taylor, *Winston Churchill*, p. 403; Elizabeth Longford and Frank Longford, "Churchill," in Lord Longford and Sir John Wheeler-Bennett, eds., *The History Makers: Leaders and Statesmen of the 20th Century* (New York: St. Martin's Press, 1973), p. 158; A. J. P. Taylor, *Politicians, Socialism and Historians* (New York: Stein and Day, 1982), p. 27.

104. Roy Howells, *Churchill's Last Years* (New York: David McKay, 1966), p. 188; and Bonham Carter, *Winston Churchill*.

105. Colville, *Winston Churchill and His Inner Circle*, p. 143; R. W. Thompson, *Winston Churchill: The Yankee Marlborough* (Garden City, N.Y.: Doubleday, 1963), p. 22; Lord Beaverbrook's remarks are in Manchester, *The Last Lion*, p. 212; for Churchill on Prince Eugene of Savoy, see John Spencer Churchill, *A Churchill Canvas* (Boston: Little, Brown, 1961), p. 258.

106. Richard Deacon, *The Cambridge Apostles: A History of Cambridge University's Elite Intellectual Secret Society.*(New York: Farrar, Straus & Giroux, 1985), p. 62; Payne, *The Great Man*, p. 114.

107. It has been reported that "Churchill was given a Private Secretary, [Edward Marsh" (Martin Gilbert, *Churchill* [Garden City, N.Y.: Doubleday, 1980], p. 25.) This is misleading; Churchill did not inherit Marsh, but rather found him. See also, Kate Fleming, *The Churchills* (New York: The Viking Press, 1975), p. 165; Christopher Hassall, *Edward Marsh: Patron of the Arts: A Biography* (London: Longmans, 1959), pp. 119 and 151. Payne, *The Great Man*, p. 114.

108. Randolph S. Churchill, *Winston Churchill*, companion vol. 2, part 2, p. 1198.

109. Trumbull Higgins, *Winston Churchill and the Dardanelles: A Dialogue in Ends and Means* (New York: Macmillan, 1963), p. 36; Colville, *Winston Churchill and His Inner Circle*, p. 24.

110. Randolph S. Churchill, *Winston Churchill*, companion vol. 2, part 3 (London: Heinemann, 1969), p. 1447; Hassall, *Edward Marsh*, p. 164.

111. Hassall, *Edward Marsh*, p. 169; Moran, *Churchill*, pp. 292–93.

112. Hassall, *Edward Marsh*, p. 142; Randolph S. Churchill, *Winston Churchill*, companion vol. 2, part 2, p. 836.

113. Hassall, *Edward Marsh*, p. 680.

114. Ibid., pp. xi, 287; Christopher Hassall, *Rupert Brooke: A Biography* (London: Faber and Faber, 1984), pp. 462–86.

115. Randolph S. Churchill, *Winston Churchill*, companion vol. 1, part I (Boston: Houghton Mifflin, 1967), pp. 625, 643. There is an abbreviated reference to this legal case in Randolph S. Churchill, *Winston Churchill*, vol. 1 (Boston: Houghton Mifflin, 1966), p. 240. In 1958, a dying Brendan Bracken recalled what was apparently a highly inexact version of this case. (Moran, *Churchill*, pp. 793–94). Bracken, however, had not yet met Churchill in 1896. A less confused, but still inexact, report is given by Brendon in *Winston Churchill* (p. 17).

116. Randolph S. Churchill, *Winston Churchill*, companion vol. 1, part I, pp. 626–28; see also, Gelven, *Winter, Friendship and Guilt*, p. 98.

117. Sadler, "The Experience of Friendship," p. 184.

118. Tillich, *Love, Power, and Justice*, p. 25; Iris Murdoch, *The Black Prince* (New York: Warner Books, 1978), p. 251; Brenton, *Friendship*, p. 135.

119. Rollo May, *Man's Search for Himself* (New York: Signet Books, 1967), p. 206; Frank Brady and W. K. Wimsatt, eds., *Samuel Johnson: Selected Poetry and Prose* (Berkeley: University of California Press), p. 239.

120. Sarah Grand, *The Heavenly Twins*, (London: William Heinemann, 1894) p. 131.

Chapter One

1. Kingsley Martin, *Father Figures: A First Volume of Autobiography: 1897–1931* (Harmondsworth: Penguin Books, 1969), p. 114. Rivers is himself dissected in a novel by Pat Barker, *The Eye in the Door* (New York: Dutton, 1994).

2. Harold Owen and John Bell, eds., *Wilfred Owen: Collected Letters* (London: Oxford University Press, 1967), p. 481n.

3. Peter de Mendelssohn, *The Age of Churchill: Heritage and Adventure 1874–1911* (New York: Alfred A. Knopf, 1961), p. 84.

Churchill did not include Lloyd George in his *Great Contemporaries* (London: Fontana Books, 1965). This revised edition is longer by several essays than the original edition of *Great Contemporaries* published in 1937 in London by Thornton Butterworth. In the 1943 edition, published by Macmillan, essays on Leon Trotsky and Franklin Roosevelt were omitted for political reasons. (Frederick Woods, *A Bibliography of the Works of Sir Winston Churchill*, 2d rev. ed. [London: Library of Imperial History, 1975], p. 80.) A relatively sympathetic 1935 essay on Adolf Hitler appears in all editions of *Great Contemporaries*. This essay was too much even for one of Churchill's most worshipful biographers. (Esmé Wingfield-Stratford, *Churchill: The Making of a Hero* [London: Victor Gollancz, 1942], p. 229.)

4. Michael Kinnear, *The Fall of Lloyd George: The Political Crisis of 1922* (London: Macmillan, 1973), p. 37; Kenneth O. Morgan, *Wales in British Politics 1868–1922*, 3d ed. (Cardiff: University of Wales Press, 1980), p. 113n; A. J. P. Taylor, *Beaverbrook* (New York: Simon and Schuster, 1972), p. 615; Trevor Wilson, ed., *The Political Diaries of C.P. Scott, 1911–1928* (Ithaca, N.Y.: Cornell University Press, 1970), p. 24.

5. Lord Boothby, "Four at Versailles," *Books and Bookmen* 18 (April 1973): 27; Donald McCormick, *The Mask of Merlin: A Critical Study of David Lloyd George* (London: Macdonald, 1963), p. 15; Kenneth O. Morgan, ed., *Lloyd George: Family Letters, 1885–1936* (Cardiff: University of Wales Press and London: Oxford University Press, 1973), p. 10.

6. A. J. P. Taylor, *English History 1914–1945* (New York: Oxford University Press, 1965), p. 137.

7. Harold Begbie, *The Mirrors of Downing Street: Some Political Reflections* (Port Washington, N.Y.: Kennikat Press, 1970), p. 4.

8. Alfred F. Havighurst, *Twentieth-Century Britain*, 2d ed. (New York: Harper & Row, 1966), p. 178.

9. Herbert Sidebotham, *Pillars of the State* (London: Nisbet, 1921), p. 79.

10. Arthur S. Link, ed., *The Papers of Woodrow Wilson*, vol. 40 (Princeton, N.J.: Princeton University Press, 1982), p. 345.

11. A. J. Sylvester, *The Real Lloyd George* (London: Cassell, 1947), p. 144.

12. Shane Leslie, *Long Shadows* (London: John Murray, 1966), p. 240; Loelia, Duchess of Westminster, *Grace and Favour* (New York: Reynal, 1961), p. 209; Kenneth Young, ed., *The Diaries of Sir Robert Bruce Lockhart*, vol. 1 (London: Macmillan, 1974), p. 370.

13. John Grigg, *Lloyd George: From Peace to War, 1912–1916* (Berkeley: University of California Press, 1985), p. 414; Robert Payne, *The Great Man: A Portrait of Winston Churchill* (New York: Coward, McCann & Geoghegan, 1974), p. 371.

14. Lord Riddell, *More Pages from My Diary: 1908–1914* (London: Country Life, 1934), p. 107.

15. John Grigg, *Lloyd George: The People's Champion 1902–1911* (Berkeley: University of California Press, 1978), pp. 128, 305; John Grigg, *Nancy Astor: A Lady Unashamed* (Boston: Little, Brown, 1980), p. 139.

16. George Dangerfield, *The Strange Death of Liberal England* (New York: Capricorn Books, 1961), p. 38.

17. Lord Beaverbrook, *Men and Power, 1917–1918* (London: Hutchinson, 1956), p. xxxvi; Lord Beaverbrook, *Politicians and the War, 1914–1916* (London: Oldbourne, 1960), p. 394; Morgan, *Wales in British Politics*, p. 277; Sir Geoffrey Shakespeare, *Let Candles Be Brought In* (London: Macdonald, 1949), p. 51.

18. Cameron Hazlehurst, *Politicians at War: July 1914 to May 1915: A Prologue to the Triumph of Lloyd George* (London: Jonathan Cape, 1971), p. 257.

19. Frank Owen, *Tempestuous Journey: Lloyd George, His Life and Times* (London: Hutchinson, 1954), p. 293.

20. W. R. P. George, *The Making of Lloyd George* (London: Faber & Faber, 1976), p. 145. See also John Grigg, *The Young Lloyd George* (London: Eyre Methuen, 1973), p. 67; Morgan, ed., *Lloyd George*, p. 14.

21. Don M. Cregier, *Bounder from Wales: Lloyd George's Career before the First World War* (Columbia: University of Missouri Press, 1976), p. 37; Grigg, *Lloyd George: The People's Champion*, pp. 129, 143; Peter Rowland, *Lloyd George* (London: Barrie & Jenkins, 1975), p. 93.

22. Grigg, *The Young Lloyd George*, p. 243.

23. A. J. P. Taylor, ed., *My Darling Pussy: The Letters of Lloyd George and Frances Stevenson 1913–41* (London: Weidenfeld and Nicolson, 1975), p. 44.

24. Grigg, *Lloyd George: The People's Champion*, p. 359.

25. Sylvester, *The Real Lloyd George*, p. 5.

26. Lady Olwen Carey Evans and Mary Garner, *Lloyd George Was My Father* (Llandysol: Gomer Press, 1985), p. 25; Frances, Countess Lloyd-George of Dwyfor, "Introduction" to Malcolm Thomson, *David Lloyd George: The Official Biography*, (London: Hutchinson, no date), pp. 14-15, 120; Frank Owen, *Tempestuous Jour-*

ney, p. 23; Sylvester, *The Real Lloyd George*, pp. 11, 272; Thomson, *David Lloyd George*, p. 100.

27. George, *The Making of Lloyd George*, p. 146; J. Hugh Edwards, *David Lloyd George: The Man and the Statesman*, vol. 1 (New York: J.H. Sears, 1929), p. 137; E. T. Raymond, *Mr. Lloyd George* (New York: George H. Doran, 1972), p. 46. "E. T. Raymond" was a pen name of E. R. Thompson.

28. Grigg, *Lloyd George: The People's Champion*, p. 90; Rowland, *Lloyd George*, p. 417; Taylor. ed., *My Darling Pussy*, pp. 196–97.

29. Earl Lloyd George, *My Father, Lloyd George* (New York: Crown, 1961), pp. 30–31; W. Watkin Davies, *Lloyd George 1863–1914* (London: Constable, 1939), pp. 11, 440; Rowland, *Lloyd George*, p. 10.

30. Davies, *Lloyd George*, p. 15.

31. Colin Cross, ed., *Life with Lloyd George: The Diary of A. J. Sylvester 1931-45* (New York: Barnes & Noble, 1975), p. 90; Earl Lloyd George, *My Father, Lloyd George*, p. 19; Sylvester, *The Real Lloyd George*, p. 6; Cregier, *Bounder from Wales*, p. 9.

32. Rowland, *Lloyd George*, p. 8; Grigg, *Lloyd George: The People's Champion*, pp. 29, 50; Davies, *Lloyd George*, pp. 20–21; Edwards, *David Lloyd George*, vol. 1, p. 26.

33. Rowland, *Lloyd George*, p. 11.

34. Regarding secondary education see Jack Jones, *The Welsh Man David: An Imaginative Presentation, Based on Fact, on the Life of David Lloyd George from 1880 to 1914* (London: Hamish Hamilton, 1944), pp. 1, 67, 197; George, *The Making of Lloyd George*, p. 162; Viscount Gwynedd, *Dame Margaret: The Life Story of His Mother* (London: George Allen & Unwin, 1947), p. 74; Morgan, *Wales in British Politics*, p. 48. Comments on Lloyd George as a lowbrow are in John Campbell, *Lloyd George: The Goat in the Wilderness 1922–1931* (London: Jonathan Cape, 1977), pp. 5, 204; Dangerfield, *The Strange Death of Liberal England*, p. 19; Begbie, *The Mirrors of Downing Street*, p. 3; Stephen Koss, *Fleet Street Radical: A. G. Gardiner and the Daily News* (Hamden, Conn.: Archon Books, 1973), p. 249; William Gerhardie, *God's Fifth Column: A Biography of the Age 1890–1940*, eds. Michael Holroyd and Robert Skidelsky (New York: Simon and Schuster, 1981), p. 314. The "yahoo" quote is from Sir John Wheeler-Bennett, *Knaves, Fools and Heroes in Europe between the Wars* (New York: St. Martin's Press, 1975), p. 173. A comment regarding his educational peers is in *The Pomp of Power* (London: Hutchinson, 1922), p. 145. See also John Buchan, *The King's Grace 1910–1935* (London: Hodder and Stoughton, 1935), p. 188.

35. On his uniqueness among cabinet members see Robert Rhodes James, *The British Revolution: British Politics, 1880–1939*, vol. 1 (London: Hamish Hamilton, 1976), p. 153; Philip W. Buck, *Amateurs and Professionals in British Politics 1918–59* (Chicago: The University of Chicago Press, 1963), p. 121. For the attitude of his colleagues see Cregier, *Bounder from Wales*, pp. 94, 111, 121. Lord Haldane's comment is in H. V. Emy, "The Land Campaign: Lloyd George as a Social Reformer, 1909-14," in A. J. P. Taylor, ed., *Lloyd George: Twelve Essays* (New York: Atheneum, 1971), p. 67; G. R. Searle, *The Quest for National Efficiency: A Study in British Politics and Political Thought, 1899–1914* (Berkeley: University of California Press, 1971), p. 249. Asquith's remarks are in Cregier, *Bounder from Wales*, p. 121; Hazlehurst, *Politicians at War*, p. 170.

36. Raymond, *Mr. Lloyd George*, p. 277; David Robin Watson, *Georges Clemenceau: A Political Biography* (New York: David McKay, 1976), pp. 226n, 400.

37. John Maynard Keynes, *Essays in Biography* (New York: W. W. Norton, 1963), p. 39.

38. Thomas A. Bailey, *Woodrow Wilson and the Lost Peace* (Chicago: Quadran-

gle Books, 1963), p. 157; Robert Lansing, *The Big Four and Others of the Peace Conference* (Boston: Houghton Mifflin, 1921), p. 103.

39. Arthur S. Link, ed., *The Papers of Woodrow Wilson*, vol. 33 (Princeton, N.J.: Princeton University Press, 1980), p. 533.

40. Burton J. Henrick, *The Life and Letters of Walter H. Page*, vol. 3 (Garden City, N.Y.: Doubleday, Page, 1925), p. 369.

41. Sir Edward Spears, "An Appreciation," in Nancy Maurice, ed., *The Maurice Case: From the Papers of Major-General Sir Frederick Maurice* (Hamden, Conn.: Archon Books, 1972), p. 41.

42. Grigg, *Lloyd George: The People's Champion*, pp. 145, 359; Cross, ed., *Life with Lloyd George*, p. 100.

43. *The Memoirs of Captain Liddell Hart*, vol. 1 (London: Cassell, 1967), pp. 339, 372-73.

44. On Lloyd George's reading and interest in books, see Thomson, *David Lloyd George*, p. 50; William Martin, *Statesmen of the War in Retrospect: 1918–1928* (New York: Minton, Balch, 1928), p. 307; Edward David, ed., *Inside Asquith's Cabinet: From the Diaries of Charles Hobhouse* (New York: St. Martin's Press, 1977), p. 230; George, *The Making of Lloyd George*, p. 69; John Grigg, "Lloyd George," in *Great Britons* (London: British Broadcasting Corporation, 1978), p. 185; Frank Owen, *Tempestuous Journey*, p. 755. Churchill's reading is discussed in Grigg, "Lloyd George," p. 185; Grigg, *Lloyd George: The People's Champion*, p. 359; Walter Henry Thompson, *Assignment: Churchill* (New York: Farrar, Straus and Young, 1955), p. 228; and Roy Howells, *Churchill's Last Years* (New York: David McKay, 1966), pp. 117-18, 199.

45. Michael G. Fry, *Lloyd George and Foreign Policy*, vol. 1 (Montréal: McGill-Queen's University Press, 1977), p. 22n; Grigg, *Lloyd George: The People's Champion*, pp. 55, 244, 285. His knowledge of contemporary literature is debated by A. J. P. Taylor, *Essays in English History* (Harmondsworth: Penguin Books, 1982), p. 256. See also Riddell, *More Pages from My Diary*, p. 128.

46. Riddell, *More Pages from My Diary*, p. 179.

47. Women's suffrage is discussed in Viscount Gwynedd, *Dame Margaret*, p. 128; Kirsty McLeod, *The Wives of Downing Street* (London: Collins, 1976), pp. 19, 195. That Margaret Lloyd George did not support even the 1918 extension of suffrage to middle-class women did not mean she had no interest in politics. She was probably the first spouse of a British prime minister to speak regularly in public (ibid., p. 20). In one by-election campaign, in Cardiganshire in 1921, she gave sixty-five speeches in support of the Coalition Liberal candidate (Morgan, *Wales in British Politics*, p. 296). She was certainly the first such spouse to build an independent political career. Utilizing the political rights of middle-class women in local elections, she became, without her husband's patronage, powerful in local government in North Wales. She was the first woman to serve as a magistrate in Wales. (Thomson, *David Lloyd George*, p. 455). She was also chairman of the Criccieth Urban District Council. (Ibid., p. 339; McLeod, *The Wives of Downing Street*, p. 203). In 1919, she gave campaign speeches in Nancy Astor's successful campaign, as a Conservative, to become the first woman to serve as a Member of Parliament (Christopher Sykes, *Nancy: The Life of Lady Astor* [London: Granada, 1979], p. 225). Otherwise, Margaret Lloyd was vigorously anti-Conservative (Lord Beaverbrook, *The Decline and Fall of Lloyd George: And Great Was the Fall Thereof* [London: Collins, 1966], p. 9n). She served as President of her local Women's Liberal Association. (Thomson, *David Lloyd George*, p. 455). In light of her political activities, her main objection to women's suffrage may have been that her husband was for it.

On Churchill and suffrage for women see Vera Brittain, *Lady into Woman: A History of Women from Victoria to Elizabeth II* (New York: Macmillan, 1953), p. 14;

Grigg, *Nancy Astor*, p. 87; Martin Pugh, *Electoral Reform in War and Peace, 1906–18* (London: Routledge and Kegan Paul, 1978), pp. 181–9, 33–34.

See also Thomson, *David Lloyd George*, p. 220; Rowland, *Lloyd George*, pp. 228, 267; Roy Douglas, *The History of the Liberal Party 1895–1970* (Madison, N.J.: Farleigh Dickinson University Press, 1971), p. 55n; David Morgan, *Suffragists and Liberals: The Politics of Woman Suffrage in England* (Totowa, N.J.: Rowman and Littlefield, 1975), p. 156; Pamela Brookes, *Women at Westminster: An Account of Women in the British Parliament, 1918–1966* (London: Peter Davies, 1967), p. 9; Kenneth O. Morgan, *Consensus and Disunity: the Lloyd George Coalition Government, 1918–1922* (Oxford: Clarendon Pres, 1986), pp. 33, 152.

48. McCormick, *The Mask of Merlin*, p. 74.

49. Brian Abel-Smith and Robert Stevens, *Lawyers and the Courts: A Sociological Study of the English Legal System, 1750–1965* (Cambridge, Mass.: Harvard University Press, 1967), pp. 67n–68n, 169, 187; Herbert du Parcq, *Life of David Lloyd George*, vol. 1 (London: Caxton, 1912), p. 43; Viscount Gwynedd, *Dame Margaret*, p. 83.

50. Oscar Browning, *Memories of Later Years* (New York: D. Appleton, 1923), pp. 46, 431; *The Journal of Arnold Bennett* (New York: The Literary Guild, 1933), p. 624; Sir Ivor Jennings; *Cabinet Government*, 3d ed. (Cambridge: Cambridge University Press, 1959), p. 187; Thomas Jones, *Lloyd George* (London: Oxford University Press, 1951), p. 267; Basil Murray, *L.G.* (London: Sampson Low, Marston, 1932), p. 52; Rowland, *Lloyd George*, p. 799. Lloyd George as a conversationalist is discussed in Thompson, *Assignment: Churchill*, p. 6; Gerhardie, *God's Fifth Column*, p. 242; Winston S. Churchill, *Thoughts and Adventures* (London: Thornton Butterworth, 1932), p. 59; and Cross, ed., *Life With Lloyd George*, p. 92.

His listening ability is described in René Kraus, *Winston Churchill: A Biography* (Philadelphia: J.B. Lippincott, 1940), pp. 221–22; Robert Boothby, *I Fight to Live* (London: Victor Gollancz, 1947), pp. 31–32; Campbell, *Lloyd George*, p. 6; Carey Evans and Garner, *Lloyd George*, pp. 44, 89; David, ed., *Inside Asquith's Cabinet*, p. 73; John Ehrman, "Lloyd George and Churchill as War Ministers," *Transactions of the Royal Historical Society*, 5th series, vol. 11, p. 104; Grigg, "Lloyd George," p. 207; Grigg, *Lloyd George: The People's Champion*, pp. 66–67, 326; Rowland, *Lloyd George*, p. 746; Arthur Salter, *Slave of the Lamp: A Public Servant's Notebook* (London: Weidenfeld & Nicolson, 1967), p. 33; The Earl of Swinton, *Sixty Years of Power: Some Memories of the Men Who Wielded It* (London: Hutchinson, 1966), pp. 42, 46; and Emil Ludwig, *Nine Etched from Life* (New York: Robert M. McBride, 1934), p. 211.

51. Jones, *Lloyd George*, p. 90; Arthur Salter, *Personality in Politics: Studies of Contemporary Statesmen* (London: Faber and Faber, 1947), p. 50; Shakespeare, *Let Candles Be Brought In*, p. 66.

52. Harold Macmillan, *The Past Masters: Politics and Politicians 1906–1939* (London: Macmillan, 1975), p. 60. See also Harold Macmillan, *Winds of Change 1914–1939* (New York: Harper & Row, 1966), p. 166.

53. Douglas, *The History of the Liberal Party*, p. 7; Michael Foot, *Debts of Honor* (New York: Harper & Row, 1981), p. 63; *Lord Riddell's Intimate Diary of the Peace Conference and After 1918–1923* (London: Victor Gollancz, 1933), p. 312; Edwards, *David Lloyd George*, vol. 1, p. 245. One of the few exceptions to this fidelity to duty on Lloyd George's part was that he appeared to avoid the House of Commons whenever his son Gwilym Lloyd George was speaking there (Cross, ed., *Life with Lloyd George*, p. 82). It may be that Lloyd George was a bad father (Leo Abse, *Private Member* [London: Macdonald, 1973], pp. 18–19). It may also be that Lloyd George did not want to steal the limelight from his son. Even his oldest son, Richard Lloyd George, eventually disinherited by his father, conceded that Lloyd George was a kind and gentle father (Earl Lloyd George, *My Father, Lloyd George*, p. 48).

54. Lord Boothby, "Political Titans," *Books and Bookmen* 20 (August 1974): 17. On Chaliapin, see Philip Ziegler, *Diana Cooper: A Biography* (New York: Harper & Row, 1987), p. 113; on House see H. Montgomery Hyde, *Lord Reading: The Life of Rufus Isaacs, First Marquess of Reading* (New York: Farrar, Straus and Giroux, 1967), p. 194.

55. Jo Vellacott, *Bertrand Russell and the Pacifists in the First World War* (New York: St. Martin's Press, 1980), pp. 65–66. Russell concluded that his host "belongs to the best 10 per cent" of humankind (ibid., p. 136). See also Bertrand Russell, *Autobiography* (London: Unwin Hyman, 1987), pp. 247, 288.

56. Taylor, ed., *My Darling Pussy*, p. 8. See also Grigg, *Lloyd George: From Peace to War*, p. 226.

57. Grigg, *Lloyd George: The People's Champion*, p. 358; L. S. Amery, "Two Great War Leaders," in Sir James Marchant, ed., *Winston Spencer Churchill: Servant of Crown and Commonwealth* (London: Cassell, 1954), pp. 66, 71; The Earl of Birkenhead, *Contemporary Personalities* (London: Cassell, 1924), p. 35; Keynes, *Essays in Biography*, p. 20; Salter, *Personality in Politics*, p. 40; Thomson, *David Lloyd George*, p. 154.

58. Swinton, *Sixty Years of Power*, p. 43.

59. Collin Brooks, "Churchill the Conversationalist," in Charles Eade, ed., *Churchill by His Contemporaries* (New York: Simon and Schuster, 1954), p. 301; Frank Harris, *Contemporary Portraits*, 3d series (New York: Frank Harris, 1920), p. 101; Manfred Weidhorn, *Sword and Pen: A Survey of the Writings of Sir Winston Churchill* (Albuquerque: University of New Mexico Press, 1974), p. 230; see also Brian Bond, ed., *Chief of Staff: The Diaries of Lieutenant-General Sir Henry Pownall*, vol. 2 (London: Leo Cooper, 1974), pp. 34, 109, 171; Sir Dingle Foot, *British Political Crises* (London: William Kimber, 1976), p. 184; David Mason, *Churchill* (London: Pan Books, 1973), p. 52; Mendelssohn, *The Age of Churchill*, p. 555; *Churchill: Taken from the Diaries of Lord Moran: The Struggle for Survival 1940–1965* (Boston: Houghton Mifflin, 1966), pp. 135, 245; Payne, *The Great Man*, p. 202; Robert Lewis Taylor, *Winston Churchill: An Informal Study of Greatness* (Garden City, N.Y.: Doubleday, 1952), p. 48; Thompson, *Assignment: Churchill*, p. 71; Wingfield-Stratford, *Churchill*, p. 92; R. W. Thompson, *Generalissimo Churchill* (London: Hodder and Stoughton, 1973), p. 81; Grigg, *Nancy Astor*, p. 87; R. H. Bruce Lockhart, *Memoirs of a British Agent* (London: Putnam, 1932), p. 222; Beaverbrook, *Politicians and the War*, p. 307; Virginia Cowles, *Winston Churchill: The Era and the Man* (New York, Grosset & Dunlap, no date), p. 9. For further comments on Churchill's inattention, see H. H. Asquith, *Letters to Venetia Stanley*, eds. Michael and Eleanor Brock (Oxford: Oxford University Press, 1985), p. 415; Martin Gilbert, *Winston S. Churchill*, companion vol. 3, part 1 (Boston: Houghton Mifflin, 1973), p. 484; Merle Miller, *Plain Speaking: An Oral Biography of Harry S. Truman* (New York: Berkeley, 1974), p. 85; Arthur Bryant, *Triumph in the West 1943–1946: Based on the Diaries and Autobiographical Notes of Field Marshal The Viscount Alanbrooke, K.G.O.M.* (London: The Reprint Society, 1960), p. 111; Moran, *Churchill*, p. 110; Hugo Vickers, *Gladys: Duchess of Marlborough* (New York: Holt, Rinehart and Winston, 1980), p. 67; Moran, *Churchill*, p. 110; Violet Bonham Carter, *Winston Churchill: An Intimate Portrait* (New York: Harcourt, Brace & World, 1965), pp. 7, 9; Mason, *Churchill*, p. 53.

60. Moran, *Churchill*, p. 112.

61. Isaiah Berlin, *Personal Impressions*, ed. Henry Hardy (Harmondsworth: Penguin Books, 1982), p. 12.

62. R. W. Thompson, *Generalissimo Churchill*, p. 181.

63. Salter, *Slave of the Lamp*, p. 33.

64. Martin Gilbert, *Winston S. Churchill*, vol. 3 (Boston: Houghton Mifflin, 1971),

pp. 383–84. There is an apparent textual misprinting of this exchange in Gilbert, *Winston S. Churchill*, companion vol. 3, part 1, p. 776. The occasion of this exchange is badly confused by Beaverbrook, *The Decline and Fall of Lloyd George*, p. 30.

65. Gilbert, *Winston S. Churchill*, vol. 3, p. 384.

66. Howells, *Churchill's Last Years*, p. 88.

67. Moran, *Churchill*, pp. 11, 136, 239, 746; Howells, *Churchill's Last Years*, p. 153; Samuel J. Hurwitz, "Winston S. Churchill," in Herman Ausubel, J. Bartlet Brebner, and Erling M. Hunt, eds., *Some Modern Historians of Britain: Essays in Honor of R. L. Schuyler* (New York: The Dryden Press, 1951), p. 321; Amery, "Two Great War Leaders," p. 71; Berlin, *Personal Impressions*, p. 13; Bonham Carter, *Winston Churchill*, p. 126; Lady Violet Bonham Carter, "Winston Churchill—As I Know Him," in Marchant, ed., *Winston Spencer Churchill*, p. 153; John Davenport and Charles J. V. Murphy, *The Lives of Winston Churchill* (New York: Charles Scribner's Sons, 1945), p. 51; Cowles, *Winston Churchill*, p. 201; Piers Brendon, *Winston Churchill: A Biography* (New York: Harper & Row, 1984), p. 124.

68. Henry Pelling, *Winston Churchill* (London: Macmillan, 1974), p. 357.

69. Churchill's self-centeredness is discussed in A. J. P. Taylor, "More Snakes Than Ladders," *The Observer*, October 24, 1976, p. 31; Howells, *Churchill's Last Years*, pp. 13, 80, 139; Frank Brady, *Onassis: An Extravagant Life* (Englewood Cliffs, N.J.: Prentice-Hall, 1977), p. 130; Willi Frischauer, *Onassis* (New York: Meredith Press, 1968), p. 14; Cowles, *Winston Churchill*, p. 4; Robert Rhodes James, "The Politician," in A. J. P. Taylor and others, *Churchill: Four Faces and the Man* (Harmondsworth: Penguin Books, 1973), p. 114; Michael Fowler, *Winston S. Churchill: Philosopher and Statesman* (Lanham, Md.: University Press of America, 1985), p. 5.

70. Rowland, *Lloyd George*, p. 593.

71. Shakespeare, *Let Candles Be Brought In*, pp. 58, 65; R. H. S. Crossman, *The Charm of Politics and Other Essays in Political Criticism* (New York: Harper & Brothers, 1958), p. 16; Sir Charles Webster, "The Chronicler," in Marchand, ed., *Winston Spencer Churchill*, p. 118; Boothby, "Four at Versailles," p. 27; John Gore, *King George V: A Personal Memoir* (London: John Murray, 1949), p. 251. These six volumes were first published in London as *War Memoirs of David Lloyd George* by Ivor Nicholson & Watson, 1933–36.

72. First published in London as *The World Crisis* in five volumes, with the third volume in two parts, by Thornton Butterworth, 1923-31; Blanche E. C. Dugdale, *Arthur James Balfour, First Earl of Balfour: 1906–1930* (London: Hutchinson, no date), p. 247.

73. Taylor, ed., *My Darling Pussy*, pp. 155, 161; Hurwitz, "Winston S. Churchill," pp. 313–14; Manfred Weidhorn, *Sir Winston Churchill* (Boston: Twayne, 1979), pp. 19, 121, 150; Weidhorn, *Sword and Pen*, pp. 7–8.

74. Earl Lloyd George, *My Father, Lloyd George*, p. 228; Amery, "Two Great War Leaders," p. 65; Bonham Carter, *Winston Churchill*, p. 130; Jennings, *Cabinet Government*, p. 123; Grigg, *Lloyd George: The People's Champion*, p. 12, 145; *Lord Riddell's Intimate Diary*, p. 206; Kenneth O. Morgan, ed., *Lloyd George*, p. 115; Alexander Mackintosh, *From Gladstone to Lloyd George: Parliament in Peace and War* (London: Hodder and Stoughton, 1921), p. 165.

75. Cross, ed., *Life with Lloyd George*, p. 26n; du Parcq, *Life of David Lloyd George*, vol. 1, p. 45.

76. Mackintosh, *From Gladstone to Lloyd George*, p. 161; Campbell, *Lloyd George*, p. 88; Grigg, *Lloyd George: The People's Champion*, p. 180.

77. Shakespeare, *Let Candles Be Brought In*, p. 48.

78. Cowles, *Winston Churchill*, p. 125.

79. Brendon, *Winston Churchill*, p. 22.

80. Sylvester, *The Real Lloyd George*, p. 5.

81. Bailey, *Woodrow Wilson and the Lost Peace*, p. 83; Liddell Hart [sic], *Colonel Lawrence: The Man behind the Legend* (New York: Dodd, Mead, 1934), p. 314.

82. *Lord Riddell's Intimate Diary*, p. 189.

83. Herbert du Parcq, *Life of David Lloyd George*, vol 1 (London: Caxton, 1912), p. 59.

84. Grigg, *Lloyd George: The People's Champion*, p. 141.

85. du Parcq, *Life of David Lloyd George*, vol 2, p. 333.

86. Sidebotham, *Pillars of the State*, p. 80.

87. Thomas Jones, *Lloyd George*, p. 259; Kenneth O. Morgan, *David Lloyd George: Welsh Radical as World Statesman* (Cardiff: University of Wales Press, 1963), pp. 11, 67; *Wales in British Politics*, p. 282; Koss, *Fleet Street Radical*, p. 192.

88. Edwards, *David Lloyd George*, vol I, p. 107.

89. Dangerfield, *The Strange Death of Liberal England*, p. 19; Alfred T. Davies, *The Lloyd George I Knew: Some Side-Lights on a Great Career* (London: Henry E. Walter, 1948), p. x.

90. Morgan, *David Lloyd George*, p. 8.

91. On anti-Welsh sentiment see Sir Charles Petrie, *A Historian Looks at His World* (London: Sidgwick & Jackson, 1972), p. 8; A. J. P. Taylor, *Essays in English History*, p. 258n; Walter Henry Thompson, *Assignment: Churchill*, p. 7; David Walder, *The Chanak Affair* (New York: Macmillan, 1969), p. 258; *Margot Asquith: An Autobiography*, vol. 2 (New York: George H. Doran, 1920), p. 251; Anthony Burgess, *Any Old Iron* (New York: Random House, 1989), pp. 7, 25, 47, 61; Richard Hughes, *The Wooden Shepherdess* (Frogmore: Triad/Panther Books, 1980), p. 209; and Evelyn Waugh, *Decline and Fall* (Harmondsworth: Penguin Books, 1983), pp. 65–66.

92. On Lloyd George's Welshness, see Kenneth O. Morgan, ed., *Lloyd George*, p. 7; George, *The Making of Lloyd George*, p. 17; Cross, ed., *Life with Lloyd George*, p. 182; Kenneth O. Morgan, *Wales in British Politics*, p. 218; Alfred T. Davies, *The Lloyd George I Knew*, p. 124.

93. Taylor, ed., *My Darling Pussy*, p. 190.

94. Kenneth O. Morgan, *Wales in British Politics*, pp. 167, 232–33, 256, 293, 301; Harold Wilson, *A Prime Minister on Prime Ministers* (New York: Summit Books, 1977), p. 138.

95. Edwards, *David Lloyd George*, vol. 1, p. 193; Kenneth O. Morgan, *Wales in British Politics*, p. 167.

96. Morgan, *David Lloyd George*, p. 8.

97. Morgan, *Wales in British Politics*, pp. 167, 178.

98. Morgan, *David Lloyd George*, p. 8; Cross, ed., *Life with Lloyd George*, p. 8.

99. Grigg, *Lloyd George: From Peace to War*, p. 110.

100. Evans and Garner, *Lloyd George*, p. 39; Robert Gathorne-Hardy, ed., *Ottoline: The Early Memoirs of Lady Ottoline Morrell* (London: Faber and Faber, 1963), p. 175; Grigg, *The Young Lloyd George*, p. 62.

101. Frank Owen, *Tempestuous Journey*, p. 721.

102. Grigg, *Lloyd George: The People's Champion*, p. 95.

103. Cross, ed., *Life with Lloyd George*, p. 136n; Jones, *Lloyd George*, p. 238; Rowland, *Lloyd George*, p. 667. The date and occasion on which Lloyd George became Father of the House are incorrectly described by E. Thornton Cook, *What Manner of Men? Our Prime Ministers in Action and Word from J. Ramsay Macdonald to Benjamin Disraeli (Lord Beaconsfield)* (London: Heath Cranton 1934), p. 64. It is also incorrect to explain the undoubted original antagonism between Churchill and Lord Winterton by Churchill's jealousy of Winterton as Father of the House, as is done by Maxwell Philip Schoenfeld, *The War Ministry of Winston Churchill* (Ames:

The Iowa State University Press, 1972), p. 29. Lloyd George still held that position, as Churchill was careful to recognize (Robert Rhodes James, ed., *Winston S. Churchill: His Complete Speeches 1897–1963*, vol. 4 [New York: Chelsea House, 1974], p. 6512). When Winterton did become Father of the House, upon Lloyd George's acceptance in 1945 of a peerage, Churchill did let Winterton have it, in intensely personal tones (Robert Rhodes James, ed., *Winston S. Churchill: His Complete Speeches 1897-1963*, vol. 7, pp. 7124, 7126–27.

104. Sigmund Neumann, *The Future in Perspective* (New York: G.P. Putnam's Sons, 1946), p. 68.

105. Regarding Churchill's constituency problems, see *War Memoirs of David Lloyd George*, vol. 3 (London: Ivor Nicholson & Watson, 1934), p. 1071; A. J. P. Taylor, *Politicians, Socialism and Historians* (New York: Stein and Day, 1982), p. 35; Ronald Lewin, *Churchill as Warlord* (New York: Scarborough Books, 1982), p. 11.

106. On Lloyd George's constituency, see Randolph S. Churchill, *Winston S. Churchill*, companion vol. 2, part 1 (London: Heinemann, 1969), p. 284; Douglas, *The History of the Liberal Party*, p. 149; Philip Guedalla, *A Gallery* (London: Hodder and Stoughton, 1924), p. 237.

107. Edwards, *David Lloyd George*, vol. 1, p. 31.

108. Stephen Koss, "Lloyd George and Nonconformity: The Last Rally," *The English Historical Review* 89 (January 1974): 78; Victor Wallace Germains, *The Tragedy of Winston Churchill* (London: Hurst & Blackett, 1931), p. 231; see also *Leon Trotsky on Britain* (New York: Monad Press, 1973), p. 57.

109. Stephen Koss, *Nonconformity in Modern British Politics* (London: B. T. Batsford, 1975), p. 135.

110. Ibid., pp. 35, 47; Cregier, *Bounder from Wales*, p. 78; Ivor Bulmer-Thomas, *The Growth of the British Party System*, vol. 1 (London: John Braker, 1965), pp. 161–62; Grigg, *Lloyd George: The People's Champion*, p. 33.

111. Asquith, *Letters to Venetia Stanley*, p. 289; Grigg, *Lloyd George: From Peace to War*, p. 177; Philip Magnus, *Kitchener: Portrait of an Imperialist* (New York: E.P. Dutton, 1959), pp. 299–300; Shakespeare, *Let Candles Be Brought In*, p. 335; The Kitchener comment is in Shakespeare, *Let Candles Be Brought In*, p. 336.

112. On alcohol and prohibition, see Beaverbrook, *The Decline and Fall of Lloyd George*, p. 65n; Raymond, *Mr. Lloyd George*, p. 338; Grigg, *Lloyd George: The People's Champion*, p. 71; Edwards, *David Lloyd George*, vol. 1, pp. 130–31; Hazlehurst, *Politicians at War*, p. 210; James Joll, *Europe Since 1870: An International History* (London: Weidenfeld and Nicolson, 1973), p. 201; Kenneth O. Morgan, ed., *Lloyd George*, pp. 176–77; E. Royston Pike, *Human Documents of the Lloyd George Era* (London: George Allen & Unwin, 1972), p. 148; Chris Wrigley, *David Lloyd George and the British Labour Movement: Peace and War* (Hassocks: The Harvester Press, 1976), pp. 107, 264. Criticism of effort to control alcohol is in Beaverbrook, *Politicians and the War*, p. 65; Buchan, *The King's Grace*, p. 159; Wrigley, *David Lloyd George and the British Labour Movement*, p. 107; The Earl of Oxford and Asquith, K.G., *Memories and Reflections 1852–1927*, vol. 2 (Boston: Little, Brown, 1928), p. 85; Peter Lowe, "The Rise to the Premiership 1914–16," in A. J. P. Taylor, ed., *Lloyd George*, p. 103. Regarding the "pledge," see Reginald Viscount Esher, *The Tragedy of Lord Kitchener* (London: John Murray, 1921), pp. 66–67; Alan Clark, ed., *"A Good Innings": The Private Papers of Viscount Lee of Fareham* (London: John Murray, 1974), p. 157; Cross, ed., *Life with Lloyd George*, p. 93n; Anthony Eden, *Facing the Dictators* (Boston: Houghton Mifflin, 1962), p. 135; A. J. P. Taylor, *English History*, p. 37. For more details, see Marvin Rintala, "Taking the Pledge: H. H. Asquith and Drink," *Biography* 16 (Spring 1993): 103–135.

113. Koss, *Nonconformity in Modern British Politics*, p. 106. Prime Minister Lloyd

George made Clifford a Companion of Honour (David M. Thompson, ed., *Nonconformity in the Nineteenth Century* [London: Routledge & Kegan Paul, 1972], p. 230).

114. Shakespeare, *Let Candles Be Brought In*, p. 13.

115. J. H. Shakespeare, "Free Churchmen and the Coalition," *The Lloyd George Liberal Magazine* 1 (February 1921): 298.

116. Koss, "Lloyd George and Nonconformity," p. 85; Koss, *Nonconformity in Modern British Politics*, p. 192.

117. Kenneth O. Morgan, "Lloyd George's Stage Army: The Coalition Liberals, 1918–22," in A. J. P. Taylor, ed., *Lloyd George*, pp. 252–53.

118. A. J. P. Taylor, ed., *My Darling Pussy*, p. 187.

119. Morgan, ed., *Lloyd George*, p. 7. For an alternative translation, see Morgan, *Wales in British Politics*, p. 185.

120. Grigg, *Lloyd George: The People's Champion*, p. 29.

121. Kinnear, *The Fall of Lloyd George*, p. 183; Grigg, *Lloyd George: The People's Champion*, pp. 29, 46, 163–164; Morgan, *Wales in British Politics*, p. 185.

122. Lloyd George's interest in Catholicism is found in Grigg, *Lloyd George: The People's Champion*, pp. 29, 123; Stephen Roskill, *Hankey: Man of Secrets*, vol. 1 (London: Collins, 1970), p. 387; Grigg, *The Young Lloyd George*, p. 246; Grigg, *Lloyd George: From Peace to War*, p. 111; McCormick, *The Mask of Merlin*, pp. 300–301.

123. Frank Owen, *Tempestuous Journey*, p. 756.

124. Morgan, ed., *Lloyd George*, p. 7; Edwards, *David Lloyd George*, vol. 1, pp. 31, 53, 91; Grigg, *Lloyd George: The People's Champion*, p. 50; Owen, *Tempestuous Journey*, p. 58; Koss, *Nonconformity in Modern British Politics*, p. 101; Viscount Gwynedd, *Dame Margaret*, p. 89; Rowland, *Lloyd George*, p. 93; George, *The Making of Lloyd George*, p. 27; Morgan, *Wales in British Politics*, p. 238.

125. J. W. C. Wand, "Our Faith," in Wand and others, *Our Way of Life: Twelve Aspects of the British Heritage* (London: Country Life, 1951), p. 13.

126. Alan Bullock, *The Life and Times of Ernest Bevin*, vol. 1 (London: Heinemann, 1960), p. 9.

127. For Margaret Lloyd George's Methodism, see Grigg, *Lloyd George: The People's Champion*, pp. 228–9; Morgan, ed., *Lloyd George*, pp. 95, 112, 129; Koss, *Nonconformity in Modern British Politics*, p. 142.

128. On Lloyd George's religious feeling, see Thomson, *David Lloyd George*, p. 437; Grigg, *Lloyd George: The People's Champion*, p. 51; Grigg, *The Young Lloyd George*, p. 34; Cross, ed., *Life with Lloyd George*, pp. 76–77, 91, 287; Frank Dilnot, *Lloyd George: The Man and His Story* (New York: Harper & Brothers, 1917), p. 56; Koss, "Lloyd George and Nonconformity," p. 77; J. Hugh Edwards, *David Lloyd George: The Man and the Statesman*, vol. 2 (New York: J.H. Sears, 1929), p. 652; Riddell, *More Pages from My Diary*, pp. 129, 213; and Young, ed., *The Diaries of Sir Robert Bruce Lockhart*, vol. 1, p. 201.

129. On sermons and political speeches see Edwards, *David Lloyd George*, vol. 2, p. 652; Koss, *Fleet Street Radical*, p. 128; Shakespeare, *Let Candles Be Brought In*, p. 54; Riddell, *More Pages from My Diary*, pp. 129–130, 155; Burgess, *Any Old Iron*, p. 96; Morgan, *Wales in British Politics*, p. 249; Thomson, *David Lloyd George*, p. 87; *The Journal of Arnold Bennett*, p. 658; Reginald Pound, *Arnold Bennett: A Biography* (New York: Harcourt, Brace, 1953), p. 270; Morgan, *Consensus and Disunity*, p. 319; W. Watkin Davies, *Lloyd George*, p. 40; du Parcq, *Life of David Lloyd George*, vol. I, pp. 45, 47; Michael Foot, *Debts of Honor*, p. 15; and Ludwig, *Nine Etched from Life*, p. 213.

130. George, *The Making of Lloyd George*, p. 105.

131. Guedalla, *A Gallery*, p. 237.

132. Herbert du Parcq, *Life of David Lloyd George*, vol. 4, p. 722.

133. Morgan, ed., *Lloyd George*, p. 115.

134. du Parcq, *Life of David Lloyd George*, vol. 1, p. 131; C. P. Snow, *Variety of Men* (London: Macmillan, 1967), p. 98; Koss, "Lloyd George and Nonconformity," p. 77; Petrie, *A Historian Looks at His World*, p. 8; Koss, *Nonconformity in Modern British Politics*, p. 10; Morgan, ed., *Lloyd George*, pp. 114–15.

135. Morgan, *Consensus and Disunity*, p. 161; Koss, *Nonconformity in Modern British Politics*, p. 101.

136. Douglas, *The History of the Liberal Party*, p. 6; Elizabeth Longford, *Jameson's Raid: The Prelude to the Boer War*, new ed. (London: Panther Books, 1982), p. 138.

137. Koss, *Nonconformity in Modern British Politics*, pp. 7, 39, 149; Kenneth O. Morgan, *Labour People: Leaders and Lieutenants, Hardie to Kinnock* (Oxford: Oxford University Press, 1987), pp. 302–3.

138. Kenneth O. Morgan, *The Age of Lloyd George* (New York: Barnes and Noble, 1971), p. 31; Grigg, *Lloyd George: From Peace to War*, p. 483; Eric Hobsbawm, *Workers: Worlds of Labor* (New York: Panther Books, 1984), pp. 33, 43; Koss, *Nonconformity in Modern British Politics*, p. 148; Morgan, *Labour People*, pp. 80, 203; Wilkinson's comment is in Morgan, *Labour People*, p. 103.

139. Koss, *Nonconformity in Modern British Politics*, p. 147.

140. Kenneth O. Morgan, *Labour People*, pp. 65–66.

141. Kenneth O. Morgan, *Wales in British Politics*, p. 213.

142. Kenneth O. Morgan, *Labour People*, p. 36; Morgan, *Wales in British Politics*, pp. 206, 254.

143. Morgan, *Consensus and Disunity*, p. 235; Morgan, *Labour People*, p. 174; J. A. Thompson and Arthur Mejia, Jr., *The Modern British Monarchy* (New York: St. Martin's Press, 1971), p. 44; Koss, *Nonconformity in Modern British Politics*, pp. 75, 77; Henry Pelling, *A Short History of the Labour Party*, 5th ed. (New York: St. Martin's Press, 1976), p. 16; Sir Dingle Foot, *British Political Crises*, p. 23; Peter Stansky, *Gladstone: A Progress in Politics* (Boston: Little, Brown, 1979), p. 183.

144. Koss, *Nonconformity in Modern British Politics*, p. 74.

145. Francis Williams, *Ernest Bevin: Portrait of a Great Englishman* (London: Hutchinson, 1952), p. 57.

146. Bullock, *The Life and Times of Ernest Bevin*, vol. 1, pp. 48, 51, 61–62, 73.

147. Ibid., pp. 3–4, 8–10, 21; Williams, *Ernest Bevin*, pp. 13–14, 21–25.

148. Chris Cook, *The Age of Alignment: Electoral Politics in Britain, 1922–1929* (Toronto: University of Toronto Press, 1975), p. 327.

149. Stephen Koss, *Asquith* (London: Allen Lane, 1976), pp. 203, 267–68; Roy Jenkins, *Asquith: Portrait of a Man and an Era* (New York: E.P. Dutton, 1966), p. 19.

150. Benjamin Disraeli, *Sybil or The Two Nations* (London: Oxford University Press, 1975), p. 109.

151. Koss, *Asquith*, p. 15; The Earl of Oxford and Asquith, *Memories and Reflections 1852-1927*, vol. 1 (Boston: Little, Brown, 1928), p. 163.

152. Rowland, *Lloyd George*, p. 797.

153. Kenneth O. Morgan, *Wales in British Politics*, p. 93.

154. Cross, ed., *Life with Lloyd George*, p. 188.

155. Grigg, *Lloyd George: The People's Champion*, pp. 142, 262; Hobsbawm, *Workers*, pp. 39, 103–30; Marvin Rintala, "Väinö Linna and the Finnish Condition," *Journal of Baltic Studies* 8 (Fall 1977): 227; Rudolph Stadelmann, *Social and Political History of the German Revolution*, trans. James G. Chastain (Athens: Ohio University Press, 1975), p. 6; and Edwards, *David Lloyd George*, vol. 1, p. 37.

156. du Parcq, *Life of David Lloyd George*, vol. 1, p. 3; Lucille Iremonger, *The Fiery Chariot: A Study of British Prime Ministers and the Search for Love* (London: Secker & Warburg, 1970), p. 191.

157. George, *The Making of Lloyd George*, pp. 80–82.

158. Kenneth O. Morgan, ed., *Lloyd George*, pp. 105-6, 137; Grigg, *Lloyd George: The People's Champion*, p. 262; Riddell, *More Pages from My Diary*, p. 141; Sylvester, *The Real Lloyd George*, pp. 4, 6, 10.

159. Grigg, *The Young Lloyd George*, p. 29; Edwards, *David Lloyd George*, vol. 1, pp. 45–46; Cross, ed., *Life with Lloyd George*, p. 82n; George, *The Making of Lloyd George*, p. 79.

160. On Lincoln, see Earl Lloyd George, *My Father, Lloyd George*, pp. 24–26; W. S. Adams, "Lloyd George and the Labour Movement," *Past and Present*, February, 1953, p. 56; Cregier, *Bounder from Wales*, p. 7; Owen, *Tempestuous Journey*, pp. 29, 669; Rowland, *Lloyd George*, p. 10; Sylvester, *The Real Lloyd George*, pp. 111–12, 130–33, 136–37; Thomson, *David Lloyd George*, pp. 59, 375; see also *Lord Riddell's Intimate Diary*, p. 226; Thomas Jones, *Lloyd George*, p. 114; Hendrick, *The Life and Letters of Walter H. Page*, vol. 3, p. 22; Riddell, *More Pages from My Diary*, p. 214; Dilnot, *Lloyd George*, pp. 192, 195; Edwards, *David Lloyd George*, vol. 1, p. 49.

161. Mark DeWolfe Howe, ed., *Holmes-Laski Letters: The Correspondence of Mr. Justice Holmes and Harold J. Laski 1916–1935*, vol. 2 (Cambridge, Mass.: Harvard University Press, 1953), p. 982; Winston S. Churchill, *A History of the English-Speaking Peoples: The Great Democracies* (New York: Dodd, Mead, 1971), pp. 176, 187, 209, 211; Giovanni Costigan, *Makers of Modern England: The Force of Individual Genius in History* (London: Macmillan, 1969), p. 246.

162. Thomas Jones, *A Diary with Letters: 1931–1950* (London: Oxford University Press, 1954), p. 236; Edwards, *David Lloyd George*, vol. 1, p. 278; du Parcq, *Life of David Lloyd George*, vol. 2, pp. 353, 412; Rowland, *Lloyd George*, p. 600; James John Davis, "Introduction" to Edwards, *David Lloyd George*, vol. 1, p. x; Sylvester, *The Real Lloyd George*, p. 137; Davies, *The Lloyd George I Knew*, p. 89.

163. Rowland, *Lloyd George*, p. 384; Sylvester, *The Real Lloyd George*, p. 130; Jones, *Lloyd George*, pp. 205, 275.

164. Walter Kaufmann, ed. and trans., *The Portable Nietzsche* (New York: The Viking Press, 1961), p. 190.

165. Trevor Wilson, ed., *The Political Diaries of C. P. Scott*, pp. 342–43, 345, 406.

Chapter Two

1. John Grigg, *The Young Lloyd George* (London: Eyre Methuen, 1973), p. 258. Lloyd George's name does not appear in the detailed study by Elizabeth Longford, *Jameson's Raid: The Prelude to the Boer War*, new ed. (London: Panther Books, 1984). There is not much reason for such an appearance. In 1897, shortly after the Jameson Raid, Lloyd George may have briefly considered traveling to South Africa, but did not do so (Grigg, *The Young Lloyd George*, p. 258). More surprising is the minor role played by Lloyd George in the monumental study by the countess of Longford's son, Thomas Pakenham, *The Boer War* (New York: Random House, 1979). Family piety may have been a factor. The countess of Longford's great-uncle was Joseph Chamberlain. A significant novelist dates Lloyd George's awakening to South Africa too early (Vera Brittain, *Honourable Estate: A Novel of Transition* [New York: Macmillan, 1936], p. 42).

2. Herbert du Parcq, *Life of David Lloyd George*, vol. II (London: Caxton, 1913), p. 216.

3. Grigg, *The Young Lloyd George*, p. 259n.

4. Ibid., p. 295.

5. J. Hugh Edwards, *David Lloyd George: The Man and the Statesman*, vol. 1 (New York: J.H. Sears, 1929), p. 220; Frank Owen, *Tempestuous Journey: Lloyd George, His Life and Times* (London: Hutchinson, 1954), p. 95; Chris Wrigley, *David Lloyd George and the British Labour Movement: Peace and War* (Hassocks: The Harvester Press, 1976), p. 3.

6. Winston S. Churchill, *A History of the English-Speaking Peoples: The Great Democracies* (New York: Dodd, Mead, 1971), pp. 372–73; Winston S. Churchill, *Great Contemporaries* (London: Fontana Books, 1965), p. 23.

7. *Speeches by the Earl of Oxford and Asquith, K.G.* (London: Hutchinson, 1928), pp. 36–44; *The Autobiography of Margot Asquith: Political Events and Celebrities* (London: Thornton Butterworth, 1933), p. 57; Roy Douglas, *The History of the Liberal Party, 1895–1970* (Madison, N.J.: Fairleigh Dickinson University Press, 1971), p. 23; du Parcq, *Life of David Lloyd George*, vol. 2, p. 320; Robert Rhodes James, *Rosebery: A Biography of Archibald Philip, Fifth Earl of Rosebery* (New York: Macmillan, 1963), pp. 410–15; David M. Thompson, ed., *Nonconformity in the Nineteenth Century* (London: Routledge & Kegan Paul, 1972), pp. 226–27; Max Beloff, *Imperial Sunset: Volume I—Britain's Liberal Empire, 1897–1921* (New York: Alfred A. Knopf, 1970), p. 78; Stephen Koss, ed., *The Pro-Boers: The Anatomy of an Antiwar Movement* (Chicago: The University of Chicago Press, 1973), p. xxxvii. Asquith's comment is in Stephen Koss, *Asquith* (London: Allen Lane, 1976), p. 54.

8. du Parcq, *Life of David Lloyd George*, vol. 2, p. 281.

9. A. J. Anthony Morris, *Radicalism against War, 1906–1914: The Advocacy of Peace and Retrenchment* (Totowa, N.J.: Rowman and Littlefield, 1972), p. 6. On the unjustness of the war, see du Parcq, *Life of David Lloyd George*, vol. 2, p. 303; See also Wrigley, *David Lloyd George and the British Labour Movement*, p. 18. For Lloyd George's description of the war as "damnable," "an infamy," and "unjust," see Owen, *Tempestuous Journey*, pp. 98 and 122; and du Parcq, *Life of David Lloyd George*, vol. 2, p. 218.

10. Pakenham, *The Boer War*, p. 258.

11. du Parcq, *Life of David Lloyd George*, vol. 2, p. 325.

12. Ibid., p. 267; Eduard Heimann, *Freedom and Order: Lessons from the War* (New York: Charles Scribner's Sons, 1947), p. 134. Even the most important scholarly critic of the economic causation of war conceded that if ever a war was economic in origin, it was the Boer War (Hans J. Morgenthau, *Politics Among Nations: The Struggle for Power and Peace*, 3d ed. [New York: Alfred A. Knopf, 1960], p. 49).

13. du Parcq, *Life of David Lloyd George*, vol. 2, p. 257.

14. Ibid., p. 216.

15. Ibid., p. 253. See also Jack Jones, *The Man David* (London: Hamish Hamilton, 1944), p. 115.

16. du Parcq, *Life of David Lloyd George*, vol. 2, p. 274.

17. Alexander Mackintosh, *From Gladstone to Lloyd George: Parliament in Peace and War* (London: Hodder and Stoughton, 1921), p. 163; Thomas Jones, *Lloyd George* (London: Oxford University Press, 1951), p. 28. See also Joyce Cary, *Prisoner of Grace* (New York: Harper & Brothers, 1952), p. 31; and du Parcq, *Life of David Lloyd George*, vol. 2, pp. 280–81, 294n; John Grigg, "Lloyd George," in *Great Britons* (London: British Broadcasting Corporation, 1978), p. 190; du Parcq, *Life of David Lloyd George*, vol. 3 (London: Caxton, 1913), p. 454; John Grigg, *Lloyd George: The People's Champion 1902–1911* (Berkeley: University of California Press, 1978), p. 60n; Philip Magnus, *Kitchener: Portrait of an Imperialist* (New York: E.P. Dutton, 1959), p. 173.

18. du Parcq, *Life of David Lloyd George*, vol. 2, p. 291.

19. Edwards, *Life of David Lloyd George*, vol. 1, pp. 208-11, 233; du Parcq, *Life of David Lloyd George*, vol. 1 (London: Caxton, 1913), p. 3; Victor Wallace Germains, *The Tragedy of Winston Churchill* (London: Hurst & Blackett, 1931), p. 44; Grigg, "Lloyd George," p. 190; Grigg, *Lloyd George*, pp. 28, 78; Robert Rhodes James, *The British Revolution: British Politics, 1880–1939*, vol. 1 (London: Hamish Hamilton, 1976), p. 194; Roy Jenkins, *Asquith: Portrait of a Man and of an Era* (New York: E.P. Dutton, 1966), p. 116; John Grigg, "Lloyd George and the Boer War," in A. J. A. Morris, ed., *Edwardian Radicalism 1900–1914: Some Aspects of British Radicalism* (London: Routledge & Kegan Paul, 1974), pp. 16, 22; Grigg, *Lloyd George: From Peace to War 1912–1916* (Berkeley: University of California Press, 1985), p. 212.

20. Harold Wilson, *A Prime Minister on Prime Ministers* (New York: Summit Books, 1977), p. 129. In a now-classic contemporary account, first published in 1900, Chamberlain is the central figure, and Salisbury does not appear, (J. A. Hobson, *The War in South Africa: Its Causes and Effects* [New York: Howard Fertig, 1969]).

21. D. H. Elletson, *The Chamberlains* (London: John Murray, 1966), p. 136.

22. Randolph S. Churchill, *Winston S. Churchill*, companion vol. 2, part 1 (London: Heinemann, 1969), p. 89.

23. Michael Hechter, *Internal Colonialism: The Celtic Fringe in British National Development, 1536–1966* (Berkeley: University of California Press, 1977), p. 246; John, Viscount Morley, *Recollections*, vol. 2 (New York: Macmillan, 1917), pp. 79, 89; The Earl of Oxford and Asquith, K.G., *Memories and Reflections 1852–1927*, vol. 1 (Boston: Little, Brown, 1928), p. 178; Stuart Cloete, *Rags of Glory* (Garden City, N.Y.: Doubleday, 1963), p. 253.

24. Pakenham, *The Boer War*, p. 493; Owen, *Tempestuous Journey*, p. 102; Elletson, *The Chamberlains*, p. 134; The Marquess of Reading, *Rufus Isaacs: First Marquess of Reading: 1860-1914* (London: Hutchinson, 1950), p. 77.

25. Elie Halevy, *The Rule of Democracy 1905–1914 (Book II)*, 2d ed., trans. I. E. Watkin (New York: Peter Smith, 1952), p. 388; Kenneth O. Morgan, *Labour People: Leaders and Lieutenants, Hardie to Kinnock* (Oxford: Oxford University Press, 1987), p. 116.

26. Emanoel Lee, *To The Bitter End: A Photographic History of the Boer War 1899–1902* (New York: Viking, 1985), p. 44.

27. Jack Jones, *The Man David*, p. 90; Edwards, *David Lloyd George*, vol. 1, p. 76; W. R. P. George, *The Making of Lloyd George* (London: Faber & Faber, 1976), p. 133; Grigg, *Lloyd George: The People's Champion*, pp. 236, 270; Grigg, *The Young Lloyd George*, p. 217; Lord Riddell, *More Pages from My Diary: 1908–1914* (London: Country Life, 1934), pp. 64, 77, 182, 217; Grigg, "Lloyd George," p. 189; du Parcq, *Life of David Lloyd George*, vol. 1, p. 158; du Parcq, *Life of David Lloyd George*, vol. 2, p. 263; Stephen Koss, *Fleet Street Radical: A. G. Gardiner and the Daily News* (Hamden, Conn.: Archon Books, 1973), pp. 117–18, 208; Emil Ludwig, *Nine Etched from Life* (New York: Robert M. McBride, 1934), p. 229; Randolph S. Churchill, *Winston S. Churchill*, companion vol. 2, part 2 (London: Heinemann, 1969), p. 263.

28. du Parcq, *Life of David Lloyd George*, vol. 2, p. 289; Grigg, "Lloyd George," p. 190; Edwards, *David Lloyd George*, vol. 1, pp. 224–28. Lloyd George's own estimate was fifty thousand (du Parcq, *Life of David Lloyd George*, vol. 4 [London: Caxton, 1913], p. 760). This is probably a relatively accurate figure. While this was one time Lloyd George surely did not stop to count the house, he had every reason to discuss privately the size of the crowd with the Birmingham police. Since one of

their own was killed, the latter had reason to be candid, privately, with the intended victim. The crowd's threats are found in du Parcq, *Life of David Lloyd George*, vol. 4, p. 760.

29. Cloete, *Rags of Glory*, pp. 543–44.

30. Lloyd George's escape in Birmingham is found in Grigg, *Lloyd George: From Peace to War*, p. 171; du Parcq, *Life of David Lloyd George*, vol. 2, pp. 288, 290, 292–93; A. G. Gardiner, *Prophets, Priests & Kings* (London: J.M. Dent & Sons, 1914), p. 130; Wilson, *A Prime Minister on Prime Ministers*, p. 144; Giovanni Costigan, *Makers of Modern England: The Force of Individual Genius in History* (London: Macmillan, 1969), p. 199; Basil Murray, *L.G.* (London: Sampson Low, Marston, 1932), p. 32. Chamberlain's response is in Julian Amery, *The Life of Joseph Chamberlain*, vol. 4 (London: Macmillan, 1951), p. 21; du Parcq, *Life of David Lloyd George*, vol. 2, p. 297; A. J. P. Taylor, *Essays in English History* (Harmondsworth: Penguin Books, 1982), p. 183; A. J. P. Taylor, "Lloyd George," in Lord Longford and Sir John Wheeler-Bennett, eds., *The History Makers: Leaders and Statesmen of the 20th Century* (New York: St. Martin's Press, 1973), p. 79. An international arms merchant, Basil Zaharoff, may also have been at work in Birmingham (Donald McCormick, *Peddler of Death: The Life and Times of Sir Basil Zaharoff* [New York: Holt, Rinehart and Winston, 1965], pp. 78–80. Others injured are discussed by Grigg, "Lloyd George," p. 191.

31. Comments on Birmingham events are found in Randolph S. Churchill, *Winston S. Churchill*, companion vol. 2, part 1, pp. 103–4.

32. Sir Charles Mallet, *Mr. Lloyd George: A Study* (London: Ernest Benn, 1930), pp. 22–23, 304–5; Jenkins, *Asquith*, p. 116; Kenneth O. Morgan, *David Lloyd George: Welsh Radical as World Statesman* (Cardiff: University of Wales Press, 1963), p. 32; Kenneth O. Morgan, *Wales in British Politics, 1868–1922*, 3d ed. (Cardiff: University of Wales Press, 1980), pp. 178–79.

33. du Parcq, *Life of David Lloyd George*, vol. 2, p. 217.

34. Lloyd George's personal and professional risks are discussed in Jenkins, *Asquith*, p. 116; Mallet, *Mr. Lloyd George*, p. 23; *Lord Riddell's Intimate Diary of the Peace Conference and After 1918–1923* (London: Victor Gollancz, 1933), p. 157; Lady Olwen Carey Evans and Mary Garner, *Lloyd George Was My Father* (Llandysul: Gomer Press, 1985), p. 21; Grigg, *Lloyd George: From Peace to War*, pp. 44–45;

35. Carey Evans and Garner, *Lloyd George*, pp. 20–21; Grigg, *Lloyd George: The People's Champion*, p. 53; Grigg, "Lloyd George and the Boer War," p. 21; Viscount Gwynedd, *Dame Margaret: The Life Story of His Mother* (London: George Allen & Unwin, 1947), pp. 6–7.

36. Earl Lloyd George, *My Father, Lloyd George* (New York: Crown, 1961), p. 70. See also Viscount Gwynedd, *Dame Margaret*, p. 118.

37. On Lloyd George's courage in speaking at Birmingham, see Lord Boothby, "Alongside Lloyd George," *Books and Bookmen* 20 (September 1975): 13; Arthur Salter, *Personality in Politics: Studies of Contemporary Statesmen* (London: Faber and Faber, 1947), p. 52; and Amery, *The Life of Joseph Chamberlain*, vol. 4, p. 20.

38. Herbert Sidebotham, *Pillars of the State* (London: Nisbet, 1921), p. 81.

39. du Parcq, *Life of David Lloyd George*, vol. 2, p. 241.

40. E. T. Raymond, *Mr. Lloyd George* (New York: George H. Doran, 1922), pp. 86–87 (E. T. Raymond was a pen name of E. R. Thompson); Lord Boothby, "Lloyd George: Promise and Fall," *Books and Bookmen* 18 (August 1973): 28; Grigg, "Lloyd George," p. 190; Jenkins, *Asquith*, p. 116; Richard Shannon, *The Crisis of Imperialism 1865–1915* (London: Granada, 1979), p. 335; Trevor Wilson, *The Myriad Faces of War: Britain and the Great War, 1914–1918* (Cambridge: Polity Press, 1986), p. 103; Cloete, *Rags of Glory*, pp. 253–54; Earl Lloyd George, *My Father, Lloyd George*, p. 77; Jack Jones, *The Man David*, p. 124.

41. Gardiner, *Prophets, Priests, & Kings*, p. 131; Magnus, *Kitchener*, p. 173; Raymond, *Mr. Lloyd George*, p. 64; Stuart Hodgson, *Portraits and Reflections* (New York: E.P. Dutton, 1929), p. 26; Ludwig, *Nine Etched from Life*, p. 214.

42. Sinclair Lewis, *It Can't Happen Here* (New York: Signet Books, 1970), p. 108; Beloff, *Imperial Sunset*, vol. 1, p. 77; Pakenham, *The Boer War*, pp. xix, 607; William Gerhardie, *God's Fifth Column: A Biography of the Age 1890–1940* (New York: Simon and Schuster, 1981), p. 93; *Recollections*, vol. 2, p. 90. World censure is the subject of Beloff, *Imperial Sunset*, vol. 1, p. 75; Eric Fischer, *The Passing of the European Age: A Study of the Transfer of Western Civilization and Its Renewal in Other Continents* (Cambridge, Mass.: Harvard University Press, 1943), p. 90; S. L. A. Marshall, *World War I* (New York: American Heritage Press, 1971), p. 22.

43. John Colville, *The Fringes of Power: 10 Downing Street Diaries 1939-1955* (New York: W.W. Norton, 1986), p. 345.

44. Randolph S. Churchill, *Winston S. Churchill*, companion vol. 2, part 1, p. 161.

45. Virginia Cowles, *Winston Churchill: The Era and the Man* (New York: Grosset & Dunlap, no date), p. 78; Halevy, *The Rule of Democracy*, p. 612; George Malcolm Thomson, *The Twelve Days: 24 July to 4 August 1914* (New York: G.P. Putnam's Sons, 1964), p. 28.

46. Pakenham, *The Boer War*, p. 536; Lee, *To the Bitter End*, p. 186; Magnus, *Kitchener*, p. 177; Alan Paton, *Hope for South Africa* (London: Pall Mall Press, 1958), p. 35.

47. Grigg, *Lloyd George: From Peace to War*, pp. 156, 170; James, *Rosebery*, p. 422; Denis Judd, *Lord Reading: Rufus Isaacs, First Marquess of Reading, Lord Chief Justice and Viceroy of India, 1860–1953* (London: Weidenfeld and Nicolson, 1982), p. 41; Longford, *Jameson's Raid*, p. 321; Philip Magnus, *King Edward the Seventh* (Harmondsworth: Penguin Books, 1979), p. 363; Magnus, *Kitchener*, pp. 177–78; André Maurois, *The Edwardian Era*, trans. Hamish Miles (New York: D. Appleton-Century, 1933), p. 137; Kenneth O. Morgan, *The Age of Lloyd George* (New York: Barnes & Noble, 1971), p. 29; Morgan, *Wales in British Politics*, p. 180. It has been argued that the concentration camp was invented by the British in South Africa (Gil Elliot, *Twentieth Century Book of the Dead* [London: Allen Lane The Penguin Press, 1972], p. 95; Gerald L. Houseman, *G.D.H. Cole* [Boston: Twayne, 1979], pp. 14–15). Since the Spanish used concentration camps in Cuba before the British used them in South Africa, the latter use would involve invention only if there was no cross-national borrowing. How Kitchener, not the most innovative of minds, came to order their use remains unclear. Early in the Boer War, Lloyd George saw the similarity between Spanish policy in Cuba and British policy in South Africa (du Parcq, *Life of David Lloyd George*, vol. 2, p. 237). The provenance of the English-language term *concentration camp* is somewhat more clear. The term was apparently first used in March 1901 by two Liberal members of Parliament, John Ellis and C. P. Scott, who simply translated *reconcentrado* (Pakenham, *The Boer War*, p. 535). Scott, also editor of the *Manchester Guardian*, seems the more likely translator. This is an unexpected byline for a journalist who was for decades not only close to Lloyd George but also the "custodian of the Liberal Conscience" (Kenneth O. Morgan, *Consensus and Disunity: The Lloyd George Coalition Government 1918–1922* [Oxford: Clarendon Press, 1986], p. 130).If the temple of British liberalism was Mancunian, its high priest was C. P. Scott. For the fate of Boers in the concentration camps see Vera Brittain, *Testament of Friendship: The Story of Winifred Holtby* (New York: Wideview Books, 1981), p. 219; Leo Marquard, *The People and Policies of South Africa*, 2d ed. (Cape Town: Oxford University Press, 1960), p. 19. For Churchill's defense see Randolph S. Churchill, *Winston S. Churchill*, companion vol. 2, part 1, p. 75. See also Lee, *To the Bitter End*, p. 186, and Pakenham, *The Boer War*, pp. 549, 608.

48. Magnus, *Kitchener*, p. 177.
49. Leon Uris, *Trinity* (New York: Bantam Books, 1979), p. 446.
50. Beloff, *Imperial Sunset*, vol. 1, p. 77. Borden's son was killed in the Boer War (Michael Barthorp, *The Anglo-Boer Wars: The British and the Afrikaners, 1815–1902* [London: Blandford Press, 1987], pp. 135, 137). Lord Methuen, Sir William Gatacre, and Sir Redvers Buller were all British generals in South Africa. Methuen was captured by the Boers; Gatacre and Buller were removed from their commands (Pakenham, The Boer War, pp. 249, 485, 583).
51. James, *The British Revolution*, vol. 1, pp. 204–5; Lee, *To the Bitter End*, p. 130; Robert Blake, Preface to Lee, *To the Bitter End*, p. ix.
52. Pakenham, *The Boer War*, pp. xxi–xxii; Elizabeth Longford, *The Pebbled Shore* (London: Weidenfeld and Nicolson, 1986), p. 293; Trevor Royle, *The Kitchener Enigma* (London: Michael Joseph, 1985), p. 187. See also Michael G. Fry, *Lloyd George and Foreign Policy*, vol. 1 (Montréal: McGill-Queens University Press, 1977), p. 57.
53. du Parcq, *Life of David Lloyd George*, vol. 2, p. 327.

Chapter Three

1. Virginia Cowles, *Winston Churchill: The Era and the Man* (New York: Grosset & Dunlap, no date), p. 78; Herbert du Parcq, *Life of David Lloyd George*, vol. 2 (London: Caxton, 1912), p. 266; Robert Rhodes James, *Churchill: A Study in Failure, 1900–1939* (Harmondsworth: Penguin Books, 1973), p. 27; Robert Rhodes James, *The British Revolution: British Politics, 1880–1939*, vol. 1 (London: Hamish Hamilton, 1976), p. 263; *Churchill: Taken from the Diaries of Lord Moran: The Struggle for Survival, 1940–1965* (Boston: Houghton-Mifflin, 1966), p. 350.
2. Ted Morgan, *Churchill: Young Man in a Hurry, 1874–1915* (New York: Simon and Schuster, 1982), p. 147. There were, nevertheless, absent members. There was no full House between 1893, when Gladstone brought up the Irish Home Rule Bill, and 3 P.M., 3 August 1914 (Barbara W. Tuchman, *The Guns of August* [New York: Bonanza Books, 1982], p. 116).
3. Descriptions of Lloyd George come from many sources. Some include: Jack Jones, *The Man David: An Imaginative Presentation, Based on Fact, of the Life of David Lloyd George from 1880–1914* (London: Hamish Hamilton, 1944), p. 131; Malcolm Thomson, *David Lloyd George: The Official Biography* (London: Hutchinson, no date), p. 154; Sir Geoffrey Shakespeare, *Let Candles Be Brought In* (London: Macdonald, 1949), pp. 38-39; Vera Brittain, *Honourable Estate: A Novel of Transition* (New York: Macmillan, 1936), p. 45; E. T. Raymond, *Mr. Lloyd George* (New York: George H. Doran, 1922), p. 337 (E. T. Raymond was a pen name of E. R. Thompson). For a surprising range in Lloyd George's reported height, see Lady Olwen Carey Evans and Mary Garner, *Lloyd George Was My Father* (Llandysul: Gomer Press, 1985), p. 28; Don M. Cregier, *Bounder from Wales: Lloyd George's Career before the First World War* (Columbia: University of Missouri Press, 1976), p. 45; Earl Lloyd George, *My Father, Lloyd George* (New York: Crown, 1961), p. 34.
4. Head size and shape are discussed in Raymond, *Mr. Lloyd George*, p. 72; Harold Begbie, *The Mirrors of Downing Street: Some Political Reflections* (Port Washington, N.Y.: Kennikat Press, 1970), p. 13; J. Hugh Edwards, *David Lloyd George: The Man and the Statesman*, vol. 2 (New York: J.H. Sears, 1929), p. 651; Alexander Mackintosh, *From Gladstone to Lloyd George: Parliament in Peace and War* (London: Hodder and Stoughton, 1921), p. 175; Lord Beaverbrook, *Men and*

Power, 1917–1918 (London: Hutchinson, 1956), pp. 44, 343. In regard to phrenology, see Giovanni Costigan, *Makers of Modern England: The Force of Individual Genius in History* (London: Macmillan, 1969), p. 240; Cregier, *Bounder from Wales*, pp. 18–19, 91; Colin Cross, ed., *Life with Lloyd George: The Diary of A. J. Sylvester 1931–45* (New York: Barnes & Noble, 1975), pp. 162, 177, 180, 183, 235, 244; Earl Lloyd George, *My Father, Lloyd George*, pp. 95–96; Donald McCormick, *The Mask of Merlin: A Critical Study of David Lloyd George* (London: Macdonald, 1963), p. 18; Peter Rowland, *Lloyd George* (London: Barrie & Jenkins, 1975), p. 748; Thomson, *David Lloyd George*, p. 68. Lloyd George was quite capable of making at least initial judgments about the intelligence and character of other persons on the basis of the size and shape, including protrusions, of their heads. He was favorably impressed by the head of Robert Nivelle, one of the French military commanders in the First World War (Frank Owen, *Tempestuous Journey: Lloyd George, His Life and Times* [London: Hutchinson, 1954], p. 388; John Terraine, "Lloyd George's Dilemma," *History* 11 [May 1961]: 357). On first meeting Neville Chamberlain, Lloyd George was negatively impressed by Chamberlain's head (Sir Dingle Foot, *British Political Crises* [London: William Kimber, 1976], p. 181; Emery Kelen, *Peace in Their Time: Men Who Led Us In and Out of War, 1914–1945* [New York: Alfred A. Knopf, 1963], p. 335; Rowland, *Lloyd George*, p. 409). This characteristic was ever-present in Lloyd George's continuing contempt for Chamberlain (John Grigg, *Lloyd George: From Peace to War, 1912–1916* (Berkeley, University of California Press, 1985), p. 492; Thomas Jones, *A Diary with Letters: 1931–1950* [London: Oxford University Press, 1954], p. 470; Owen, *Tempestuous Journey*, p. 744; C. P. Snow, *Variety of Men* [London: Macmillan, 1967], p. 108). To Lloyd George, Chamberlain was literally a pinhead (David Walder, *The Chanak Affair* [New York: Macmillan, 1969], p. 328). Lloyd George arranged to meet C. P. Snow because, from a distance, Snow's head seemed interesting (Snow, *Variety of Men*, pp. 92–93). The single major exception to Lloyd George's faith in phrenology was Andrew Bonar Law (Owen, *Tempestuous Journey*, p. 133). Lord Beaverbrook, also a phrenologist, made the same exception (Lord Beaverbrook, *Politicians and the War 1914–1916* [London: Oldbourne, 1960], p. 258; Eric Hiscock, *The Bells of Hell Go Ting-A-Ling-A-Ling: An Autobiographical Fragment without Maps* [London: Arlington Books, 1976], p. 116). There appears to be no scientific basis for phrenology. (Morris Ginsberg, *Essays in Sociology and Social Philosophy* [Harmondsworth: Penguin Books, 1968], p. 183; John Liggett, *The Human Face* [New York: Stein and Day, 1974], pp. 7, 212).

5. Cross, ed., *Life with Lloyd George*, p. 67; Michael G. Fry, *Lloyd George and Foreign Policy*, vol. 1 [Montréal: McGill-Queen's University Press, 1977], p. 14; Shakespeare, *Let Candles Be Brought In*, p. 38; Creiger, *Bounder from Wales*, p. 45.

6. Lord Beaverbrook: *The Decline and Fall of Lloyd George: And Great Was the Fall Thereof* (London: Collins, 1966), p. 304; John Grigg, *The Young Lloyd George* (London: Eyre Methuen, 1973), p. 210; Thomas Jones, *Lloyd George* (London: Oxford University Press, 1951), p. 264; Shakespeare, *Let Candles Be Brought In*, pp. 39, 64; Owen, *Tempestuous Journey*, p. 275; A. L. Rowse, *The Churchills: The Story of a Family* (New York: Harper & Row, 1966), p. 429; Cross, ed., *Life with Lloyd George*, pp. 36, 59; Kenneth Young, ed., *The Diaries of Sir Robert Bruce Lockhart*, vol. 1 (London: Macmillan, 1974), p. 165. Lloyd George was so fond of Handel's music that, as he was about to succeed H. H. Asquith as prime minister, he attended a performance of "Elijah" with Margot Asquith (Grigg, *Lloyd George: From Peace to War*, p. 413).

7. A. P. Herbert, *Independent Member* (Garden City, N.Y.: Doubleday, 1951), p. 41; Thomson, *David Lloyd George*, p. 154; John Masters, *Now, God Be Thanked*

(New York: McGraw-Hill, 1979), p. 488; John Colville, *The Fringes of Power: 10 Downing Street Diaries, 1939–1955* (New York: W.W. Norton, 1986), p. 106; John Grigg, *Lloyd George: The People's Champion, 1902–1911* (Berkeley: University of California Press, 1978), p. 67; Arthur Salter, *Personality in Politics: Studies of Contemporary Statesmen* (London: Faber and Faber, 1947), p. 58.

8. Masters, *Now, God Be Thanked*, pp. 488–89; E. Royston Pike, *Human Documents of the Lloyd George Era* (London: George Allen & Unwin, 1972), p. 8; Mackintosh, *From Gladstone to Lloyd George*, p. 175; A. J. P. Taylor, *Essays in English History* (Harmondsworth: Penguin Books, 1982), p. 261; L. S. Amery, "Two Great War Leaders," in Sir James Marchant, ed., *Winston Spencer Churchill: Servant of Crown and Commonwealth* (London: Cassell, 1954), p. 68; Rowland, *Lloyd George*, p. 155; Thomson, *David Lloyd George*, pp. 110, 219; J. B. Priestley, *The Edwardians* (New York: Harper & Row, 1970), p. 114.

9. Randolph S. Churchill, *Winston S. Churchill*, companion vol. 2, part 1 (London: Heinemann, 1969), p. 12; Rowland, *Lloyd George*, p. 155; Robert Rhodes James, ed., *Winston S. Churchill: His Complete Speeches, 1897–1963*, vol. 1 (New York: Chelsea House, 1974), p. 65; Julian Amery, *The Life of Joseph Chamberlain*, vol. 4 (London: Macmillan, 1951), p. 30; James C. Humes, *Churchill: Speaker of the Century* (New York: Scarborough Books, 1982), p. 78; William Manchester, *The Last Lion: Winston Spencer Churchill: Visions of Glory 1874–1932* (Boston: Little, Brown, 1983), p. 342; Rowland, *Lloyd George*, p. 151; René Kraus, *Winston Churchill: A Biography* (Philadelphia: J.B. Lippincott, 1940), p. 113; Winston S. Churchill, *My Early Life: A Roving Commission* (New York: Charles Scribner's Sons, 1963), p. 366.

10. du Parcq, *Life of David Lloyd George*, vol. 1 (London: Caxton, 1912), p. 43; J. Hugh Edwards, *David Lloyd George: The Man and the Statesman*, vol. 1 (New York: J.H. Sears, 1929), p. 73; Grigg, *The Young Lloyd George*, p. 45; Owen, *Tempestuous Journey*, p. 41; David Lloyd George, *Where Are We Going?* (New York: George H. Doran, 1923), p. 343; Randolph S. Churchill, *Winston S. Churchill*, vol. 2 (Boston: Houghton-Mifflin, 1967), p. 3.

11. Randolph S. Churchill, *Winston S. Churchill*, companion vol. 2, part 1, p. 20; John Colville, *Winston Churchill and His Inner Circle* (New York: Wyndham Books, 1981), p. 11; Randolph S. Churchill, *Winston S. Churchill*, vol. 2, pp. 1, 3–4. There is confused chronology in Ephesian, *Winston Churchill* (London: Mills & Boon, 1927), p. 81. Ephesian was a pen name of C. E. Bechhofer-Roberts.

12. Cowles, *Winston Churchill*, p. 79; Winston S. Churchill, *My Early Life*, p. 365; Hugh Martin, *Battle: The Life Story of the Rt. Hon. Winston S. Churchill* (London: Sampson Low, Marston, 1932), p. 54; Kate Fleming, *The Churchills* (New York: The Viking Press, 1975), p. 162; A. MacCallum Scott, *Winston Spencer Churchill* (London: Methuen, 1905), p. 110. Major John Seely had been elected Conservative member for the Isle of Wight in 1900 while on active military service in South Africa, but did not return to Britain until several months after Churchill's maiden speech (J. E. B. Seely, *Adventure* [London: William Heinemann, 1931], pp. 83, 86). Churchill had carried Seely's orders to South Africa (ibid., pp. 59, 106). After Seely assumed his seat in the House of Commons, he and Churchill cooperated closely for several years (Arthur C. Murray, *Master and Brother: Murrays of Elibank* [London: John Murray, 1945], p. 131; Scott, *Winston Spencer Churchill*, p. 211). Seely and Churchill had first met at Harrow (Seely, *Adventure*, p. 7).

13. Piers Brendon, *Winston Churchill: A Biography* (New York: Harper & Row, 1984), p. 41; Randolph S. Churchill, *Winston S. Churchill*, vol. 1 (Boston: Houghton-Mifflin, 1966), p. 204; Morgan, *Churchill*, p. 60; Robert Payne, *The Great Man: A Portrait of Winston Churchill* (New York: Coward & McCann & Geoghegan, 1974), p. 70. Erroneous reports of Churchill's height made him even shorter (Humes, *Churchill*, p. xiii; Payne, *The Great Man*, p. 236).

14. Anthony Storr, "The Man," in A. J. P. Taylor and others, *Churchill: Four Faces and the Man* (Harmondsworth: Penguin Books, 1973), p. 210; Fleming, *The Churchills*, p. 161; Roy Howells, *Churchill's Last Years* (New York: David McKay, 1966), p. 74; Morgan, *Churchill*, p. 237; Mary Soames, *Clementine Churchill: The Biography of a Marriage* (Boston: Houghton Mifflin, 1979), p. 67; Mary Soames, *Family Album: A Personal Selection from Four Generations of Churchills* (Boston: Houghton Mifflin, 1982), photograph 69; Ephesian, *Winston Churchill*, p. 234; Kraus, *Winston Churchill*, p. 111.

15. Wilfrid Scawen Blunt, *My Diaries: Being a Personal Narrative of Events, 1888–1914* (New York: Alfred A. Knopf, 1932), p. 74; Storr, "The Man," p. 211; Manchester, *The Last Lion*, p. 17; Cowles, *Winston Churchill*, p. 42; Humes, *Churchill*, p. 30; Moran, *Churchill*, pp. 197–98.

16. Winston Churchill, *Savrola* (London: Hodder and Stoughton, 1915), p. 34.

17. Violet Bonham Carter, *Winston Churchill: An Intimate Portrait* (New York: Harcourt, Brace & World, 1965), p. 64; Rowse, *The Churchills*, p. 429; Herbert Sidebotham, *Pillars of the State* (London: Nisbet, 1921), p. 144; R. W. Thompson, *Winston Churchill: The Yankee Marlborough* (Garden City, N.Y.: Doubleday, 1963), p. 95; Beaverbrook, *The Decline and Fall of Lloyd George*, p. 48; John Spencer Churchill, *A Churchill Canvas* (Boston: Little, Brown, 1961), p. 63; Walter Henry Thompson, *Assignment: Churchill* (New York: Farrar, Straus and Young, 1955), p. 273; Kenneth Young, *Churchill and Beaverbrook: A Study in Friendship and Politics* (New York: James H. Heineman, 1966), p. 28; Cecil Roberts, *The Growing Boy: Being the First Book of an Autobiography, 1892–1908* (London: Hodder and Stoughton, 1967), p. 107; Randolph S. Churchill, *Winston S. Churchill*, companion vol. 1 (Boston: Houghton-Mifflin, 1967), p. 950; Cowles, *Winston Churchill*, p. 80; Ephesian, *Winston Churchill*, p. 85; Robert Lewis Taylor, *Winston Churchill: An Informal Study of Greatness* (Garden City, N.Y.: Doubleday, 1952), p. 216; Martin, *Battle*, p. 54; Moran, *Churchill*, p. 831; Maxwell Philip Schoenfeld, *The War Ministry of Winston Churchill* (Ames: The Iowa State University Press, 1972), p. 18.

18. J. B. Atkins, *Incidents and Reflections* (London: Christophers, 1947), p. 130.

19. Randolph S. Churchill, *Winston S. Churchill*, companion vol. 1, part 2, pp. 818, 950.

20. Kraus, *Winston Churchill*, p. 113; Louis Adamic, *Dinner at the White House* (New York: Harper & Brothers, 1946), pp. 29, 31, 57; Humes, *Churchill*, pp. vii, xiii, 42–43, 167, 189; Martin, *Battle*, p. 84; Moran, *Churchill*, pp. 660, 830; Payne, *The Great Man*, p. 202; Lucy Masterman, "Churchill: The Liberal Phase—Part I," *History Today* 14 (November 1964): 741; Esmé Wingfield-Stratford, *Churchill: The Making of a Hero* (London: Victor Gollancz, 1942), p. 247; Leo Abse, *Private Member* (London: Macdonald, 1973), p. 60.

21. Randolph S. Churchill, *Winston S. Churchill*, companion vol. 1, part 2, p. 1191; Randolph S. Churchill, *Winston S. Churchill*, companion vol. 2, part 1, pp. 55–56, 408.

22. Randolph S. Churchill, *Winston S. Churchill*, vol. 2, p. 11; Randolph S. Churchill, *Winston S. Churchill*, companion vol. 2, part 1, pp. 12–13, 15; Jack Fishman, *My Darling Clementine: The Story of Lady Churchill* (New York: David McKay, 1963), p. 22; Morgan, *Churchill*, p. 149; Bonham Carter, *Winston Churchill*, pp. 63–64; Ralph G. Martin, *Jennie: The Life of Lady Randolph Churchill*, vol. 2 (New York: New American Library, 1972), p. 251; Begbie, *The Mirrors of Downing Street*, p. 105; Princess Bibesco, *Sir Winston Churchill: Master of Courage*, trans. Vladimir Kean (London: Robert Hale, 1957), p. 90; Brendon, *Winston Churchill*, p. 58; Collin Brooks, "Churchill the Conversationalist," in Charles Eade, ed., *Churchill by his Contemporaries* (New York: Simon and Schuster, 1954), p. 300; Colville, *The Fringes of Power*, p. 341; Colville, *Winston Churchill and His Inner Circle*, p. 113;

Olivia Coolidge, *Winston Churchill and the Story of Two World Wars* (Boston: Houghton Mifflin, 1960), pp. 18, 26, 36, 145; Cowles, *Winston Churchill*, pp. 9, 42; John Davenport and Charles J.V. Murphy, *The Lives of Winston Churchill* (New York: Charles Scribner's Sons, 1945), p. 3; Ephesian, *Winston Churchill*, pp. 27, 136; Fleming, *The Churchills*, p. 158; A. G. Gardiner, *Pillars of Society* (London: J.M. Dent & Sons, 1916), p. 158; Frank Harris, *Contemporary Portraits*, 3d series (New York: Frank Harris, 1920), p. 90; Humes, *Churchill*, pp. vii, xiii, 42–43, 81, 167, 189, 196, 255; James, *Churchill*, pp. 5, 30, 36; Elizabeth Longford, *Winston Churchill* (London: Sidgwick & Jackson, 1974), p. 36; Mackintosh, *From Gladstone to Lloyd George*, p. 221; Hugh Martin, *Battle*, pp. 14, 84; David Mason, *Churchill* (London: Pan Books, 1973), p. 85; Moran, *Winston Churchill*, pp. 12, 132, 314, 473, 487, 571, 660; Morgan, *Winston Churchill*, p. 171; Elizabeth Nel, *Mr.Churchill's Secretary* (New York: Coward McCann, 1958), p. 27; Payne, *The Great Man*, pp. 74, 110, 233; Henry Pelling, *Winston Churchill* (London: Macmillan, 1974), pp. 50, 62; Stephen Roskill, *Churchill and the Admirals* (New York: William Morrow, 1978), pp. 223–24; Arthur Salter, *Slave of the Lamp: A Public Servant's Notebook* (London: Weidenfeld & Nicolson, 1967), pp. 42, 139; James Stuart, *Within the Fringe: An Autobiography* (London: The Bodley Head, 1967), pp. 121, 125, 148; R. W. Thompson, *Winston Churchill*, p. 95; Walter Henry Thompson, *Assignment: Churchill*, pp. 183–84; Malcolm Thomson, *Churchill: His Life and Times* (London: Odhams, 1965), p. 15; Harold Wilson, *A Prime Minister on Prime Ministers* (New York: Summit Books, 1977), p. 245; Robert Lewis Taylor, *Winston Churchill*, pp. 321-22, 426; Sarah Churchill, *Keep on Dancing*, ed. Paul Medlicott (New York: Coward, McCann & Geoghegan, 1981), p. 45; Robert Rhodes James, "The Politician," in A. J. P. Taylor and others, *Churchill*, p. 60; Michael Foot, *Aneurin Bevan: A Biography*, vol. 2 (New York: Atheneum, 1974), p. 245; Peter de Mendelssohn, *The Age of Churchill: Heritage and Adventure, 1874–1911* (New York: Alfred A. Knopf, 1961), p. 534; Masters, *Now, God Be Thanked*, p. 144; H. G. Wells, *Men Like Gods* (New York: Grosset & Dunlap, 1923), pp. 97–98, 100, 104; *The Boston Globe TV Week*, 16–22 January 1983, p. 2; Kraus, *Winston Churchill*, pp. 42-43; Gerald Pawle, *The War and Colonel Warden* (New York: Alfred A. Knopf, 1963), p. 159.

23. Bibesco, *Sir Winston Churchill*, pp. 90–91; Frank Brennand, *The Young Churchill* (London: New English Library, 1972), p. 34; Earl Winterton, "Churchill the Parliamentarian," in Eade, ed., *Churchill by His Contemporaries*, pp. 62–63; Grigg, *Lloyd George*, p. 173; Masterman, "Churchill," pp. 745, 747; Mendelssohn, *The Age of Churchill*, p. 455; Costigan, *Makers of Modern England*, p. 259.

24. Robert Lewis Taylor, *Winston Churchill*, p. 100; Walter Henry Thompson, *Assignment: Churchill*, p. 183; Walter Henry Thompson, "Guarding Mr. Churchill," in Eade, ed., *Churchill by His Contemporaries*, p. 206.

25. Cowles, *Winston Churchill*, p. 81; Payne, *The Great Man*, p. 109; Hugh Martin, *Battle*, p. 54; Stephen R. Graubard, *Burke, Disraeli, and Churchill: The Politics of Perseverance* (Cambridge, Mass: Harvard University Press, 1961), p. 178; Ephesian, *Winston Churchill*, p. 88; James, ed., *Winston S. Churchill*, vol. 1, pp. 65–70; Amery, *The Life of Joseph Chamberlain*, vol. 4, p. 30; Churchill, *Winston S. Churchill*, companion vol. 2, part 1, p. 19.

26. Philip Guedalla, *Mr. Churchill* (New York: Reynal & Hitchcock, 1942), p. 94; Payne, *The Great Man*, p. 108.

27. Morgan, *Churchill*, p. 148; Churchill, *Winston S. Churchill*, companion vol. 2, part 1, pp. 68–69; Ephesian, *Winston Churchill*, p. 85; Humes, *Churchill*, p. 77; Hugh Martin, *Battle*, p. 54; Pelling, *Winston Churchill*, p. 76; Rowland, *Lloyd George*, p. 151; Thomson, *Churchill*, p. 82; Churchill, *My Early Life*, p. 366.

28. Cowles, *Winston Churchill*, p. 5.

29. The claim, by Walter Henry Thompson, *Assignment: Churchill*, pp. 182–83,

that Churchill wrote all his speeches is exaggerated. It was probably true until the Second World War began. It was essentially true of House of Commons speeches even during that war (Colville, *The Fringes of Power*, p. 365). The text of those speeches was frequently altered by his staff before being printed in Hansard (ibid., pp. 258, 397, 421, 520, 527). After the Second World War, many of Churchill's speeches, including at least some in the House of Commons, were written by his staff (ibid., pp. 367, 649, 695). See also Moran, *Churchill*, p. 7; Brendon, *Winston Churchill*, p. 36; Humes, *Churchill*, pp. 64–65, 121; Pelling, *Winston Churchill*, p. 300; R. W. Thompson, *Winston Churchill*, p. 122; Viscount Samuel, "The Campbell-Bannerman-Asquith Government," in Marchant, ed., *Winston Spencer Churchill*, p. 49; Reed Whittemore, "Churchill and the Limitations of Myth," *Yale Review* 44 (December 1954): 249; Alan Clark, ed., *"A Good Innings": The Private Papers of Viscount Lee of Fareham* (London: John Murray, 1974), p. 120; Storr, "The Man," p. 238; George Malcolm Thomson, *Vote of Censure* (New York: Stein and Day, 1968), p. 205.

30. A. J. P. Taylor, *English History, 1914-1945* (New York: Oxford University Press, 1965), p. 482; A. J. P. Taylor, *Essays in English History*, p. 261; Sir Dingle Foot, *British Political Crises*, p. 147; Victor Wallace Germains, *The Tragedy of Winston Churchill* (London: Hurst & Blackett, 1931), p. 47; Martin Gilbert, *Winston S. Churchill*, vol. 6 (Boston: Houghton Mifflin, 1983), p. 164; Morgan, *Churchill*, p. 174; Pelling, *Winston Churchill*, p. 85; Storr, "The Man," p. 238; Brendon, *Winston Churchill*, p. 36; Alec Douglas-Home, *The Way the Wind Blows: An Autobiography* (New York: Quadrangle/The New York Times Book Co., 1976), p. 49; Robert H. Pilpel, *Churchill in America, 1895–1961: An Affectionate Portrait* (New York: Harcourt Brace Jovanovich, 1976), p. 150; Henry W. Nevinson, *More Changes More Chances* (New York: Harcourt, Brace, no date), p. 370; John H. Peck, "The Working Day," *The Atlantic* 215 (March 1965): 74.

31. Moran, *Churchill*, pp. 456–57; Fishman, *My Darling Clementine*, p. 85; Mason, *Churchill*, p. 83.

32. Sir John Smyth, *The Only Enemy: An Autobiography* (London: Hutchinson, 1959), p. 285; Harold Balfour, *Wings over Westminster* (London: Hutchinson, 1973), p. 79; The Earl of Swinton, *Sixty Years of Power: Some Memories of the Men Who Wielded It* (London: Hutchinson, 1966), pp. 131–32; Woodrow Wyatt, *Into the Dangerous World* (London: George Weidenfeld & Nicolson, 1952), pp. 109–10.

33. Germains, *The Tragedy of Winston Churchill*, p. 278; A. P. Herbert, "The Master of Words," in Marchant, ed., *Winston Spencer Churchill*, p. 101; Pelling, *Winston Churchill*, p. 642; Priestley, *The Edwardians*, p. 42; Moran, *Churchill*, p. 392.

34. Harold Macmillan, *The Past Masters: Politics and Politicians, 1906-1939* (London: Macmillan, 1975), p. 56; Owen, *Tempestuous Journey*, p. 98; Lord Riddell, *More Pages from My Diary: 1908-1914* (London: Country Life, 1934), p. 94; Snow, *Variety of Men*, pp. 99–100; John Campbell, *Lloyd George: The Goat in the Wilderness, 1922-1931* (London: Jonathan Cape, 1977), pp. 120, 236; James, *Churchill*, p. 29; Michael Foot, *Aneurin Bevan*, vol. 2, p. 249; Pierre Maillaud, *The English Way* (New York: Oxford University Press, 1946), p. 79; Salter, *Slave of the Lamp*, p. 54; Snow, *Variety of Men*, p. 100; Wilson, *A Prime Minister on Prime Ministers*, p. 138.

35. J. H. Grainger, *Character and Style in English Politics* (Cambridge: Cambridge University Press, 1969), p. 3.

36. James, "The Politician," p. 105; John Ehrman, "Lloyd George and Churchill as War Ministers," *Transactions of the Royal Historical Society*, 5th series, vol. 11, p. 104; Brendon, *Winston Churchill*, p. 173; Winifred Holtby, *Letters to a Friend*,

eds. Alice Holtby and Jean McWilliam (New York: Macmillan, 1938), pp. 245–46; Christopher Sykes, *Evelyn Waugh: A Biography* (Boston: Little, Brown, 1975), p. 443; Grainger, *Character and Style in English Politics*, p. 239.

37. Moran, *Churchill*, pp. 13, 650, 831.

38. James, "The Politician," p. 109.

39. Moran, *Churchill*, p. 641.

40. Ibid., pp. 13, 831.

41. Walter Henry Thompson, *Assignment: Churchill*, p. 185.

42. James, ed., *Winston S. Churchill*, vol. 1, p. 66.

43. Ibid., p. 65; Humes, *Churchill*, p. 79; Morgan, *Churchill*, p. 148. For a less accurate report of Chamberlain's response, see Cowles, *Winston Churchill*, p. 80.

44. James, ed., *Winston S. Churchill*, vol. 1, pp. 68–69; Manchester, *The Last Lion*, p. 343.

45. Scott, *Winston Spencer Churchill*, p. 112; Payne, *The Great Man*, p. 108; A. L. Rowse, "Churchill's Place in History," in Eade, ed., *Churchill by His Contemporaries*, p. 421.

46. Frederick Woods, ed., *Young Winston's Wars: The Original Dispatches of Winston S. Churchill, War Correspondent, 1897–1900* (London: Leo Cooper, 1972), p. 117.

47. Ibid., p. 161.

48. Scott, *Winston Spencer Churchill*, p. 111.

49. James, ed., *Winston S. Churchill*, vol. 1, pp. 69–70; Herbert Leslie Stewart, *Winged Worlds: Sir Winston Churchill as Writer and Speaker* (New York: Bouregy & Curl, 1954), p. 10.

50. Mackintosh, *From Gladstone to Lloyd George*, p. 222; Wingfield-Stratford, *Churchill*, p. 78.

51. Lady Algernon Gordon Lennox, ed., *The Diary of Lord Bertie of Thame, 1914–1918*, vol. 2 (London: Hodder & Stoughton, 1924), p. 270; R. G. Menzies, "Churchill and the Commonwealth," in Marchant, ed., *Winston Spencer Churchill*, p. 94; Janet Adam Smith, *John Buchan: A Biography* (Boston: Little, Brown, 1965), pp. 110–11, 157; James, ed., *Winston S. Churchill*, vol. 1, pp. 297–99.

52. Jones, *The Man David*, pp. 120–21; Winston S. Churchill, *My Early Life*, p. 367; Grigg, *Lloyd George*, p. 64. The Bar of the House of Commons is a line on the carpet where each member entering the Chamber of the House bows to the speaker. (Sir Harry Boyne, *The Houses of Parliament* [New York: Larousse, 1981], p. 31). Nonmembers are not permitted inside the Bar, hence the name. The Bar is not, as mistakenly assumed by Kraus (*Winston Churchill*, p. 114), a barroom. Lloyd George and Churchill were not consuming alcohol when they met. Alcohol was served in the members' smoking room (Boyne, *The Houses of Parliament*, p. 48). Lloyd George and Churchill were not, however, in the smoking room, as reported by Cowles (*Winston Churchill*, p. 82), when they met.

53. Lloyd George's memory of the exchange is found in Cross, ed., *Life with Lloyd George*, p. 88. Churchill's recollection is from Churchill, *My Early Life*, p. 367.

Chapter Four

1. Virginia Cowles, *Winston Churchill: The Era and the Man* (New York: Grosset & Dunlap, no date), p. 82; Frank Owen, *Tempestuous Journey: Lloyd George, His Life and Times* (London: Hutchinson, 1954), p. 109.; Ivor Bulmer-Thomas, *The Growth of the British Party System*, vol. 1 (London: John Baker, 1965), p. 164; Earl

Lloyd George, *My Father, Lloyd George* (New York: Crown, 1961), pp. 79, 177–78; Philip Guedalla, *Mr. Churchill* (New York: Reynal & Hitchcock, 1942), p. 123.

2. Randolph S. Churchill, *Winston S. Churchill*, companion vol. 2, part 2 (London: Heinemann, 1969), p. 1024.

3. Winston S. Churchill, *My Early Life: A Roving Commission* (New York: Charles Scribner's Sons, 1963), p. 367; Colin Cross, ed., *Life with Lloyd George: The Diary of A. J. Sylvester 1931–45* (New York: Barnes & Noble, 1975), p. 139; Giovanni Costigan, *Makers of Modern England: The Force of Individual Genius in History* (London: Macmillan, 1969), p. 197; Thomas Jones, *Lloyd George* (London: Oxford University Press, 1951), p. 1; Lloyd George, *My Father, Lloyd George*, p. 79, Malcolm Thomson, *Churchill: His Life and Times* (London: Odhams, 1965), p. 104; Peter de Mendelssohn, *The Age of Churchill: Heritage and Adventure, 1874–1911* (New York: Alfred A. Knopf, 1961), p. 437; Harold Nicolson, *Diaries and Letters, 1939–1945*, ed. Nigel Nicolson (New York: Atheneum, 1967), p. 164; Frances Stevenson, *Lloyd George: A Diary*, ed. A. J. P. Taylor (London: Hutchinson, 1971), p. 253.

4. John Colville, *Winston Churchill and His Inner Circle* (New York: Wyndham Books, 1981), p. 19.

5. John Grigg, *Lloyd George: From Peace to War, 1912–1916* (Berkeley: University of California Press, 1985), p. 136; W. Watkin Davies, *Lloyd George 1863–914* (London: Constable, 1939), p. 439; Peter Rowland, *Lloyd George* (London: Barrie & Jenkins, 1975), p. 239; Frances Lloyd George, *The Years that are Past* (London: Hutchinson, 1967), p. 60. Lloyd George's comment is from Stephen Koss, *Asquith* (London: Allen Lane, 1976), p. 153.

6. Jack Fishman, *My Darling Clementine: The Story of Lady Churchill* (New York: David McKay, 1963), p. 31; John Grigg, *Lloyd George: The People's Champion, 1902–1911* (Berkeley: University of California Press, 1978), pp. 65, 144–45; John Spencer Churchill, *A Churchill Canvas* (Boston: Little, Brown, 1961), p. 39.

7. Randolph S. Churchill, *Winston S. Churchill*, companion vol. 2, part 1 (London: Heinemann, 1969), p. 281; Piers Brendon, *Winston Churchill: A Biography* (New York: Harper & Row, 1984), p. 90; Maxwell P. Schoenfeld, *Sir Winston Churchill: His Life and Times*, 2d ed. (Malabar, Fla: Robert E. Krieger, 1986), p. 41; V. G. Trukhanovsky, *Winston Churchill* (Moscow: Progress Publishers, 1978), p. 143; Manfred Weidhorn, *Sir Winston Churchill* (Boston: Twayne, 1979), p. 122; David Walder, *The Chanak Affair* (New York: Macmillan, 1969), p. 326; Martin Gilbert, *Winston Churchill*, vol. 5 (Boston: Houghton Mifflin, 1977), p. 144; Andrew Barrow, *Gossip: A History of High Society from 1920 to 1970* (New York: Coward, McCann & Geoghegan, 1979), p. 92; Michael Thornton, *Royal Feud: The Dark Side of the Love Story of the Century* (New York: Simon and Schuster, 1985), p. 178; Cross, ed., *Life with Lloyd George*, p. 233; Rowland, *Lloyd George*, pp. 369, 758; A. J. Sylvester, *The Real Lloyd George* (London: Cassell, 1947), p. 252; Grigg, *Lloyd George: From Peace to War*, p. 397; A. J. P. Taylor, ed., *My Darling Pussy: The Letters of Lloyd George and Frances Stevenson, 1913–41* (London: Weidenfeld and Nicolson, 1975), p. 11; Stevenson, *Lloyd George*, p. 292.

8. Rowland, *Lloyd George*, p. 531; Barrow, *Gossip*, p. 5; Mary Soames, *Clementine Churchill: The Biography of a Marriage* (Boston: Houghton Mifflin, 1979), p. 265; Violet Bonham Carter, *Winston Churchill: An Intimate Portrait* (New York: Harcourt, Brace & World, 1965), p. 97.

9. Cross, ed., *Life with Lloyd George*, p. 138.

10. Ibid., p. 139.

11. Gilbert, *Winston S. Churchill*, vol. 5, p. 698; Stevenson, *Lloyd George*, p. 322.

12. Sir Geoffrey Shakespeare, *Let Candles Be Brought In* (London: Macdonald, 1949), p. 64. This was in addition to a painting by Churchill done *circa* 1927 in the south of France, also given to Lloyd George, which eventually passed out of the Lloyd George family. (David Coombs, ed., *Churchill: His Paintings* [Cleveland: World,

1967], pp. 84, 115; Kenneth Young, ed., *The Diaries of Sir Robert Bruce Lockhart*, vol. 1 [London: Macmillan, 1974], p. 353). The Marrakesh painting's later fate is unknown. Also unknown is the fate of the wedding gift, a silver fruit basket, of David and Margaret Lloyd George to Winston and Clementine Churchill. (Fishman, *My Darling Clementine*, p. 19). It was not among the items probated after the deaths of the Churchills. (Grigg, *Lloyd George*, p. 164n).

13. Rowland, *Lloyd George*, p. 245n.

14. Fishman, *My Darling Clementine*, pp. 15–18; Randolph S. Churchill, *Winston S. Churchill*, vol. 2 (Boston: Houghton Mifflin, 1967), p. 265; Soames, *Clementine Churchill*, p. 66; Grigg, *Lloyd George*, pp. 163, 164n; St. Margaret's Church was aptly chosen for a fashionable fictional wedding by Evelyn Waugh, *(Decline and Fall* [Harmondsworth: Penguin Books, 1983], p. 149). For the guest's comment, see Nicholas Mosley, *Julian Grenfell: His Life and the Times of His Death 1888–1915* (London: Weidenfeld and Nicolson, 1976), p. 175.

15. Fishman, *My Darling Clementine*, pp. 18–19.

16. Published in two volumes in London by Gollancz in 1938.

17. Cross, ed., *Life with Lloyd George*, pp. 186, 190; Gilbert, *Winston S. Churchill*, vol. 5, p. 897.

18. Viscount Gwynedd, *Dame Margaret: The Life Story of His Mother* (London: George Allen & Unwin, 1947), pp. 157, 196; Cross, ed., *Life with Lloyd George*, p. 191; Kirsty McLeod, *The Wives of Downing Street* (London: Collins, 1976), p. 205; Rowland, *Lloyd George*, p. 748.

19. William A. Sadler, Jr., *Existence and Love: A New Approach in Existential Phenomenology* (New York: Charles Scribner's Sons, 1969), p. 333; Lloyd George, *My Father, Lloyd George*, p. 139; Joseph P. Lash, *Roosevelt and Churchill 1939–1941: The Partnership That Saved the West* (New York: W.W. Norton, 1976), p. 54.

20. Robert J. Scally, *The Origins of the Lloyd George Coalition: The Politics of Social-Imperialism, 1900–1918* (Princeton, N.J.: Princeton University Press, 1975), p. 280.

21. V. I. Lenin, *"Left-Wing" Communism, an Infantile Disorder* (Moscow: Progress, 1975), p. 68.

22. Bonham Carter, *Winston Churchill*, p. 108; Victor Wallace Germains, *The Tragedy of Winston Churchill* (London: Hurst & Blackett, 1931), p. 112; Grigg, *Lloyd George*, p. 136; Cameron Hazlehurst, *Politicians at War: July 1914 to May 1915: A Prologue to the Triumph of Lloyd George* (London: Jonathan Cape, 1971), p. 205; Frances Lloyd George, *The Years That Are Past*, p. 59; William Manchester, *The Last Lion: Winston Spencer Churchill: Visions of Glory, 1874–1932* (Boston: Little, Brown, 1983), p. 344; E. T. Raymond, *Mr. Lloyd George* (New York: George H. Doran, 1922), p. 113 (E. T. Raymond was a pen name of E. R. Thompson); Viscount Samuel, "The Campbell-Bannerman-Asquith Government," in Sir James Marchant, ed., *Winston Spencer Churchill: Servant of Crown and Commonwealth* (London: Cassell, 1954), p. 51; Esmé Wingfield-Stratford, *Churchill: The Making of a Hero* (London: Victor Gollancz, 1942), p. 112; Mendelssohn, *The Age of Churchill*, p. 443.

23. Lloyd George, *My Father, Lloyd George*, p. 182; Rowland, *Lloyd George*, p. 208.

24. Kenneth O. Morgan, ed., *Lloyd George: Family Letters, 1885–1936* (Cardiff: University of Wales Press and London: Oxford University Press, 1972), p. 183; Trevor Wilson, ed., *The Political Diaries of C. P. Scott 1911–1928* (Ithaca, N.Y.: Cornell University Press, 1970), p. 195; Owen, *Tempestuous Journey*, pp. 221, 255, 289; Lord Riddell, *More Pages from My Diary: 1908–1914* (London: Country Life, 1934), p. 25; Malcolm Thomson, *David Lloyd George: The Official Biography* (London: Hutchinson, no date), p. 205; Bonham Carter, *Winston Churchill*, p. 331; Cowles, *Winston Churchill*, p. 204; The Earl of Oxford and Asquith, K.G., *Memories and*

Reflections, 1852–1927, vol. 2 (Boston: Little, Brown, 1928), p. 122; Martin Gilbert, *Winston S. Churchill*, vol. 3 (Boston: Houghton Mifflin, 1971), p. 570; Martin Gilbert, *Winston S. Churchill*, companion vol. 3, part 2 (Boston: Houghton Mifflin, 1973), p. 1271.

25. Gilbert, *Winston S. Churchill*, vol. 3, p. 622.

26. Gilbert, *Winston S. Churchill*, companion vol. 3, part 2, pp. 1517–18; Grigg, *Lloyd George: From Peace to War*, p. 362; Koss, *Asquith*, p. 254; Frances Lloyd George, *The Years That Are Past*, pp. 86, 90; Thomson, *David Lloyd George*, p. 257; Germains, *The Tragedy of Winston Churchill*, p. 250.

27. Gilbert, *Winston S. Churchill*, vol. 3, p. 622; Gilbert, *Winston S. Churchill*, companion vol. 3, part 2, p. 1345.

28. Lord Beaverbrook, *Politicians and the War 1914–1916* (London: Oldbourne, 1960), pp. 234–35; Gilbert, *Winston S. Churchill*, companion vol. 3, part 2, pp. 1409, 1485–86.

29. Gilbert, *Winston S. Churchill*, vol. 3, p. 816; Wilson, ed., *The Political Diaries of C. P. Scott*, p. 235; Frank Brennand, *The Young Churchill* (London: New English Library, 1972), p. 70; Winston S. Churchill, *The World Crisis, 1911-1918*, vol. 2 (London: Odhams, 1938), p. 1141; Ephesian, *Winston Churchill* (London: Mills & Boon, 1927), p. 209 (Ephesian was a pen name of C. E. Bechhofer-Roberts); Hugh Martin, *Battle: The Life Story of the Rt. Hon. Winston S. Churchill* (London: Sampson Low, Marston, 1932), p. 149; Lord Beaverbrook, *Men and Power, 1917–1918* (London: Hutchinson, 1956), pp. 114, 127, 131; Beaverbrook, *Politicians and the War*, pp. 526, 529; *War Memoirs of David Lloyd George*, vol. 3 (London: Ivor Nicolson & Watson, 1934), pp. 1067–68; Elizabeth Longford, *Winston Churchill* (London: Sidgwick & Jackson, 1974), p. 68; Rowland, *Lloyd George*, p. 373; Thomson, *David Lloyd George*, p. 265.

30. Gilbert, *Winston S. Churchill*, companion vol. 3, part 2, p. 1545.

31. Anita Leslie, *Lady Randolph Churchill: The Story of Jennie Jerome* (New York: Lancer Books, 1969), p. 427; Winston S. Churchill, *The World Crisis*, vol. 2, pp. 1144, 1208; Lady Algernon Gordon Lennox, ed., *The Diary of Lord Bertie of Thame, 1914–1918*, vol. 2 (London: Hodder and Stoughton, 1924), p. 156.

32. Earl Lloyd George, *My Father, Lloyd George*, p. 181.

33. Beaverbrook, *Men and Power*, p. 121; Owen, *Tempestuous Journey*, p. 352.

34. Roy Douglas, *The History of the Liberal Party, 1895–1970* (Madison: Fairleigh Dickinson University Press, 1971), p. 107; Winston S. Churchill, *The World Crisis*, vol. 2, pp. 1144, 1170; Trukhanovsky, *Winston Churchill*, p. 136; Kenneth Young, *Churchill and Beaverbrook: A Study in Friendship and Politics* (New York: James H. Heineman, 1966), p. 46; Bulmer-Thomas, *The Growth of the British Party System*, vol. 1, p. 231; Henry Pelling, *Winston Churchill* (London: Macmillan, 1974), p. 228; Rowland, *Lloyd George*, p. 409.

35. Cecil Roberts, *The Years of Promise: Being the Second Book of an Autobiography, 1908–1919* (London: Hodder and Stoughton, 1968), p. 147; Beaverbrook, *Men and Power*, pp. 63, 139; Paul Guinn, *British Strategy and Politics 1914 to 1918* (Oxford: Clarendon Press, 1965), p. 240; John P. Mackintosh, *The British Cabinet*, 2d ed. (London: Methuen, 1968), p. 396; Owen, *Tempestuous Journey*, p. 415; *War Memoirs of David Lloyd George*, vol. 3, pp. 1068, 1070, 1072;Kenneth O. Morgan, "Lloyd George's Premiership: A Study in 'Prime Ministerial Government,'" *Historical Journal* 13 (1970): 137.

36. R. W. Thompson, *Winston Churchill: The Yankee Marlborough* (Garden City, N.Y.: Doubleday, 1963), p. 182.

37. Alan Clark, ed., *"A Good Innings": The Private Papers of Viscount Lee of Fareham* (London: John Murray, 1974), p. 170.

38. Winston S. Churchill, *The World Crisis*, vol. 2, pp. 1176–77.

39. Donald McCormick, *The Mask of Merlin: A Critical Study of David Lloyd George* (London: Macdonald, 1963), p. 287; Martin, *Battle*, p. 155; Lloyd George, *My Father, Lloyd George*, p. 177.

40. Beaverbrook, *Men and Power*, pp. 138–39.

41. Winston S. Churchill, *The World Crisis*, vol. 2, p. 1209; Cowles, *Winston Churchill*, p. 229; Guedalla, *Mr. Churchill*, p. 202; A. L. Rowse, *The Churchills: The Story of a Family* (New York: Harper & Row, 1966), p. 486; Walder, *The Chanak Affair*, p. 64; Wingfield-Stratford, *Churchill*, p. 195.

42. Beaverbrook, *Men and Power*, pp. 325–26; *Lord Riddell's Intimate Diary of the Peace Conference and After, 1918–1923* (London: Victor Gollancz, 1933), pp. 203, 260; Arthur Salter, *Personality in Politics: Studies of Contemporary Statesmen* (London: Faber and Faber, 1947), pp. 101–2; Arthur Salter, *Slave of the Lamp: A Public Servant's Notebook* (London: Weidenfeld & Nicolson, 1967), p. 31; Robert Rhodes James, *Churchill: A Study in Failure, 1900–1939* (Harmondsworth: Penguin Books, 1973), p. 191.

43. Rowland, *Lloyd George*, p. 587; Walder, *The Chanak Affair*, p. 329.

44. Lord Beaverbrook, *The Decline and Fall of Lloyd George: And Great Was the Fall Thereof* (London: Collins, 1966), p. 204. The Order of Companions of Honour had been recently created to reward service of national importance.

45. Kenneth O. Morgan, *The Age of Lloyd George* (New York: Barnes & Noble, 1971), p. 98.

46. Chris Cook, *The Age of Alignment: Electoral Politics in Britain, 1922–1929* (Toronto: University of Toronto Press, 1975), p. 218.

47. Frances, Countess Lloyd-George of Dwyfor, "Introduction" to Thomson, *David Lloyd George*, p. 26.

48. Frances Donaldson, *The Marconi Scandal* (New York: Harcourt, Brace & World, 1962), pp. 53–54; Randolph S. Churchill, *Winston S. Churchill*, vol. 2, p. 538.

49. Grigg, *Lloyd George: From Peace to War*, p. 48; Donaldson, *The Marconi Scandal*, pp. 54, 75; The Marquess of Reading, *Rufus Isaacs: First Marquess of Reading: 1860–1919* (London: Hutchinson, 1950), pp. 228, 236–37.

50. Cowles, *Winston Churchill*, p. 165; Frank Dilnot, *Lloyd George: The Man and His Story* (New York: Harper & Brothers, 1917), pp. 164–65; J. H. Grainger, *Character and Style in English Politics* (Cambridge: Cambridge University Press, 1969), pp. 148–49; Harold Wilson, *A Prime Minister on Prime Ministers* (New York: Summit Books, 1977), p. 147.

51. Edward David, ed., *Inside Asquith's Cabinet: From the Diaries of Charles Hobhouse* (New York: St. Martin's Press, 1977), p. 139.

52. Morgan, *Wales in British Politics*, pp. 175–76; Donaldson, *The Marconi Scandal*, p. 127.

53. Cowles, *Winston Churchill*, p. 165; Grigg, *Lloyd George: The People's Champion*, p. 357.

54. Robert Rhodes James, ed., *Winston S. Churchill: His Complete Speeches, 1897–1963*, vol. 2 (New York: Chelsea House, 1974), p. 2120.

55. Ibid., p. 2121.

56. Earl Lloyd George, *My Father, Lloyd George*, p. 180; Randolph S. Churchill, *Winston S. Churchill*, vol. 2, p. 536; Randolph S. Churchill, *Winston S. Churchill*, companion vol. 2, part 3 (London: Heinemann, 1969), pp. 1740, 1747; Gilbert, *Winston S. Churchill*, vol. 3, p. 623n; H. Montgomery Hyde, *Lord Reading: The Life of Rufus Isaacs, First Marquess of Reading* (New York: Farrar, Straus and Giroux, 1967), pp. 141–42; Lucille Iremonger, *The Fiery Chariot: A Study of British Prime Ministers and the Search for Love* (London: Secker & Warburg, 1970), p. 206; McCormick, *The Mask of Merlin*, p. 232; Owen, *Tempestuous Journey*, pp. 231–32;

Pelling, *Winston Churchill*, p. 176; Rowland, *Lloyd George*, p. 265; Grigg, *Lloyd George: From Peace to War*, p. 55; Thomson, *David Lloyd George*, p. 217; Donaldson, *The Marconi Scandal*, p. 97; Riddell, *More Pages from My Diary*, pp. 146, 162.

57. Randolph S. Churchill, *Winston S. Churchill*, vol. 2, p. 536; Owen, *Tempestuous Journey*, p. 231.

58. Gilbert, *Winston S. Churchill*, vol. 3, p. 623n; Reading, *Rufus Isaacs*, pp. 259–60; Owen, *Tempestuous Journey*, p. 238.

59. Cregier, *Bounder from Wales*, p. 206; Owen, *Tempestuous Journey*, p. 232; Riddell, *More Pages from My Diary*, pp. 131, 139.

60. Taylor, ed., *My Darling Pussy*, p. 4; George Dangerfield, *The Strange Death of Liberal England* (New York: Capricorn Books, 1961), p. 272.

61. Ted Morgan, *Churchill: Young Man in a Hurry, 1874–1915* (New York: Simon and Schuster, 1982), p. 562; C. P. Snow, *Variety of Men* (London: Macmillan, 1967), p. 97.

62. Lloyd George, *The Years That Are Past*, p. 54.

63. Ford Madox Ford, *Return to Yesterday* (New York: Horace Liveright, 1932), p. 356.

64. Morgan, *Churchill*, p. 357; Cowles, *Winston Churchill*, p. 165; James, *Churchill*, p. 68; Snow, *Variety of Men*, p. 127.

65. Bonham Carter, *Winston Churchill*, p. 116; Lady Violet Bonham Carter, "Winston Churchill—As I Know Him," in Marchant, ed., *Winston Spencer Churchill*, p. 159; Pelling, *Winston Churchill*, p. 415; Shakespeare, *Let Candles Be Brought In*, p. 67.

66. Winston Churchill, *Savrola* (London: Hodder and Stoughton, 1915), p. 41.

67. Arno J. Mayer, "Winston Churchill: Power Politician and Counter-Revolutionary," in Kurt H. Wolff and Barrington Moore, Jr., eds., *The Critical Spirit: Essays in Honor of Herbert Marcuse* (Boston: Beacon Press, 1967), pp. 329–30.

68. Taylor, ed., *My Darling Pussy*, p. 233n; Anthony Storr, "The Man," in A. J. P. Taylor and others, *Churchill: Four Faces and the Man* (Harmondsworth: Penguin Books, 1973), p. 242; James, *Churchill*, p. 358; Randolph S. Churchill, *Winston S. Churchill*, vol. 2, pp. 539–40.

69. Earl Lloyd George, *My Father, Lloyd George*, p. 32; Riddell, *More Pages from My Diary*, p. 165; Scally, *The Origins of the Lloyd George Coalition*, p. 245; Taylor, ed., *My Darling Pussy*, p. 175.

70. Joyce Cary, *Prisoner of Grace* (New York: Harper & Brothers, 1952), p. 160.

71. Ibid., p. 92; Herbert du Parcq, *Life of David Lloyd George*, vol. 4 (London: Caxton, 1913), p. 822.

72. Riddell, *More Pages from My Diary*, p. 190. See also Churchill, *Winston S. Churchill*, vol. 2, p. 640; Cregier, *Bounder from Wales*, p. 224.

73. Earl Lloyd George, *My Father, Lloyd George*, p. 185.

74. Gilbert, *Winston S. Churchill*, companion vol. 3, part 2, p. 1482; Gilbert, *Winston S. Churchill*, vol. 3, p. 751.

75. Morgan, *Churchill*, p. 357.

76. Laurence Thompson, *1940: Year of Legend, Year of History* (London: Collins, 1966), p. 152; Thompson, *Winston Churchill*, p. 102.

77. Young, *Churchill and Beaverbrook*, p. 100; Salter, *Slave of the Lamp*, p. 30; Stevenson, *Lloyd George*, p. 324; Taylor, ed., *My Darling Pussy*, p. 211.

78. Countess Lloyd-George of Dwyfor, "Introduction," p. 16.

79. R. W. Thompson, *Winston Churchill*, p. 154; Longford, *Winston Churchill*, p. 41; Mendelssohn, *The Age of Churchill*, p. 488; John Campbell, *Lloyd George: The Goat in the Wilderness, 1922–1931* (London: Jonathan Cape, 1977), pp. 102, 104.

80. R. W. Thompson, *Winston Churchill*, p. 218.

81. *The Memoirs of Captain Liddell Hart*, vol. 1, p. 374. See also Robert Booth-

by, *I Fight To Live* (London: Victor Gollancz, 1947), p. 45; Lord Boothby, "Political Titans," *Books and Bookmen* 20 (August 1974): 18.

82. John Davenport and Charles J. V. Murphy, *The Lives of Winston Churchill* (New York: Charles Scribner's Sons, 1945), p. 35; Neil Ferrier, ed., *Churchill: The Man of the Century* (no place: no publisher, 1955), p. 16; René Kraus, *Winston Churchill: A Biography* (Philadelphia: J. B. Lippincott, 1940), p. 137; Morgan, *Churchill*, p. 316; Thompson, *Winston Churchill*, pp. 17, 111, 171; Cowles, *Winston Churchill*, pp. 121, 138–39; Grigg, *Lloyd George*, p. 64; Kenneth O. Morgan, "Lloyd George's Stage Army: The Coalition Liberals, 1918–22," in A. J. P. Taylor, ed., *Lloyd George: Twelve Essays* (New York: Atheneum, 1971), p. 232; Maxwell Philip Schoenfeld, *The War Ministry of Winston Churchill* (Ames: The Iowa State University Press, 1972), p. 26; Walder, *The Chanak Affair*, p. 288; Cowles, *Winston Churchill*, p. 121; *The Memoirs of Captain Liddell Hart*, vol. 1 (London: Cassell, 1967), p. 374; Olivia Coolidge, *Winston Churchill and the Story of Two World Wars* (Boston: Houghton Mifflin, 1960), p. 35; Manfred Weidhorn, *Sword and Pen: A Survey of the Writings of Sir Winston Churchill* (Albuquerque: University of New Mexico Press, 1974), p. 239.

83. Cregier, *Bounder from Wales*, pp. 86–87.

84. Herbert du Parcq, *Life of David Lloyd George*, vol. II (London: Caxton, 1912), p. 266; Grigg, *Lloyd George*, p. 64.

85. James C. Humes, *Churchill: Speaker of the Century* (New York: Scarborough Books, 1982), p. 116; Mendelssohn, *The Age of Churchill*, p. 572; Grigg, Lloyd George, pp. 64–65; David, ed., *Inside Asquith's Cabinet*, p. 121.

86. The year 1903 is mistakenly reported by A. J. P. Taylor, "The Statesman," in Taylor and others, *Churchill*, p. 14.

87. Davenport and Murphy, *The Lives of Winston Churchill*, p. 15; Ephesian, *Winston Churchill*, p. 114; Guedalla, *Mr. Churchill*, pp. 104–5; Alfred F. Havighurst, *Twentieth-Century Britain*, 2d ed. (New York: Harper & Row, 1966), p. 75; Humes, *Churchill*, p. 102; Martin, *Battle*, p. 68, Mendelssohn, *The Age of Churchill*, pp. 274–75; Owen, *Tempestuous Journey*, p. 139; Rowse, *The Churchills*, p. 437; Schoenfeld, *Sir Winston Churchill*, p. 15; A. MacCallum Scott, *Winston Spencer Churchill* (London: Methuen, 1905), pp. 216–17; Thomson, *Churchill*, p. 85; Wingfield-Stratford, *Churchill*, p. 91; Robert Rhodes James, *Victor Cazalet: A Portrait* (London: Hamish Hamilton, 1976), p. 115; Kraus, *Winston Churchill*, p. 129; Manchester, *The Last Lion*, pp. 363–64.

88. Herbert du Parcq, *Life of David Lloyd George*, vol. 3 (London: Caxton, 1912), p. 435. See also Cregier, *Bounder from Wales*, p. 87; Earl Lloyd George, *My Father, Lloyd George*, pp. 178–79.

89. Thelma Cazalet-Keir, *From the Wings* (London: The Bodley Head, 1967), p. 52.

90. Robert Rhodes James, ed., *Winston S. Churchill: His Complete Speeches 1897–1963*, vol. 7 (New York: Chelsea House, 1974), p. 7137.

91. Grigg, *Lloyd George*, p. 66.

92. Cowles, *Winston Churchill*, p. 121; Davies, *Lloyd George*, p. 287; Mendelssohn, *The Age of Churchill*, p. 609; Arthur C. Murray, *Master and Brother: Murrays of Elibank* (London: John Murray, 1945), p. 40.

93. Scally, *The Origins of the Lloyd George Coalition*, p. 258; *Editorial: The Memoirs of Colin R. Coote* (London: Eyre & Spottiswoode, 1965), p. 310; David, ed., *Inside Asquith's Cabinet*, p. 7.

94. Kenneth O. Morgan, *Wales in British Politics*, pp. 259–60.

95. C. J. Lowe and M. L. Dockrill, *The Mirage of Power*, vol. 3 (London: Routledge & Kegan Paul, 1972), pp. 702, 705.

96. Vera Brittain, *Born 1925: A Novel of Youth* (London: Virago Press, 1982),

pp. 366–67; Willie Morris, *Terrains of the Heart and Other Essays on Home* (Oxford, Miss.: Yoknapatawpha Press, 1981), p. 188.

97. Humes, *Churchill*, p. 247. A few months after his father's death Gwilym Lloyd George was asked by the leader of the Conservative party to sit on the opposition front bench. When Lloyd George *fils* said he could only sit there as a Liberal, Churchill snapped, "And what the hell else should you sit as?" (Douglas, *The History of the Liberal Party*, p. 249).

98. *Churchill: Taken from the Diaries of Lord Moran: The Struggle for Survival 1940–1965* (Boston: Houghton Mifflin, 1966), p. 728.

99. Ibid., p. 350.

100. Humes, *Churchill*, p. 238.

101. R. W. Thompson, *Winston Churchill*, p. 171.

102. Grigg, *Lloyd George: The People's Champion*, p. 64.

103. Earl Schenk Miers, *The Story of Winston Churchill* (New York: Wonder Books, 1965), p. 23.

Chapter Five

1. Frank Dilnot, *Lloyd George: The Man and His Story* (New York: Harper & Brothers, 1917), p. 74. In 1908, when the new president of the Board of Trade first received cabinet rank, British law still obliged him to resign his parliamentary seat to stand for reelection. (Randolph S. Churchill, *Winston S. Churchill*, companion vol. 2, part 2 [London: Heinemann, 1969], p. 764; Roy Douglas, *The History of the Liberal Party, 1895–1970* [Madison, N.J.: Fairleigh Dickinson University Press, 1971], p. 43; John Grigg, *Lloyd George: The People's Champion, 1892–1911* [Berkeley: University of California Press, 1978], p. 164). The new chancellor of the exchequer campaigned energetically for his friend (Randolph S. Churchill, *Winston S. Churchill*, vol. 2 [Boston: Houghton Mifflin, 1967], p. 251; Herbert du Parcq, *Life of David Lloyd George*, vol. 2 (London: Caxton, 1913), p. 506; Ted Morgan, *Churchill: Young Man in a Hurry, 1874–1915* [New York: Simon and Schuster, 1982], p. 222). The chancellor thereby violated the convention that cabinet members did not campaign in by-elections (Hugh Martin, *Battle: The Life Story of the Rt. Hon. Winston S. Churchill* [London: Sampson Low, Marston, 1932], p. 76). For this violation the chancellor was vigorously attacked by the leader of the Conservative party, A. J. Balfour (H. A. Taylor, *Jix: Viscount Brentford* [London: Stanley Paul, 1933], pp. 87, 91–92).

2. Ephesian, *Winston Churchill*, 3d ed. [London: Mills & Boon, 1927], p. 146. Ephesian was a pen name of C. E. Bechhofer-Roberts.

3. Randolph S. Churchill, *Winston S. Churchill*, companion vol. 2, part 2, p. 887.

4. Grigg, *Lloyd George: The People's Champion*, pp. 190, 192–93; Thomas Jones, *Lloyd George* (London: Oxford University Press, 1951), p. 36; Robert Speaight, *The Life of Hilaire Belloc* (New York: Farrar, Straus & Cudahy, 1957), p. 233; Sir Harry Boyne, *The Houses of Parliament* (New York: Larousse, 1981), p. 58; Sir Austen Chamberlain, *Politics from Inside: An Epistolary Chronicle, 1906–1914* (New Haven: Yale University Press, 1937), pp. 135–36, 176–77; Alan Clark, ed., *"A Good Innings": The Private Papers of Viscount Lee of Fareham* (London: John Murray, 1974), pp. 102–3; J. Hugh Edwards, *David Lloyd George: The Man and the Statesman*, vol. 1 (New York: J.H. Sears, 1929), p. 308; Grigg, *Lloyd George: The People's Champion*, p. 190; Elie Halevy, *The Rule of Democracy, 1905–1914 (Book 1)*, trans. E. I. Watkin, 2d ed. (New York: Peter Smith, 1952), p. 290; Jack Jones, *The Man David*

(London: Hamish Hamilton, 1944), p. 159. Gladstone's first budget speech as chancellor, in 1853, was equally long (Peter Stansky, *Gladstone: A Progress in Politics* [Boston: Little, Brown, 1979], p. 74).

5. Ephesian, *Winston Churchill*, p. 146; Virginia Cowles, *Winston Churchill: The Era and the Man* [New York: Grosset & Dunlap, no date], p. 128; Don M. Cregier, *Bounder from Wales: Lloyd George's Career before the First World War* (Columbia: University of Missouri Press, 1976), p. 125.

6. Chamberlain, *Politics from Inside*, p. 178; Alexander Mackintosh, *From Gladstone to Lloyd George: Parliament in Peace and War* (London: Hodder and Stoughton, 1921), p. 167; A. J. A. Morris, *C. P. Trevelyan, 1870–1958: Portrait of a Radical* (New York: St. Martin's Press, 1979), p. 79; Arthur C. Murray, *Master and Brother: Murrays of Elibank* (London: John Murray, 1945), p. 19; Peter Rowland, *Lloyd George* (London: Barrie & Jenkins, 1975), p. 216; Cregier, *Bounder from Wales*, p. 125; John Grigg, *Lloyd George: From Peace to War, 1912–1916* (Berkeley: University of California Press, 1985), p. 104; Bruce K. Murray, "The Politics of the 'People's Budget,'" *The Historical Journal* 16 (September 1973): 565; A. J. P. Taylor, *Essays in English History* (Harmondsworth: Penguin Books, 1982), p. 260.

7. Grigg, *Lloyd George: From Peace to War*, p. 268.

8. Edwards, *David Lloyd George*, vol. 1, p. 309.

9. Blanche E. C. Dugdale, *Arthur James Balfour, First Earl of Balfour, 1906–1930* (London: Hutchinson, no date), p. 40; John Grigg, "Lloyd George," in *Great Britons* (London: British Broadcasting Corporation, 1978), p. 193.

10. Churchill, *Winston S. Churchill*, vol. 2, p. 311; Edwards, *David Lloyd George*, vol. 1, pp. 303, 309, 330.

11. William Logue, *Léon Blum: The Formative Years, 1872–1914* (DeKalb: Northern Illinois University Press, 1973), p. 144.

12. Edwards, *David Lloyd George*, vol. 1, pp. 116, 307.

13. Karl de Schweinitz, *England's Road to Social Security: From the Statute of Laborers in 1349 to the Beveridge Report of 1942* (New York: A.S. Barnes, 1975), p. 201.

14. J. L. Talmon, *The Myth of the Nation and the Vision of Revolution: The Origins of Ideological Polarisation in the Twentieth Century* (London: Secker & Warburg, 1981), pp. 100–101; Cameron Hazlehurst, *Politicians at War: July 1914 to May 1915: A Prologue to the Triumph of Lloyd George* (London: Jonathan Cape, 1971), p. 18.

15. Herbert du Parcq, *Life of David Lloyd George*, vol. 4 (London: Caxton, 1913), p. 677; J. Hugh Edwards, *David Lloyd George: The Man and the Statesman*, vol. 2 (New York: J.H. Sears, 1929), p. 644; E. Royston Pike, *Human Documents of the Lloyd George Era* (London: George Allen & Unwin, 1972), p. 105.

16. Thomas Jones, *A Diary with Letters, 1931–1950* (London: Oxford University Press, 1954), p. 146.

17. William Manchester, *The Last Lion: Winston Spencer Churchill: Visions of Glory, 1874–1932* (Boston: Little, Brown, 1983), p. 408.

18. Violet Bonham Carter, *Winston Churchill: An Intimate Portrait* (New York: Harcourt, Brace & World, 1965), p. 129; Peter Fraser, *Joseph Chamberlain: Architect of Democracy* (New York: A.S. Barnes, 1967), p. 295; Grigg, *Lloyd George: From Peace to War*, p. 71; Halevy, *The Rule of Democracy*, p. 364.

19. Cregier, *Bounder from Wales*, p. 118; Basil Murray, *L.G.* (London: Sampson Low, Marston, 1932), p. 54; E. T. Raymond, *Mr. Lloyd George* (New York: George H. Doran, 1922), p. 124 (E. T. Raymond was a pen name of E. R. Thompson); Malcolm Thomson, *David Lloyd George: The Official Biography* (London: Hutchinson, no date), p. 183; Edwards, *David Lloyd George*, vol. 1, pp. 316–17; Grigg, *Lloyd George: The People's Champion*, p. 177.

20. Malcolm Thomson, *David Lloyd George*, p. 185; Robert J. Scally, *The Origins of the Lloyd George Coalition: The Politics of Social-Imperialism, 1900–1918* (Princeton, N.J.: Princeton University Press, 1975), p. 153.

21. Stephen Koss, *Fleet Street Radical: A. G. Gardiner and the Daily News* (Hamden, Conn.: Archon Books, 1973), p. 43.

22. Grigg, *Lloyd George: The People's Champion*, p. 200. See also Robert Rhodes James, *Rosebery: A Biography of Archibald Philip, Fifth Earl of Rosebery* (New York: Macmillan, 1963), p. 465.

23. Grigg, *Lloyd George: The People's Champion*, p. 158.

24. Lord Riddell, *More Pages from My Diary, 1908–1914* (London: Country Life, 1934), p. 76.

25. Grigg, *Lloyd George: The People's Champion*, p. 236; Countess Lloyd-George of Dwyfor, "Introduction" to Malcolm Thomson, *David Lloyd George*, p. 19.

26. Giovanni Costigan, *Makers of Modern England: The Force of Individual Genius in History* (London: Macmillan, 1969), p. 250; Scally, *The Origins of the Lloyd George Coalition*, p. 151; Douglas, *The History of the Liberal Party*, p. 40; Grigg, *Lloyd George: The People's Champion*, p. 134; Grigg, *Lloyd George: From Peace to War*, p. 105.

27. Grigg, *Lloyd George: The People's Champion*, pp. 202, 218; Churchill, *Winston S. Churchill*, vol. 2, p. 312; Robert Rhodes James, ed., *Winston S. Churchill: His Complete Speeches, 1897–1963*, vol. 2 (New York: Chelsea House, 1974), p. 1346; Kenneth Rose, *The Later Cecils* (New York: Harper & Row, 1975), p. 76. Prime Minister Asquith was present at only 202 of these divisions (*The Autobiography of Margot Asquith: Political Events and Celebrities* [London: Thornton Butterworth, 1933], p. 123); see also Raymond, *Mr. Lloyd George*, p. 124; Ephesian, *Winston Churchill*, p. 147; Brian Gardner, *Churchill in his Time: A Study in a Reputation, 1939–1945* (London: Methuen, 1968), p. 296; Jones, *The Man David*, p. 160; Peter de Mendelssohn, *The Age of Churchill: Heritage and Adventure, 1874–1911* (New York: Alfred A. Knopf, 1961), p. 486; Owen, *Tempestuous Journey*, p. 173; Cregier, *Bounder from Wales*, p. 126.

28. G. D. H. Cole and Raymond Postgate, *The Common People, 1746–1946* (London: Methuen, 1949), p. 465; Dangerfield, *The Strange Death of Liberal England*, p. 20; Rose, *The Later Cecils*, p. 76; Paul Thompson, *The Edwardians* (London: Granada, 1979), p. 249; Manfred Weidhorn, *Sir Winston Churchill* (Boston: Twayne, 1979), p. 113; Douglas, *The History of the Liberal Party*, p. 44; Grigg, *Lloyd George: The People's Champion*, p. 231; G. H. L. LeMay, *The Victorian Constitution: Conventions, Usages and Contingencies* (New York: St. Martin's Press, 1979), p. 195. This may have been the best-attended meeting ever of the House of Lords (*The Autobiography of Margot Asquith*, p. 130).

29. Bonham Carter, *Winston Churchill*, p. 147; Frank Brennand, *The Young Churchill* (London: New English Library, 1972), p. 39; Mendelssohn, *The Age of Churchill*, p. 453; Lord Montagu of Beaulieu, *More Equal Than Others: The Changing Fortunes of the British and European Aristocracies* (London: Michael Joseph, 1970), pp. 163–64; Esmé Wingfield-Stratford, *Churchill: The Making of a Hero* (London: Victor Gollancz, 1942), p. 123.

30. Winston Spencer Churchill, *The People's Rights* (New York: Taplinger, 1971), p. 99; Churchill, *Winston S. Churchill*, vol. 2, p. 327; Douglas, *The History of the Liberal Party*, p. 47; Sir Almeric Fitzroy, *Memoirs*, vol. 1 (London: Hutchinson, 1925), p. 401; Grigg, *Lloyd George*, p. 254.

31. Negative: Grigg, *Lloyd George: From Peace to War*, p. 160n; LeMay, *The Victorian Constitution*, p. 193; affirmative: Cole and Postgate, *The Common People*, p. 465; Cowles, *Winston Churchill*, p. 134; Douglas, *The History of the Liberal Party*, p. 44; Edwards, *David Lloyd George*, vol. 1, p. 320; H. Montgomery Hyde, *Lord*

Reading: The Life of Rufus Isaacs, First Marquess of Reading (New York: Farrar, Straus & Giroux, 1967), p. 76; André Maurois, The Edwardian Era, trans. Hamish Miles (New York: D. Appleton-Century, 1933), pp. 306, 308, 310; Scally, The Origins of the Lloyd George Coalition, p. 146; Murray, L.G., pp. 54–55; question mark: Henry Pelling, A Short History of the Labour Party, 5th ed. (New York: St. Martin's Press, 1976), p. 23.

32. Randolph S. Churchill, Winston S. Churchill, vol. 2, p. 312.

33. Grigg, Lloyd George: The People's Champion, p. 203; du Parcq, Life of David Lloyd George, vol. 4, p. 683. Although he had four thousand listeners, the hall at Limehouse would not hold all those who came to hear the chancellor (Douglas, The History of the Liberal Party, p. 42). Lloyd George gave another, shorter, speech to those who had not been able to hear his first speech. In this seldom-noticed coda, he concluded that "with your help we can brush the Lords like chaff before us" (Grigg, Lloyd George: The People's Champion, p. 208; David B. Strother, ed., Modern British Eloquence [New York: Funk & Wagnalls, 1969], p. 417). Lloyd George later gave pride of place among his speeches to Limehouse. (Lord Riddell's Intimate Diary of the Peace Conference and After, 1918–1923 [London: Victor Gollancz, 1933], p. 156. The impact of the Limehouse speech is nevertheless exaggerated by Malcolm Thomson (David Lloyd George, p. 186).

34. du Parcq, Life of David Lloyd George, vol. 4, pp. 697, 705–6.

35. Ibid., p. 715; Grigg, Lloyd George: The People's Champion, p. 220; Arthur C. Murray, Master and Brother, p. 45; Basil Murray, L.G., p. 55.

36. Churchill, Winston S. Churchill, vol. 2, p. 346.

37. Churchill, Winston S. Churchill, companion vol. 2, part 2, p. 1032.

38. Ibid., pp. 330–31, 336, 347; Churchill, Winston S. Churchill, companion vol. 2, part 2, pp. 1031, 1099; Elizabeth Longford, Elizabeth R: A Biography (London: Weidenfeld and Nicolson, 1983), p. 18; Wilfrid Scawen Blunt, My Diaries: Being a Personal Narrative of Events, 1888–1914 (New York: Alfred A. Knopf, 1932), p. 712; Elizabeth Longford, A Pilgrimage of Passion: The Life of Wilfrid Scawen Blunt (New York: Alfred A. Knopf, 1980), p. 384; Lord Riddell, More Pages from My Diary, p. 22. Not all who received Churchill's assurances of ennoblement appear on Prime Minister Asquith's list of 249 potential nominees, although the name of John Strange Churchill does there appear (Roy Jenkins, Asquith: Portrait of a Man and an Era [New York: E.P. Dutton, 1966], pp. 534–37.

39. Montagu, More Equal Than Others, p. 163.

40. Churchill, Winston S. Churchill, vol. 2, p. 324, 331; Churchill, Winston S. Churchill, companion vol. 2, part 2, p. 968; Grigg, Lloyd George: The People's Champion, p. 245. For Churchill's comment on Asquith, see Churchill, Winston S. Churchill, vol. 2, p. 332.

41. Randolph S. Churchill, Winston S. Churchill, vol. 2, p. 348; Dangerfield, The Strange Death of Liberal England, p. 65; LeMay, The Victorian Constitution, p. 212; Rose, The Later Cecils, p. 79. The same margin, but a different total, was reported by John Viscount Morley in Recollections (vol. 2 [New York: Macmillan, 1917], p. 356). There was no fear of inaction by the House of Lords because of poor attendance, a quorum in the House of Lords being three members (Boyne, The Houses of Parliament, p. 58).

42. Marvin Rintala, "Two Compromises: Victorian and Bismarckian," Government and Opposition 3 (Spring 1968): 207–221; Kinley Roby, The King, The Press and the People: A Study of Edward VII (London: Barrie & Jenkins, 1975), p. 303.

43. Philip W. Buck, Amateurs and Professionals in British Politics, 1918–59 (Chicago: The University of Chicago Press, 1963), p. 55. Among those who barely missed Buck's cutoff point before accepting a peerage was Hugh Dalton (Kenneth O. Morgan, Labour People: Leaders and Lieutenants, Hardie to Kinnock [Oxford:

Oxford University Press, 1987], p. 129). The prime minister at Buck's cutoff point, Harold Macmillan, waited until 1984, when he was ninety, to become earl of Stockton. Among those who barely missed Buck's beginning point, there was H. H. Asquith, who, in 1916, while still prime minister, described the ritual of becoming a member of the House of Lords as "the very stupidest of the many stupid ceremonies that we have" (Arthur S. Link, ed., *The Papers of Woodrow Wilson*, vol. 38 [Princeton, N.J.: Princeton University Press, 1982], p. 256). In 1925, at seventy-two and having been rejected by his constituents, he went gratefully to the House of Lords as earl of Oxford and Asquith. (Koss, *Fleet Street Radical*, p. 301). Among the few exceptions to Bennett's hypothesis was Neville Chamberlain, who while dying in late 1940 declined Prime Minister Churchill's offer of the Garter, as he had earlier declined a peerage, because "I prefer to die plain 'Mr. Chamberlain' like my father before me, unadorned by any title" (Colville, *The Fringes of Power*, p. 257). Joseph Chamberlain would, at least at that moment, have been proud of his son.

44. James, ed., *Winston S. Churchill*, vol. 1, pp. 713, 717–18.

45. Stephen Koss, *Asquith* (London: Allen Lane, 1976), p. 109.

46. Churchill, *Winston S. Churchill*, companion vol. 2, part 2, p. 900.

47. Blunt, *My Diaries*, p. 689.

48. Rowland, *Lloyd George*, p. 190.

49. du Parcq, *Life of David Lloyd George*, vol. 4, p. 638.

50. D. A. Hamer, *Liberal Politics in the Age of Gladstone and Rosebery: A Study in Leadership and Policy* (Oxford: Clarendon Press, 1972), p. 193; Manchester, *The Last Lion*, p. 341.

51. Edwards, *David Lloyd George*, vol. 1, pp. 320–21.

52. Churchill, *The People's Rights*, especially pp. 23, 37.

53. John Gore, *King George V: A Personal Memoir* (London: John Murray, 1949), p. 2.

54. Philip Magnus, *King Edward the Seventh* (Harmondsworth: Penguin Books, 1979), p. 473.

55. Edward David, ed., *Inside Asquith's Cabinet: From the Diaries of Charles Hobhouse* (New York: St. Martin's Press, 1977), p. 91; Cregier, *Bounder from Wales*, pp. 111, 169; Edward, Duke of Windsor, "Reflections of a One-Time Prince of Wales," *McCall's* 96 (June 1969): 107; John Colville, *Winston Churchill and His Inner Circle* (New York: Wyndham Books, 1981), p. 26; Ted Morgan, *Churchill*, p. 235; Bonham Carter, *Winston Churchill*, p. 147; Owen, *Tempestuous Journey*, p. 179; A.L. Rowse, *The Churchills: The Story of a Family* (New York: Harper & Row, 1966), p. 456.

56. Bonham Carter, *Winston Churchill*, p. 146; Owen, *Tempestuous Journey*, p. 187.

57. Henry Pelling, *Winston Churchill* (London: Macmillan, 1974), p. 18; Robert Blake, *Disraeli* (Garden City, N.Y.: Anchor Books, 1968), p. 658; Andrew Barrow, *Gossip: A History of High Society from 1920 to 1970* (New York: Coward, McCann & Geoghegan, 1979), pp. 57–58, 146; John Spencer Churchill, *A Churchill Canvas* (Boston: Little, Brown, 1961), p. 20. When Churchill was born there, Blenheim had ninety servants (John Davenport and Charles J. V. Murphy, *The Lives of Winston Churchill* [New York: Charles Scribner's Sons, 1945], p. 7).

58. Elizabeth Longford, *Winston Churchill* (London: Sidgwick & Jackson, 1974), p. 15; Robert Rhodes James, *Lord Randolph Churchill: Winston Churchill's Father* (New York: A.S. Barnes, 1960), p. 111; Harold Nicolson, *King George V: His Life and Reign* (London: Constable, 1952), p. 39.

59. Pelling, *Winston Churchill*, p. 20; James Leutze, ed., *The London Observer: The Journal of General Raymond E. Lee, 1940–1941* (London: Hutchinson, 1972), p. 376; Earl Schenk Miers, *The Story of Winston Churchill* (New York: Wonder Books, 1965), p. 11; Robert H. Pilpel, *Churchill in America, 1895–1961: An Affectionate*

Portrait (New York: Harcourt Brace Jovanovich, 1976), p. 14; Rose, *The Later Cecils*, p. 104; Taylor, *English History*, p. 172n; Judith M. Hughes, *Emotion and High Politics: Personal Relations at the Summit in Late Nineteenth-Century Britain and Germany* (Berkeley: University of California Press, 1983), p. 95; Manchester, *The Last Lion*, pp. 80, 130; Simon Winchester, *Their Noble Lordships: Class and Power in Modern Britain* (New York: Random House, 1982), pp. 15-16.

60. R. F. Foster, *Lord Randolph Churchill: A Political Life* (Oxford: Clarendon Press, 1982), pp. 349, 374, 379; Kate Fleming, *The Churchills* (New York: The Viking Press, 1975), p. 144.

61. Randolph S. Churchill, *Winston S. Churchill*, companion vol. 1, part 2 (Boston: Houghton Mifflin, 1967), p. 869.

62. Hugh Trevor-Roper, ed., *Final Entries 1945: The Diaries of Joseph Goebbels*, trans. Richard Barry (New York: G.P. Putnam's Sons, 1978), p. 76.

63. Pelling, *Winston Churchill*, p. 327.

64. Montagu, *More Equal Than Others*, p. 141; Longford, *Winston Churchill*, p. 15; Robert Payne, *The Great Man: A Portrait of Winston Churchill* (New York: Coward, McCann & Geoghegan, 1974), p. 59; Randolph S. Churchill, *Twenty-One Years* (Boston: Houghton Mifflin, 1945), p. 5; Ephesian, *Winston Churchill*, p. 15n; Pelling, *Winston Churchill*, p. 20; Cecil Roberts, *One Year of Life: Some Autobiographical Pages* (New York: Macmillan, 1952), p. 45n.

65. Randolph S. Churchill, *Winston S. Churchill*, companion vol. 1, part 1 (Boston: Houghton Mifflin, 1967), p. 166; Ted Morgan, *Churchill*, p. 43.

66. Costigan, *Makers of Modern England*, p. 260; Wingfield-Stratford, *Churchill*, p. 102; Ted Morgan, *Churchill*, p. 233.

67. Tom Clarke, *Northcliffe in History: An Intimate Study of Press Power* (London: Hutchinson, 1950), p. 58; The Marquess of Reading, *Rufus Isaacs: First Marquess of Reading: 1860–1914* (London: Hutchinson, 1950), p. 11.

68. Rowse, *The Churchills*, p. 428.

69. Davenport and Murphy, *The Lives of Winston Churchill*, pp. 86–87; Payne, *The Great Man*, p. 348; Olivia Coolidge, *Winston Churchill and the Story of Two World Wars* (Boston: Houghton Mifflin, 1960), p. 260; Arthur Krock, "Randolph—Without the Boast of Heraldry, the Pomp of Pow'r," in Kay Halle, ed., *The Grand Original: Portraits of Randolph Churchill by his Friends* (Boston: Houghton Mifflin, 1971), p. 178; Winchester, *Their Noble Lordships*, p. 49; Tom Cullen, *Maundy Gregory: Purveyor of Honours* (London: The Bodley Head, 1974), p. 28; Churchill, *A Churchill Canvas*, p. 238; Pelling, *Winston Churchill*, p. 557; Mary Soames, *Clementine Churchill: The Biography of a Marriage* (Boston: Houghton Mifflin, 1979), pp. 433, 571, 668; Malcolm Thomson, *Churchill: His Life and Times* (London: Oldhams Books, 1965), pp. 397, 408; Chartwell Manor in Kent was the home of Clementine and Winston Churchill for more than forty years.

70. *Churchill: Taken from the Diaries of Lord Moran: The Struggle for Survival, 1940–1965* (Boston: Houghton Mifflin, 1966), pp. 401–8.

71. James, ed., *Winston S. Churchill*, vol. 1, p. 716.

72. Colville, *Winston Churchill and His Inner Circle*, p. 70. Bracken nevertheless accepted a viscountcy from Churchill, though he refused to take his seat in the House of Lords.

73. John Colville, *The Fringes of Power: 10 Downing Street Diaries, 1939–1955* (New York: W.W. Norton, 1986), p. 675.

74. Moran, *Winston Churchill*, pp. 430–431; Payne, *The Great Man*, pp. 357–58; Malcolm Thomson, *Churchill*, p. 442.

75. Colville, *The Fringes of Power*, p. 311.

76. Ibid., p. 709; Piers Brendon, *Winston Churchill: A Biography* (New York: Harper & Row, 1984), p. 220; Costigan, *Makers of Modern England*, p. 302; Pelling,

Winston Churchill, p. 643; A. J. P. Taylor, *Essays in English History*, p. 295. There is an imprecise report in Ivor Bulmer-Thomas, *The Growth of the British Party System* (vol. 2 [London: John Baker, 1965], p. 204).

77. Moran, *Churchill*, p. 425.

78. Colin Cross, ed., *Life with Lloyd George: The Diary of A. J. Sylvester 1931–45* (New York: Barnes & Noble, 1975), p. 288; A. J. Sylvester, *The Real Lloyd George* (London: Cassell, 1947), p. 287; Costigan, *Makers of Modern England*, p. 239; Cregier, *Bounder from Wales*, p. 18; John Ehrman, "Lloyd George and Churchill as War Ministers," *Transactions of the Royal Historical Society*, 5th series, vol. 11, p. 102; Frances, Countess Lloyd-George of Dwyfor, "Introduction" to Thomson, *David Lloyd George*, p. 17; C. P. Snow, *Variety of Men* (London: Macmillan, 1967), p. 96; Taylor, *Essays in English History*, p. 257; A. J. P. Taylor, "Lloyd George," in Lord Longford and Sir John Wheeler-Bennett, eds., *The History Makers: Leaders and Statesmen of the 20th Century* (New York: St. Martin's Press, 1973), p. 80; R. W. Thompson, *Winston Churchill: The Yankee Marlborough* (Garden City, N.Y.: Doubleday, 1963), p. 154.

79. Martin Gilbert, *Winston S. Churchill*, vol. 5 (Boston: Houghton Mifflin, 1977), p. 1054; Harold Nicolson, *Diaries and Letters, 1930–1939*, ed. Nigel Nicolson (New York: Atheneum, 1968), p. 394.

80. Countess Lloyd-George of Dwyfor, "Introduction," p. 17; *Lord Riddell's Intimate Diary*, p. 287; Snow, *Variety of Men*, p. 96. Allowing only Churchill to use his first name may have been an assertion of independence from other politicians by Lloyd George. In premodern cultures knowing a person's name gave one power over that person (T. D. Weldon, *The Vocabulary of Politics* [Baltimore, Md.: Penguin Books, 1960], p. 18). The familiarity permitted Churchill was an acknowledgment by Lloyd George of interdependence.

81. Lord Beaverbrook, *The Decline and Fall of Lloyd George: And Great Was the Fall Thereof* (London: Collins, 1966), p. 303; David, ed., *Inside Asquith's Cabinet*, p. 273; Lord Hankey, *Politics, Trials and Errors* (Chicago: Henry Regnery, 1950), p. 1; Taylor, *English History*, p. 5n; Wilson Harris, *J. A. Spender* (London: Cassell, 1946), p. 95.

82. While Lloyd George was prime minister the house in which he had been born was purchased by one of his followers, Sir Graham Wood, to be preserved "as a place of national interest for all time" (*The Lloyd George Liberal Magazine* 1 [July 1921]: 626). There is no perpetuity in politics. The house, at what was then 5 New York Place, no longer stands. Lloyd George would have been pleased that it was replaced by modern public housing. He might even have been amused by a plaque on that housing, at 32 Wadeson Road, honoring, incorrectly, the "Earl of Dwyfor" (John Grigg, *The Young Lloyd George* [London: Eyre Methuen, 1973], p. 23). As late as 1954 there was not even an incorrect marker (Owen, *Tempestuous Journey*, p. 14). At that silence Lloyd George would probably have smiled, and commented on the difficulty of locating even the most famous, and humblest, of birthplaces.

83. Lloyd George's brother was known throughout his lifetime of 102 years as William George. While in his nineties, William George published a masterpiece of sibling rivalry, *My Brother and I* (London: Eyre & Spottiswoode, 1958); Lloyd George's sister was known until her marriage as Mary Ellen George.

84. Cross., ed., *Life with Lloyd George*, pp. 337–38.

85. Cook, *What Manner of Men?*, p. 54; W. Watkin Davies, *Lloyd George, 1863–1914* (London: Constable, 1939), p. 20; Herbert du Parcq, *Life of David Lloyd George*, vol. 1 (London: Caxton, 1912), pp. 23–24; Edwards, *David Lloyd George*, vol. 1, p. 25; Grigg, *Lloyd George: The People's Champion*, pp. 12–13; Jones, *Lloyd George*, p. 3; Raymond, *Mr. Lloyd George*, p. 21; Rowland, *Lloyd George*, p. 9.

86. Raymond, *Mr. Lloyd George*, p. 47; Grigg, *Lloyd George: The People's Champion*, p. 13.

87. du Parcq, *Life of David Lloyd George*, vol. 4, pp. 637, 685; Pike, *Human Documents of the Lloyd George Era*, p. 107.

88. Grigg, *Lloyd George: From Peace to War*, p. 291.

89. Sir Geoffrey Shakespeare, *Let Candles Be Brought In* (London: Macdonald, 1949), pp. 50, 67; Halevy, *The Rule of Democracy*, p. 237; James C. Humes, *Churchill: Speaker of the Century* (New York: Stein and Day, 1982), pp. 113, 118; Edwards, *David Lloyd George*, vol. 1, p. 17; Emil Ludwig, *Nine Etched from Life* (New York: Robert M. McBride, 1934), p. 207; Taylor, *Essays in English History*, p. 266; Manchester, *The Last Lion*, p. 405; Koss, *Fleet Street Radical*, p. 131; V. G. Trukhanovsky, *Winston Churchill* (Moscow: Progress Publishers, 1978), p. 80.

90. Costigan, *Makers of Modern England*, p. 198.

91. Wilson, *A Prime Minister on Prime Ministers*, p. 138.

92. Paul Addison, "Lloyd George and Compromise Peace in the Second World War," in A. J. P. Taylor, ed., *Lloyd George: Twelve Essays* (New York: Atheneum, 1971), p. 365; Campbell, *Lloyd George*, p. 4; Grigg, *Lloyd George: From Peace to War*, p. 292; Cregier, *Bounder from Wales*, p. 7; George Malcolm Thomson, *The Prime Ministers: From Robert Walpole to Margaret Thatcher* (London: Nationwide Book Service, 1980), pp. xxi–xxii.

93. du Parcq, *Life of David Lloyd George*, vol. 1, p. 14; Grigg, *The Young Lloyd George*, p. 31; Viscount Gwynedd, *Dame Margaret: The Life Story of His Mother* (London: George Allen & Unwin, 1947), p. 74; Thomas Jones, *Lloyd George*, p. 2; Raymond, *Mr. Lloyd George*, pp. 13, 26, 29.

94. Edwards, *David Lloyd George*, vol. 1, pp. 61, 183; Malcolm Thomson, *David Lloyd George*, p. 59; Cregier, *Bounder from Wales*, p. 92; Brian Abel-Smith and Robert Stevens, *Lawyers and the Courts: A Sociological Study of the English Legal System, 1750–1965* (Cambridge, Mass.: Harvard University Press, 1967), p. 230; du Parcq, *Life of David Lloyd George*, vol. 4, p. 646; the Earl of Swinton, *Sixty Years of Power: Some Memories of the Men Who Wielded It* (London: Hutchinson, 1966), pp. 44–45; Taylor, *Essays in English History*, p. 255; Edwards, *David Lloyd George*, vol. 1, p. 46; Malcolm Thomson, *David Lloyd George*, p. 69; Cook, *What Manner of Men?*, p. 60.

95. Disraeli was apprenticed in his youth to a firm of solicitors, but never became a solicitor. Blake, *Disraeli*, p. 17.

96. Anthony Sampson, *The Changing Anatomy of Britain* (New York: Vintage Books, 1984), p. 161; Taylor, *Essays in English History*, p. 255.

97. Grigg, *Lloyd George: The People's Champion*, p. 20; Rowland, *Lloyd George*, pp. 745, 790. This farm was a beehive of activity. Honey was sold from it in pots labeled "From the apiary of the Right Hon. D. Lloyd George, O.M., M.P." (Thomas Jones, *Lloyd George*, p. 274). Also, Lloyd George personally sold, at a roadside stall, the farm's apples (Thelma Cazalet-Keir, *From the Wings* [London: The Bodley Head, 1967], p. 59). From the farm came potatoes for which Lloyd George accepted a first-prize check for twenty-five shillings from the Chiddingford Agricultural Association (Barrow, *Gossip*, p. 64). Lloyd George received, while visiting Adolf Hitler, nightly telephonic reports of farm activities (Thomas Jones, *A Diary with Letters*, p. 255). See also Alfred T. Davies, *The Lloyd George I Knew: Some Side-Lights on a Great Career* (London: Henry E. Walter, 1948), p. 115.

98. W. R. P. George, *The Making of Lloyd George* (London: Faber & Faber, 1971), p. 105.

99. V. I. Lenin, *"Left-Wing" Communism: An Infantile Disorder* (Moscow: Progress, 1975), p. 70.

100. Ibid., p. 66.

101. A. G. Gardiner, *Prophets, Priests, & Kings* (London: J.M. Dent & Sons, 1914), p. 136.

102. Grigg, *Lloyd George: The People's Champion*, p. 360; Campbell, *Lloyd George*, p. 285; *Leon Trotsky on Britain* (New York: Monad Press, 1973), pp. 188–89; Koss, *Fleet Street Radical*, p. 189.

103. Stansky, *Gladstone*, p. 178; Cook, *What Manner of Men?*, p. 53; Edwards, *David Lloyd George*, vol. 1, p. 37; Ludwig, *Nine Etched from Life*, p. 213.

104. Riddell, *More Pages from My Diary*, p. 133; Edwards, *David Lloyd George*, vol. 1, p. 45; Elie Halevy, *The Rule of Democracy, 1905–1914 (Book 2)*, 2d ed., trans. E. I. Watkin (New York: Peter Smith, 1952), p. 469; Chamberlain, *Politics from Inside*, p. 533; Sir Dingle Foot, *British Political Crises* (London: William Kimber, 1976), p. 78; Grigg, *Lloyd George: The People's Champion*, p. 242; Chris Wrigley, *David Lloyd George and the British Labour Movement: Peace and War* (Hassocks: The Harvester Press, 1976), pp. 31–32; Ludwig, *Nine Etched from Life*, p. 208.

105. du Parcq, *Life of David Lloyd George*, vol. 4, p. 742.

106. Riddell, *More Pages from My Diary*, pp. 179–80; Grigg, *Lloyd George: From Peace to War*, p. 102; Paul Johnson, *Modern Times: The World from the Twenties to the Eighties* (New York: Harper Colophon Books, 1985), p. 163; Kenneth O. Morgan, *Consensus and Disunity: The Lloyd George Coalition Government, 1918–1922* (Oxford: Clarendon Press, 1986), pp. 157–58.

107. Riddell, *More Pages from My Diary*, pp. 63–64.

108. Robert Eccleshall, *British Liberalism: Liberal Thought from the 1640s to 1980s* (London: Longman, 1986), p. 186; Grigg, *Lloyd George: From Peace to War*, p. 39; Kenneth O. Morgan, *The Age of Lloyd George* (New York: Barnes & Noble, 1971), p. 37; Kenneth O. Morgan, "Lloyd George's Premiership: A Study in 'Prime Ministerial Government,'" *The Historical Journal* 13 (1970): 140; Wrigley, *David Lloyd George and the British Labour Movement*, p. 4.

109. Campbell, *Lloyd George*, p. 98; Hamer, *Liberal Politics*, p. 328; Kenneth O. Morgan, *David Lloyd George: Welsh Radical as World Statesman* (Cardiff: University of Wales Press, 1963), p. 71; Kenneth O. Morgan, *Wales in British Politics, 1868–1922*, 3d ed. (Cardiff: University of Wales Press, 1980), p. 211; Taylor, "Lloyd George," p. 79; Wrigley, *David Lloyd George and the British Labour Movement*, p. 3; Grigg, *Lloyd George: From Peace to War*, p. 292.

110. F. L. Carsten, *War against War: British and German Radical Movements in the First World War* (Berkeley: University of California Press, 1982), p. 61. A decade later Kirkwood, now a Labor member of Parliament, was describing Lloyd George as the real leader of the Labor Party (Frances Stevenson, *Lloyd George: A Diary*, ed., A. J. P. Taylor [London: Hutchinson, 1971], pp. 244–45). Even later, Kirkwood died as Baron Kirkwood.

111. W. S. Adams, "Lloyd George and the Labour Movement," *Past and Present* 3 (February 1953): 56.

112. Wrigley, *David Lloyd George and the British Labour Movement*, p. 61.

113. Pike, *Human Documents of the Lloyd George Era*, p. 9.

114. Beatrice Webb, *Our Partnership*, eds. Barbara Drake and Margaret I. Cole (Cambridge: Cambridge University Press, 1975), p. 474.

115. Lord Taylor of Mansfield, *Uphill All the Way: A Miner's Struggle* (London: Sidgwick & Jackson, 1972), pp. 132, 161; Pamela Brookes, *Women at Westminster: An Account of Women in the British Parliament, 1918–1966* (London: Peter Davies, 1967), p. 159; Thomson, *David Lloyd George*, p. 179.

116. Flora Thompson, *Lark Rise to Candleford: A Trilogy* (Harmondsworth: Penguin Books, 1984), p. 97. Thompson's characters were not alone in prematurely ennobling Lloyd George (Grigg, *Lloyd George: The People's Champion*, p. 89).

117. George Dangerfield, *The Strange Death of Liberal England* (New York: Capricorn Books, 1961), p. 311.

118. Riddell, *More Pages from My Diary*, p. 141.

119. Grigg, "Lloyd George," p. 197; Wrigley, *David Lloyd George and the British Labour Movement*, pp. 22, 25; Iain McLean, *Keir Hardie* (London: Allen Lane, 1975), p. 99; Taylor, *Essays in English History*, p. 274; Cross, ed., *Life with Lloyd George*, p. 24.

120. Bulmer-Thomas, *The Growth of the British Party System*, p. 75; Rowland, *Lloyd George*, p. 691; Taylor, "Lloyd George," p. 87; A. J. P. Taylor, ed., *My Darling Pussy: The Letters of Lloyd George and Frances Stevenson 1913–1941* (London: Weidenfeld and Nicolson, 1975), p. 151; Taylor, *Essays in English History*, p. 278; Kenneth O. Morgan, "Lloyd George's Stage Army: The Coalition Liberals, 1918-22," in A. J. P. Taylor, ed., *Lloyd George: Twelve Essays* (New York: Atheneum, 1971), p. 254; R. H. Gretton, *A Modern History of the English People, 1880–1922* (New York: Lincoln Macveagh, The Dial Press, 1930), p. 870.

121. Campbell, *Lloyd George*, p. 152.

122. Riddell, *More Pages from My Diary*, p. 155; *Lord Riddell's Intimate Diary*, p. 139.

123. Raymond, *Mr. Lloyd George*, p. 297; Viscount Gwynedd, *Dame Margaret*, p. 177; Sir Frederick Ponsonby, *Reflections of Three Reigns* (New York: E.P. Dutton, 1952), p. 464; Taylor, *Essays in English History*, p. 257; Robert Rhodes James, *Memoirs of a Conservative: J. C. C. Davidson's Memoirs and Papers, 1910-37* (New York: Macmillan, 1970), p. 67; Cross, ed., *Life with Lloyd George*, pp. 184, 187; Thomas Jones, *Lloyd George*, p. 258. While a minister of the Crown, he often attended sessions of the House of Lords that interested him, lounging on the steps of the throne. (Grigg, *Lloyd George: The People's Champion*, p. 106n).

124. Thomas Jones, *Lloyd George*, p. 259; Rowland, *Lloyd George*, pp. 795–96; Shakespeare, *Let Candles Be Brought In*, p. 46; Sylvester, *The Real Lloyd George*, pp. 303–4.

125. Cross, ed., *Life with Lloyd George*, p. 313; Thomas Jones, *Lloyd George*, p. 260.

126. Cross, ed., *Life with Lloyd George*, pp. 333–34; Sylvester, *The Real Lloyd George*, p. 303.

127. Sylvester, *The Real Lloyd George*, pp. 306–7.

128. Sir Iain Moncreiffe, "Foreword" to Montagu, *More Equal Than Others*, p. 15.

129. Costigan, *Makers of Modern England*, p. 241; Davies, *The Lloyd George I Knew*, pp. 115–16; Thomas Jones, *Lloyd George*, p. 260; McCormick, *The Mask of Merlin*, p. 300; Owen, *Tempestuous Journey*, p. 755; Rowland, *Lloyd George*, p. 796; Grigg, *Lloyd George: The People's Champion*, p. 262; Taylor, *Beaverbrook*, p. 562.

130. Cross, ed., *Life with Lloyd George*, p. 313; Rowland, *Lloyd George*, p. 790; Viscount Gwynedd, *Dame Margaret*, p. 177.

131. The official registry entry of Lloyd George's death gives his occupation as "Earl Lloyd-George of Dwyfor O.M. Retired M.P." To describe these social roles as occupations would have amused the deceased. Their juxtaposition would not have amused him.

132. Long before his death, at a state funeral in Westminster Abbey, Lloyd George responded negatively to a suggestion that someday he, too, would be buried there: "I shall rest beneath the trees of my own home" (Ludwig, *Nine Etched from Life*, p. 250).

133. Hugh Dalton, *High Tide and After: Memoirs 1945–1960* (London: Frederick Muller, 1962), p. 100; McCormick, *The Mask of Merlin*, p. 300.

134. Viscount Gwynedd, *Dame Margaret*, p. 171.

135. F. W. S. Craig, ed., *British Electoral Facts, 1885–1975* (London: Macmillan, 1976), pp. 51, 133; Morgan, ed., *Lloyd George*, p. 95n; Douglas, *The History of the Liberal Party*, p. 248; Alan Sked and Chris Cook, *Post-War Britain: A Political History*, 2d ed. (Harmondsworth: Penguin Books, 1984), p. 16; Thomson, *David Lloyd*

George, p. 410. Carnarvon Boroughs disappeared as a constituency in the 1948 redistribution of seats (Craig, ed., *British Electoral Facts*, p. 147; Cross, ed., *Life with Lloyd George*, pp. 330–31; George, *The Making of Lloyd George*, p. 156; Grigg, *The Young Lloyd George*, p. 81).

136. Douglas, *The History of the Liberal Party*, p. 247. Another passionate partisan of a single chamber, Georges Clemenceau, also eventually went to the other house, but at least Clemenceau lived to enjoy being a senator (Theodore Zeldin, *France, 1848–1945: Politics & Anger* (Oxford: Oxford University Press, 1982), p. 337.

137. Humes, *Churchill*, p. 253; Robert Rhodes James, ed., *Winston S. Churchill: His Complete Speeches, 1897–1963*, vol. 8 (New York: Chelsea House, 1974), pp. 8642–45; Boyne, *The Houses of Parliament*, pp. 36, 39.

Chapter Six

1. Ivor Bulmer-Thomas, *The Growth of the British Party System*, vol. 1 (London: John Baker, 1965), p. 199; Colin Cross, ed., *Life with Lloyd George: The Diary of A. J. Sylvester, 1931–45* (New York: Barnes & Noble, 1975), p. 96n; George Dangerfield, *The Strange Death of Liberal England* (New York: Capricorn Books, 1961), p. 276; George Malcolm Thomson, *The Prime Ministers: From Robert Walpole to Margaret Thatcher* (London: Nationwide Book Service, 1980), p. 189; Malcolm Thomson, *Churchill: His Life and Times* (London: Odhams, 1965), p. 121; Esmé Wingfield-Stratford, *Churchill: The Making of a Hero* (London: Victor Gollancz, 1942), p. 126; William Gerhardie, *God's Fifth Column: A Biography of the Age, 1890–1940*, eds. Michael Holroyd and Robert Skidelsky (New York: Simon and Schuster, 1981), pp. 169, 239, 296; Ted Morgan, *Churchill: Young Man in a Hurry, 1874–1915* (New York: Simon & Schuster, 1982), p. 134; Basil Murray, *L.G.* (London: Sampson Low, Marston, 1932), p. 51; Virginia Cowles, *Winston Churchill: The Era and the Man* (New York: Grosset & Dunlap, no date), p. 126; B. H. Liddell Hart, *History of the First World War* (London: Pan Books, 1972), p. 15; The Earl of Swinton, *Sixty Years of Power: Some Memories of the Men Who Wielded It* (London: Hutchinson, 1966), p. 46; Frank Owen, *Tempestuous Journey: Lloyd George, His Life and Times* (London: Hutchinson, 1954), p. 290; Frank Brennand, *The Young Churchill* (London: New English Library, 1972), p. 47; Hugh Martin, *Battle: The Life Story of the Rt. Hon. Winston S. Churchill* (London: Sampson Low, Marston, 1932), p. 90; William Martin, *Statesmen of the War in Retrospect: 1918–1928* (New York: Minton, Balch, 1928), pp. 299, 305; Trevor Royle, *The Kitchener Enigma* (London: Michael Joseph, 1985), p. 285; Robert J. Scally, *The Origins of the Lloyd George Coalition: The Politics of Social-Imperialism, 1900–1918* (Princeton, N.J.: Princeton University Press, 1975), p. 251.

2. Gerhardie, *God's Fifth Column*, p. 235; Donald McCormick, *The Mask of Merlin: A Critical Study of David Lloyd George* (London: Macdonald, 1963), p. 103; E. T. Raymond, *Mr. Lloyd George* (New York: George H. Doran, 1922), p. 342. E.T. Raymond was the pen name of E. R. Thompson.

3. Henry W. Nevinson, "Lloyd George: The Leader of British Liberals," *Foreign Affairs* 9 (April 1931): 462.

4. J. H. Grainger, *Character and Style in English Politics* (Cambridge: Cambridge University Press, 1969), p. 153.

5. Herbert du Parcq, *Life of David Lloyd George*, vol. 2 (London: Caxton, 1912), p. 214; John Grigg, "Lloyd George," in *Great Britons* (London: British Broadcasting Corporation, 1978), p. 190; John Grigg, *Lloyd George: From Peace to War, 1912–1916* (Berkeley: University of California Press, 1985), p. 128; John Grigg, *The Young*

Lloyd George (London: Eyre Methuen, 1973), p. 44; Trevor Wilson, *The Downfall of the Liberal Party, 1914–1935* (Ithaca, N.Y.: Cornell University Press, 1966), p. 36; John Grigg, "Lloyd George and the Boer War," in A. J. A. Morris, ed., *Edwardian Radicalism, 1900–1914: Some Aspects of British Radicalism* (London: Routledge & Kegan Paul, 1974), p. 13; Thomas Jones, *Lloyd George* (London: Oxford University Press, 1951), p. 27.

6. Don M. Cregier, *Bounder from Wales: Lloyd George's Career before the First World War* (Columbia: University of Missouri Press, 1976), pp. 64, 226; Michael G. Fry, *Lloyd George and Foreign Policy*, vol. 1 (Montréal: McGill-Queen's University Press, 1977), p. 24; John Grigg, *Lloyd George: The People's Champion, 1902–1911* (Berkeley: University of California Press, 1978), p. 354; Kenneth O. Morgan, *David Lloyd George: Welsh Radical as World Statesman* (Cardiff: University of Wales Press, 1963), p. 32; Kenneth O. Morgan, ed., *Lloyd George: Family Letters, 1885–1936* (Cardiff: University of Wales Press and London: Oxford University Press, 1973), p. 120; Malcolm Thomson, *David Lloyd George: The Official Biography* (London: Hutchinson, no date), pp. 67, 127–28, 179, 227.

7. Marvin Rintala, "Chronicler of a Generation: Vera Brittain's Testament," *Journal of Political and Military Sociology* 12 (Spring 1984): 23–35.

8. Trumbull Higgins, *Winston Churchill and the Dardanelles: A Dialogue in Ends and Means* (New York: Macmillan, 1963), p. 243.

9. Sir Dingle Foot, *British Political Crises* (London: William Kimber, 1976), p. 55; Fry, *Lloyd George and Foreign Policy*, vol. 1, p. 42.

10. A. J. P. Taylor, "Lloyd George," in Lord Longford and Sir John Wheeler-Bennett, eds., *The History Makers: Leaders and Statesmen of the 20th Century* (New York: St. Martin's Press, 1973), p. 78.

11. Raymond, *Mr. Lloyd George*, p. 35; A. J. Anthony Morris, *Radicalism Against War, 1906–1914: The Advocacy of Peace and Retrenchment* (Totowa, N.J.: Rowman and Littlefield, 1972), p. 337.

12. Grigg, *Lloyd George: From Peace to War*, p. 184.

13. *The Memoirs of Captain Liddell Hart*, vol. 2 (London: Cassell, 1965), p. 260.

14. Sir Geoffrey Shakespeare, *Let Candles Be Brought In* (London: Macdonald, 1949), pp. 57–58.

15. Piers Brendon, *Winston Churchill: A Biography* (New York: Harper & Row, 1984), p. 193; Martin Gilbert, *Churchill* (Garden City, N.Y.: Doubleday, 1980), p. 84; Walter Henry Thompson, *Assignment: Churchill* (New York: Farrar, Straus and Young, 1955), pp. 32, 56–57, 83, 129, 157, 188; Walter H. Thompson, "Guarding Mr. Churchill," in Charles Eade, ed., *Churchill by His Contemporaries* (New York: Simon and Schuster, 1954), p. 207. As prime minister, Churchill enjoyed going to his revolver pit in the woods behind Chequers (John Colville, *Footprints in Time* [London: Collins, 1976], p. 130; John Colville, *The Fringes of Power: 10 Downing Street Diaries 1939-1955* [New York: W.W. Norton, 1986], p. 585).

16. W. R. P. George, *The Making of Lloyd George* (London: Faber & Faber, 1976), p. 114.

17. du Parcq, *Life of David Lloyd George*, vol. 2, p. 257.

18. The Earl of Birkenhead, *Contemporary Personalities* (London: Cassell, 1924), p. 165; Lord Beaverbrook, *Politicians and the War, 1914–1916* (London: Oldbourne, 1960), p. 510.

19. John Maynard Keynes, *Essays in Biography* (New York: W.W. Norton, 1963), p. 35; Sir Charles Mallet, *Mr. Lloyd George: A Study* (London: Ernest Benn, 1930), p. 43; Jones, *Lloyd George*, p. 46; Grigg, *The Young Lloyd George*, p. 259; Tom Clarke, *Northcliffe in History: An Intimate Study of Press Power* (London: Hutchinson, 1950), p. 94; Herbert Sidebotham, *Pillars of the State* (London: Nisbet, 1921), p. 92.

20. J. Hugh Edwards, *David Lloyd George: The Man and the Statesman*, vol. II (New York: J.H. Sears, 1929), p. 371; Basil Murray, *L.G.*, p. 62.

21. L. S. Amery, "Two Great War Leaders," in Sir James Marchant, ed., *Winston Spencer Churchill: Servant of Crown and Commonwealth* (London: Cassell, 1954), p. 56.

22. Kenneth O. Morgan, ed., *Lloyd George*, p. 33.

23. Trevor Wilson, ed., *The Political Diaries of C. P. Scott 1911–1928* (Ithaca, N.Y.: Cornell University Press, 1970), p. 39.

24. Oscar Browning, *Memories of Later Years* (New York: D. Appleton, 1923), p. 47.

25. Herbert du Parcq, *Life of David Lloyd George*, vol. 3 (London: Caxton, 1913), p. 439.

26. Ibid., p. 604.

27. Cregier, *Bounder from Wales*, pp. 221, 225; Fry, *Lloyd George and Foreign Policy*, vol. 1, pp. 173–74; Owen, *Tempestuous Journey*, p. 254.

28. John St. Loe Strachey, *The Adventure of Living: A Subjective Autobiography (1860–1922)* (New York: G.P. Putnam's Sons, 1922), p. 454.

29. Dangerfield, *The Strange Death of Liberal England*, p. 408.

30. Violet Bonham Carter, *Winston Churchill: An Intimate Portrait* (New York: Harcourt, Brace & World, 1965), p. 245; Lord Riddell, *More Pages from My Diary: 1908–1914* (London: Country Life, 1934), p. 219.

31. Morgan, ed., *Lloyd George*, p. 167.

32. Peter Lowe, "The Rise to the Premiership, 1914–16," in A. J. P. Taylor, ed., *Lloyd George: Twelve Essays* (New York: Atheneum, 1971), p. 96.

33. Scally, *The Origins of the Lloyd George Coalition*, pp. 251–52.

34. Kenneth O. Morgan, *The Age of Lloyd George* (New York: Barnes and Noble, 1971), p. 54.

35. Frances Lloyd George, *The Years That Are Past* (London: Hutchinson, 1967), p. 73; Stephen Koss, *Nonconformity in Modern British Politics* (London: B.T. Batsford, 1975), p. 127; Taylor, "Lloyd George," p. 81.

36. Cameron Hazlehurst, *Politicians at War: July 1914 to May 1915: A Prologue to the Triumph of Lloyd George* (London: Jonathan Cape, 1971), p. 34; Roland N. Stromberg, *Redemption by War: The Intellectuals and 1914* (Lawrence: The Regents Press of Kansas, 1982), p. 182; Joyce Cary, *Prisoner of Grace* (New York: Harper & Brothers, 1952), p. 196; John Gore, *King George V: A Personal Memoir* (London: John Murray, 1949), p. 156.

37. *After All: The Autobiography of Norman Angell* (New York: Farrar, Straus and Young, no date), pp. 181–82, 185; Wilfrid Scawen Blunt, *My Diaries: Being a Personal Narrative of Events, 1888–1914* (New York: Alfred A. Knopf, 1932), p. 844; Stephen Koss, *Asquith* (London: Allen Lane, 1976), p. 157; A. J. A. Morris, *C. P. Trevelyan, 1870–1958: Portrait of a Radical* (New York: St. Martin's Press, 1979), p. 115; Morris, *Radicalism against War*, pp. 404, 406; H. A. Taylor, *Robert Donald* (London: Stanley Paul, no date), pp. 23, 25; George Malcolm Thomson, *The Twelve Days: 24 July to 4 August 1914* (New York: G.P. Putnam's Sons, 1964), pp. 157–58.

38. E. Thornton Cook, *What Manner of Men? Our Prime Ministers in Action and Word from J. Ramsay Macdonald to Benjamin Disraeli (Lord Beaconsfield)* (London: Heath Cranton, 1934), p. 62; Murray, *L.G.*, pp. 64–65; Owen, *Tempestuous Journey*, p. 263; *The Pomp of Power* (London: Hutchinson, 1922), p. 20; Hazlehurst, *Politicians at War*, p. 85; Koss, *Asquith*, p. 157.

39. Alan Bullock, *The Life and Times of Ernest Bevin*, vol. 1 (London: Heinemann, 1960), p. 45; Morris, *Radicalism against War*, pp. 413–14; Merle Fainsod, *International Socialism and the World War* (Garden City, N.Y.: Doubleday, 1969).

40. Alan Clark, ed., *"A Good Innings": The Private Papers of Viscount Lee of Fareham* (London: John Murray, 1974), p. 127.

41. Robert Rhodes James, *Churchill: A Study in Failure, 1900–1939* (Harmondsworth: Penguin Books, 1973), p. 67; Wilson, *The Downfall of the Liberal Party*, p. 49; Stephen Koss, *Fleet Street Radical: A. G. Gardiner and the Daily News* (Hamden, Conn.: Archon Books, 1973), pp. 147–48; Morris, *Radicalism against War*, pp. 404, 409–10; Fry, *Lloyd George and Foreign Policy*, vol. 1, p. 191; Hazlehurst, *Politicians at War*, p. 86; Koss, *Asquith*, p. 157.

42. Hazlehurst, *Politicians at War*, p. 36; Koss, *Asquith*, p. 157; Koss, *Fleet Street Radical*, p. 147; Morgan, *The Age of Lloyd George*, p. 52; Morris, *Radicalism against War*, p. 418; H. H. Asquith, *Letters to Venetia Stanley*, eds., Michael Brock and Eleanor Brock (Oxford: Oxford University Press, 1985), p. 146.

43. Hazlehurst, *Politicians at War*, p. 34; Morris, *C. P. Trevelyan*, pp. 115–17; Koss, *Nonconformity in Modern British Politics*, pp. 126–27.

44. Winston Spencer Churchill, *Liberalism and the Social Problem* (London: Hodder & Stoughton, 1909), p. 67; Robert Rhodes James, ed., *Winston S. Churchill: His Complete Speeches 1897–1963*, vol. 1 (New York: Chelsea House, 1974), p. 671; R. W. Thompson, *Winston Churchill: The Yankee Marlborough* (Garden City, N.Y.: Doubleday, 1963), p. 210.

45. Paul Barton Johnson, *Land Fit for Heroes: The Planning of British Reconstruction, 1916–1919* (Chicago: The University of Chicago Press, 1968), p. 237; Morgan, *The Age of Lloyd George*, pp. 58, 109; Wilson, *The Downfall of the Liberal Party*, pp. 23–24.

46. Roy Douglas, *The History of the Liberal Party, 1895–1970* (Madison, N.J.: Fairleigh Dickinson University Press, 1971), pp. 96–97, 130, 241; Max Beloff, *Imperial Sunset*, vol. 1 (New York: Alfred A. Knopf, 1970), p. 248; Edward David, "The Liberal Party Divided, 1916–1918," *The Historical Journal* 13 (1970): 531; John Campbell, *Lloyd George: The Goat in the Wilderness, 1922–1931* (London: Jonathan Cape, 1977), p. 8; Koss, *Fleet Street Radical*, p. 156; Hazlehurst, *Politicians at War*, pp. 286–88; Morgan, *The Age of Lloyd George*, p. 75; Chris Cook, *The Age of Alignment: Electoral Politics in Britain, 1922–1929* (Toronto: University of Toronto Press, 1975), p. 8; Iain McLean, *Keir Hardie* (London: Allen Lane, 1975), p. 170.

47. Douglas, *The History of the Liberal Party*, p. 93.

48. Morris, *Radicalism against War*, p. 417.

49. Marvin Rintala, *The Constitution of Silence: Essays on Generational Themes* (Westport: Greenwood Press, 1979), p. 37.

50. Osbert Sitwell, *Great Morning* (London: Macmillan, 1948), p. 298.

51. Grigg, *Lloyd George: From Peace to War*, p. 209n; John Wilson, *CB: A Life of Sir Henry Campbell-Bannerman* (New York: St. Martin's Press, 1974), pp. 244, 435, 456; Roy Jenkins, *Nine Men of Power* (New York: British Book Centre, 1974), p. 65.

52. Lord Boothby, "Founder of the Welfare State," *Books and Bookmen* 17 (September 1972): 17.

53. Douglas, *The History of the Liberal Party*, p. 93.

54. John P. Mackintosh, *The British Cabinet*, 2d ed. (London: Methuen, 1968), p. 343; A. J. P. Taylor, *Essays in English History* (Harmondsworth: Penguin Books, 1982), p. 222; George Macaulay Trevelyan, *Grey of Fallodon* (London: Longmans, Green, 1937), p. 262n.

55. Mackintosh, *The British Cabinet*, pp. 373, 388; The Earl of Oxford and Asquith, K.G., *Memories and Reflections, 1852–1927*, vol. 2 (Boston: Little, Brown, 1928), p. 238; Raymond, *Mr. Lloyd George*, pp. 15–16; Patrick Gordon Walker, *The Cabinet: Political Authority in Britain* (New York: Basic Books, 1970), p. 87; Humphry Berkeley, *The Power of the Prime Minister* (New York: Chilmark Press, 1968), p. 46.

56. The Earl of Oxford and Asquith, K.G., *Fifty Years of British Parliament*, vol. 1 (Boston: Little, Brown, 1926), p. 11.

57. Barbara W. Tuchman, *The Guns of August* (New York: Bonanza Books, 1982), p. 52.

58. Asquith, *Letters to Venetia Stanley*, p. 123.

59. Ibid., p. 125; Hazlehurst, *Politicians at War*, p. 33; Morris, *Radicalism against War*, p. 395; Peter Rowland, *Lloyd George* (London: Barrie & Jenkins, 1975), p. 282; Oxford and Asquith, *Memories and Reflections*, vol. 2, p. 11.

60. Stephen R. Graubard, *Burke, Disraeli, and Churchill: The Politics of Perseverance* (Cambridge, Mass.: Harvard University Press, 1961), p. 185; John Evelyn Wrench, *Geoffrey Dawson and Our Times* (London: Hutchinson, 1955), p. 104; Liddell Hart, *History of the First World War*, p. 26; Robert Payne, *The Great Man: A Portrait of Winston Churchill* (New York: Coward, McCann & Geoghegan, 1974), p. 143; Mary Soames, *Clementine Churchill: The Biography of a Marriage* (Boston: Houghton Mifflin, 1979), p. 136; Winston S. Churchill, *The World Crisis, 1911–1918*, vol. 1 (London: Odhams, 1938), pp. 161, 173; Cregier, *Bounder from Wales*, p. 244; Reginald Viscount Esher, *The Tragedy of Lord Kitchener* (London: John Murray, 1921), p. 21; Roy Jenkins, *Asquith: Portrait of a Man and an Era* (New York: E.P. Dutton, 1966), p. 325; C. J. Loew and M. L. Dockrill, *The Mirage of Power*, vol. 3 (London: Routledge & Kegan Paul, 1972), p. 492; Owen, *Tempestuous Journey*, p. 262; Rowland, *Lloyd George*, p. 281; Wilson, ed., *The Political Diaries of C. P. Scott*, p. 93; Wingfield-Stratford, *Churchill*, pp. 144–45.

61. Morris, *Radicalism against War*, p. 404; Hazlehurst, *Politicians at War*, p. 85; Beaverbrook, *Politicians and the War*, p. 17; A. J. P. Taylor, *Beaverbrook* (New York: Simon and Schuster, 1972), p. 83.

62. Tuchman, *The Guns of August*, p. 91; Wrench, *Geoffrey Dawson and Our Times*, p. 105; Hazlehurst, *Politicians at War*, pp. 87, 90; Winston S. Churchill, *The World Crisis*, vol. 1, p. 176; Cregier, *Bounder from Wales*, p. 249; Blanche E. P. Dugdale, *Arthur James Balfour, First Earl of Balfour: 1906–1930* (London: Hutchinson, no date), p. 84; David Mason, *Churchill* (London: Pan Books, 1973), p. 21; Koss, *Asquith*, p. 158; Oxford and Asquith, *Memories and Reflections*, vol. 2, p. 12.

63. Bulmer-Thomas, *The Growth of the British Party System*, vol. 1, pp. 221–22.

64. Asquith, *Letters to Venetia Stanley*, p. 146.

65. Morris, *Radicalism against War*, p. 398; Cregier, *Bounder from Wales*, p. 251.

66. Koss, *Asquith*, p. 159; Kenneth O. Morgan, *David Lloyd George*, p. 50; Arthur C. Murray, *Master and Brother: Murrays of Elibank* (London: John Murray, 1945), p. 120; Edwards, *David Lloyd George*, vol. II, p. 391; George Malcolm Thomson, *The Twelve Days*, p. 170.

67. Edwards, *David Lloyd George*, vol. II, pp. 381, 383; Bonham Carter, *Winston Churchill*, p. 249; M.L. Dockrill, "David Lloyd George and Foreign Policy before 1914," in A.J.P. Taylor, ed., *Lloyd George*, pp. 28, 30; Jones, *Lloyd George*, p. 48; William Manchester, *The Last Lion: Winston Spencer Churchill: Visions of Glory 1874–1932* (Boston: Little, Brown, 1983), pp. 469, 472; Arthur C. Murray, *Master and Brother*, p. 119; Henry Pelling, *Winston Churchill* (London: Macmillan, 1974), p. 177; Raymond, *Mr. Lloyd George*, p. 170; Malcolm Thomson, *David Lloyd George*, p. 230; Wrench, *Geoffrey Dawson and Our Times*, p. 105.

68. Tuchman, *The Guns of August*, pp. 94, 113; Victor Wallace Germains, *The Tragedy of Winston Churchill* (London: Hurst & Blackett, 1931), p. 277; Foot, *British Political Crises*, p. 57; Gerhardie, *God's Fifth Column*, p. 296; Beaverbrook, *Politicians and the War*, p. 23; Viscount Samuel, "The Campbell-Bannerman-Asquith Government," in Marchant, ed., *Winston Spencer Churchill*, p. 53; Scally, *The Origins of the Lloyd George Coalition*, p. 18; David Walder, *The Chanak Affair* (New York: Macmillan, 1969), p. 20; Manchester, *The Last Lion*, p. 473.

69. Fry, *Lloyd George and Foreign Policy*, vol. I, p. 185; Kenneth O. Morgan, *The Age of Lloyd George*, p. 53; Kenneth O. Morgan, ed., *Lloyd George*, p. 167.

70. Fry, *Lloyd George and Foreign Policy*, vol. I, p. 205; Hazlehurst, *Politicians*

at War, p. 117; Chris Wrigley, *David Lloyd George and the British Labour Movement: Peace and War* (Hassocks: The Harvester Press, 1976), p. 81.

71. Kenneth O. Morgan, ed., *Lloyd George*, p. 167.

72. Ibid.; *War Memoirs of David Lloyd George*, vol. I (London: Ivor Nicholson & Watson, 1933), p. 66.

73. Mackintosh, *The British Cabinet*, p. 342; Tuchman, *The Guns of August*, p. 115; Hazlehurst, *Politicians at War*, p. 68.

74. Hazlehurst, *Politicians at War*, pp. 64, 68-69; Wilson, ed., *The Political Diaries of C.P. Scott*, p. 92; Rowland, *Lloyd George*, p. 281.

75. Martin Gilbert, *Winston S. Churchill*, companion vol. III, part 2 (Boston: Houghton Mifflin, 1973), p. 1201.

76. Arthur C. Murray, *Master and Brother*, p. 122; Martin Gilbert, *Winston S. Churchill*, companion vol. III, part 1 (Boston: Houghton Mifflin, 1973), pp. 6-7, 12-13, 294; Gilbert, *Winston S. Churchill*, companion vol. III, part 2, p. 1592; Stephen Roskill, *Churchill and the Admirals* (New York: William Morrow, 1978), pp. 26-27. During the Second World War Churchill considered sending British troops into the neutral Irish Free State, and ordered the Royal Navy to make frequent use of neutral Turkish territorial waters. Roskill, *Churchill and the Admirals*, pp. 122, 328.

77. Elie Halevy, *The Rule of Democracy, 1905-1914 (Book I)*, trans. E.I. Watkin, 2nd ed. (New York: Peter Smith, 1952), p. 43; George Malcolm Thomson, *The Twelve Days*, p. 185.

78. B. H. Liddell Hart, *Strategy*, 2d rev. ed. (New York: The New American Library, 1974), p. 187; Martin Gilbert, *Winston S. Churchill*, vol. 3 (Boston: Houghton Mifflin, 1971), p. 25; Gilbert, *Winston S. Churchill*, companion vol. 3, part 2, p. 923; Wingfield-Stratford, *Churchill*, p. 145.

79. Beaverbrook, *Politicians and the War*, p. 25; Hugh Martin, *Battle*, p. 106.

80. Wilson, ed., *The Political Diaries of C. P. Scott*, pp. 99, 103; Edward David, ed., *Inside Asquith's Cabinet: From the Diaries of Charles Hobhouse* (New York: St. Martin's Press, 1977), p. 179.

81. Oxford and Asquith, *Memories and Reflections*, vol. 2, pp. 10–11.

82. Gilbert, *Winston S. Churchill*, vol. 3, p. 27.

83. *The Autobiography of Margot Asquith: Political Events and Celebrities* (London: Thornton Butterworth, 1933), p. 196; John Buchan, *The King's Grace, 1910–1935* (London: Hodder & Stoughton, 1935), p. 113.

84. Gilbert, *Winston S. Churchill*, vol. 3, p. 31; Soames, *Clementine Churchill*, p. 137.

85. James, ed., *Winston S. Churchill*, vol. 1, p. 82.

86. Soames, *Clementine Churchill*, pp. 94, 137; Gilbert, *Winston S. Churchill*, vol. 3, p. 31.

87. Gilbert, *Winston S. Churchill*, vol. 3, p. 31.

88. Gilbert, *Winston S. Churchill*, companion vol. 2, part 1, p. 400.

89. Gilbert, *Winston S. Churchill*, vol. 3, p. 475.

90. A. L. Rowse, *The Churchills: The Story of a Family* (New York: Harper & Row, 1966), p. 486.

91. Germains, *The Tragedy of Winston Churchill*, p. 277; Wilson, ed., *The Political Diaries of C. P. Scott*, p. 108.

92. A. J. P. Taylor, *Essays in English History*, p. 269; Gilbert, *Winston S. Churchill*, vol. 3, p. 23; Stephen E. Koss, *Sir John Brunner: Radical Plutocrat, 1842–1919* (Cambridge: Cambridge University Press, 1970), p. 270; Ted Morgan, *Churchill*, p. 392 Beaverbrook, *Politicians and the War*, pp. 22–23; Grigg, *Lloyd George: From Peace to War*, p. 142; Koss, *Fleet Street Radical*, p. 150; Mackintosh, *The British Cabinet*, p. 331; Morris, *Radicalism against War*, p. 401; Dugdale, *Arthur James Balfour*, p. 86.

93. Fry, *Lloyd George and Foreign Policy*, vol. 1, p. 184; Hazlehurst, *Politicians at War*, pp. 52, 60–61, 121; Rowland, *Lloyd George*, p. 282; Tuchman, *The Guns of August*, p. 94; Winston S. Churchill, *The World Crisis*, vol. 1, p. 174; Dockrill, "David Lloyd George and Foreign Policy," p. 27; Jenkins, *Asquith*, p. 326; Koss, *Asquith*, pp. 156–57; Morris, *Radicalism against War*, p. 390.

94. A. J. P. Taylor, "Lloyd George," p. 81; A. J. P. Taylor, *Essays in English History*, p. 269.

95. Hazlehurst, *Politicians at War*, p. 103.

96. Gilbert, *Winston S. Churchill*, vol. 3, p. 23; Hazlehurst, *Politicians at War*, pp. 63–64, 307, 321–26.

97. Hazlehurst, *Politicians at War*, p. 108; Fry, *Lloyd George and Foreign Policy*, vol. 1, p. 204.

98. James, *Churchill*, p. 66.

99. Manchester, *The Last Lion*, p. 471.

100. Winston Churchill, *Savrola* (London: Hodder & Stoughton, 1915), p. 37.

101. Randolph S. Churchill, *Winston S. Churchill*, vol. 2 (Boston: Houghton Mifflin, 1967), p. 702.

102. Ibid; Randolph S. Churchill, *Winston S. Churchill*, companion vol. 2, part 3 (London: Heinemann, 1969), p. 1997. See also Countess Lloyd-George of Dwyfor, "Introduction" to Malcolm Thomson, *David Lloyd George*, p. 16; Owen, *Tempestuous Journey*, p. 265.

103. Churchill, *Winston S. Churchill*, vol. 2, p. 701; Churchill, *Winston S. Churchill*, companion vol. 2, part 3, p. 1996; Countess Lloyd-George of Dwyfor, "Introduction," p. 16. See also Fry, *Lloyd George and Foreign Policy*, vol. 1, p. 204n; Earl Lloyd George, *My Father, Lloyd George* (New York: Crown, 1961), p. 143; Owen, *Tempestuous Journey*, p. 265.

104. Earl Lloyd George, *My Father, Lloyd George*, p. 143.

105. Churchill, *Winston S. Churchill*, vol. 2, p. 704.

106. Grigg, *Lloyd George: From Peace to War*, pp. 162, 165–66, 169–70.

107. *The Collected Poems of Wilfred Owen*, ed. C. Day Lewis (New York: New Directions, 1964), pp. 41–42.

108. Grigg, *Lloyd George: From Peace to War*, p. 169.

109. Cross, ed., *Life with Lloyd George*, p. 114.

110. Winston S. Churchill, *The World Crisis*, vol. 1, p. 222; Gilbert, *Winston S. Churchill*, vol. 3, p. 55.

111. Winston S. Churchill, *The World Crisis*, vol. 1, p. 223.

112. Leslie D. Weatherhead, *In Quest of a Kingdom* (New York: Abingdon Press, 1944), p. 70. Weatherhead, a prominent Nonconformist clergyman and a British pioneer in religious psychology, was well known to Lloyd George (Horton Davies, *Varieties of English Preaching 1900–1960* [London: SCM Press, 1963], pp. 140–47; see also Lady Olwen Carey Evans and Mary Garner, *Lloyd George Was My Father* (Llandysul: Gomer Press, 1985), p. 78; J. Glenn Gray, *The Warriors: Reflections on Men in Battle* (New York: Harper & Row, 1967), p. 95; Harold Balfour, *Wings over Westminster* (London: Hutchinson, 1973), p. 192.

Chapter Seven

1. Sir Dingle Foot, *British Political Crises* (London: William Kimber, 1976), p. 178.

2. John P. Mackintosh, *The British Cabinet*, 2d ed. (London: Methuen, 1968), p. 572.

3. Robert Rhodes James, ed., *Winston S. Churchill: His Complete Speeches 1897–1963*, vol. 2 (New York: Chelsea House, 1974), p. 1688.

4. Maxwell P. Schoenfeld, *Sir Winston Churchill: His Life and Times*, 2d ed. (Malabar, Fla.: Robert E. Krieger, 1986), p. 71.

5. Foot, *British Political Crises*, p. 57.

6. Laurence Thompson, *1940: Year of Legend, Year of History* (London: Collins, 1966), p. 166n.

7. Foot, *British Political Crises*, p. 10; Alan Campbell Johnson, *Viscount Halifax: A Biography* (London: Robert Hale, 1941), p. 557; Kenneth Young, "Off the Ball—or, Churchill Ill-considered," *Encounter* 26 (February 1966): 96.

8. Manfred Weidhorn, *Sword and Pen: A Survey of the Writings of Sir Winston Churchill* (Albuquerque: University of New Mexico Press, 1974), p. 219.

9. Joseph P. Lash, *Roosevelt and Churchill, 1939–1941: The Partnership That Saved the West* (New York: W.W. Norton, 1976), p. 195.

10. Henry Pelling, *Winston Churchill* (London: Macmillan, 1974), pp. 397, 433.

11. Ibid., p. 437; Lord Boothby, "War Lord of Parliament," *Books and Bookmen* 19 (April 1974): 24; John Colville, *The Fringes of Power: 10 Downing Street Diaries, 1939–1955* (New York: W.W. Norton, 1986), p. 123; Kate Fleming, *The Churchills* (New York: The Viking Press, 1975), p. 191; Martin Gilbert, *Winston S. Churchill*, vol. 4 (Boston: Houghton Mifflin, 1983), p. 313; J. M. Lee, *The Churchill Coalition, 1940–1945* (London: Batsford, 1980), p. 31; Ronald Lewin, *Churchill as Warlord* (New York: Scarborough Books, 1982), p. 10; Elizabeth Longford, *Elizabeth R: A Biography* (London: Weidenfeld and Nicolson, 1983), p. 86; Mackintosh, *The British Cabinet*, p. 423; A. J. P. Taylor, *Essays in English History* (Harmondsworth: Penguin Books, 1982), p. 286; Michael Thornton, *Royal Feud: The Dark Side of the Love Story of the Century* (New York: Simon and Schuster, 1985), p. 200; A. J. P. Taylor, *Beaverbrook* (New York: Simon and Schuster, 1972), p. 410; Robert Blake, *Disraeli* (Garden City, N.Y.: Doubleday, 1968), p. 348; Piers Brendon, *Winston Churchill: A Biography* (New York: Harper & Row, 1984), p. 141; *The Art of the Possible: The Memoirs of Lord Butler* (Harmondsworth: Penguin Books, 1973), pp. 84–85; James C. Humes, *Churchill: Speaker of the Century* (New York: Scarborough Books, 1982), p. 184; Roy Jenkins, *Nine Men of Power* (New York: British Book Centre, 1974), p. 152; Maxwell Philip Schoenfeld, *The War Ministry of Winston Churchill* (Ames: The Iowa State University Press, 1972), p. 9; The Earl of Birkenhead, *Halifax: The Life of Lord Halifax* (London: Hamish Hamilton, 1965), p. 453; Hugh Dalton, *The Fateful Years: Memoirs, 1931–1945* (London: Frederick Muller, 1957), p. 307; Alec Douglas-Home, *The Way the Wind Blows: An Autobiography* (New York: Quadrangle, 1976), p. 75; Brian Gardner, *Churchill in His Time: A Study in a Reputation, 1939–1945* (London: Methuen, 1968), p. 35; A. J. P. Taylor, *English History 1914-1945* (New York: Oxford University Press, 1965), p. 473; Thompson, *1940*, pp. 83–84. For a mistaken argument that the Labor party was responsible for Churchill's succession to Chamberlain, see Edward Hyams, *The New Statesman: The History of the First Fifty Years 1913–1963* (London: Longmans, 1963), p. 222.

12. Laurence Thompson, *1940*, p. 93; Taylor, *English History*, p. 472.

13. René Kraus, *The Men around Churchill* (Philadelphia: J.B. Lippincott, 1941), pp. 24–25.

14. Lewin, *Churchill as Warlord*, pp. 41–42; Taylor, *Beaverbrook*, p. 409; Jenkins, *Nine Men of Power*, pp. 135, 153.

15. Cecil King, "Political Pot-pourri," *Books and Bookmen* 21 (November 1974): 15.

16. Evelyn Waugh, *Brideshead Revisited: The Sacred and Profane Memories of Captain Charles Ryder* (Boston: Little, Brown, 1945), p. 331. Coming from Waugh, this approached praise. His fictional description of Churchill is much harsher (Evelyn Waugh, *Men at Arms: A Novel* [Boston: Little, Brown, 1952], pp. 242–43). His private judgment of Churchill was much harsher still. (Mark Amory, ed., *The Letters of Evelyn Waugh* [New Haven: Ticknor & Fields, 1980], p. 630).

17. James Stuart, *Within the Fringe: An Autobiography* (London: The Bodley Head, 1967), p. 97; Birkenhead, *Halifax*, pp. 130–31, 456, 458–59, 464, 501, 510, 536, 538, 551.

18. Johnson, *Viscount Halifax*, p. 61.

19. John Grigg, *Nancy Astor: A Lady Unashamed* (Boston: Little, Brown, 1980), p. 153; Ronald Tree, *When the Moon Was High: Memoirs of Peace and War 1897–1942* (London: Macmillan, 1975), p. 78; Foot, *British Political Crises*, p. 161; Robert Rhodes James, "The Politician," in A. J. P. Taylor and others, *Churchill: Four Faces and the Man* (Harmondsworth: Penguin Books, 1973), p. 100; Pelling, *Winston Churchill*, p. 386.

20. Taylor, *Beaverbrook*, p. 386.

21. Joel Colton, *Léon Blum: Humanist in Politics* (Cambridge, Mass.: The MIT Press, 1974), p. 306.

22. Violet Bonham Carter, "Introduction" to Eugen Spier, *Focus: A Footnote to the History of the Thirties* (London: Oswald Wolff, 1963), p. 9; Violet Bonham Carter, "Winston Churchill—as I Know Him," in Sir James Marchant, ed., *Winston Spencer Churchill: Servant of Crown and Commonwealth* (London: Cassell, 1954), p. 154; Harold Wilson, *A Prime Minister on Prime Ministers* (New York: Summit Books, 1977), p. 287; Hugh Martin, *Battle: The Life Story of the Rt. Hon. Winston S. Churchill* (London: Sampson Low, Marston, 1932), pp. 236–37; Colville, *The Fringes of Power*, pp. 321, 431.

23. Johnson, *Viscount Halifax*, p. 556.

24. Vera Brittain, *Testament of Experience: An Autobiographical Story of the Years 1925–1950* (New York: Wideview Books, 1981), p. 250; Gilbert, *Winston S. Churchill*, vol. 6, p. 285.

25. Pelling, *Winston Churchill*, p. 438; A. J. P. Taylor, "The Statesman," in Taylor and others, *Churchill: Four Faces and the Man* (Harmondsworth: Penguin Books, 1973), p. 33; Alfred F. Havighurst, *Twentieth-Century Britain*, 2d ed. (New York: Harper & Row, 1966), p. 292; Gilbert, *Winston S. Churchill*, vol. 6, p. 239.

26. André Beaufre, *1940: The Fall of France*, trans. Desmond Flower (New York: Alfred A. Knopf, 1968), p. 174; Butler, *The Art of the Possible*, p. 83; B. H. Liddell Hart, "Churchill in War: A Study of His Capacity and Performance in the Military Sphere," *Encounter* 26 (April 1966): 17; Basil Liddell Hart, "The Military Strategist," in Taylor and others, *Churchill*, p. 187; Arthur Marwick, *Britain in the Century of Total War: War, Peace and Social Change, 1900–1967* (Harmondsworth: Penguin Books, 1970), p. 272; Schoenfeld, *The War Ministry of Winston Churchill*, p. 8; Charles Stuart, ed., *The Reith Diaries* (London: Collins, 1975), p. 284; Taylor, *English History*, p. 47; A. J. P. Taylor, *The War Lords* (Harmondsworth: Penguin Books, 1981), p. 72; Colville, *The Fringes of Power*, p. 96.

27. Taylor, *Essays in English History*, pp. 290, 296; J. L. Moulton, *A Study of Warfare in Three Dimensions: The Norwegian Campaign of 1940* (Athens: The Ohio University Press, 1967), pp. 70–71; R. W. Thompson, *Winston Churchill: The Yankee Marlborough* (Garden City, N.Y.: Doubleday, 1963), p. 269; Lord Hankey, *Politics, Trials and Errors* (Chicago: Henry Regnery, 1950), pp. 61, 72–79; Stephen Roskill, *Churchill and the Admirals* (New York: William Morrow, 1978), pp. 96–97.

28. Colville, *The Fringes of Power*, p. 65; Jukka Nevakivi, *The Appeal That Was Never Made: The Allies, Scandinavia and the Finnish Winter War, 1939–1940* (Montréal: McGill-Queen's University Press, 1976), pp. 107–8; Virginia Cowles, *Winston Churchill: The Era and the Man* (New York: Grosset & Dunlap, no date), p. 315n; Brittain, *Testament of Experience*, p. 247; R. W. Thompson, *Winston Churchill*, p. 267.

29. Roskill, *Churchill and the Admirals*, pp. 98–99; Gilbert, *Winston S. Churchill*, vol. 6, p. 274; Lewin, *Churchill as Warlord*, p. 25; Lord Altrincham, "Churchill in

International Affairs," in Charles Eade, ed., *Churchill by His Contemporaries* (New York: Simon and Schuster, 1954), p. 233; Boothby, "War Lord of Parliament," p. 24; Taylor, *Beaverbrook*, p. 408.

30. Gilbert, *Winston S. Churchill*, vol. 6, pp. 224, 287.

31. Harold Macmillan, *The Blast of War, 1939–1945* (New York: Harper & Row, 1968), p. 52; Harold Nicolson, *Diaries and Letters, 1939–1945*, ed. Nigel Nicolson (New York: Atheneum, 1967), p. 70.

32. Roskill, *Churchill and the Admirals*, p. 106; Macmillan, *The Blast of War*, p. 54.

33. Nicolson, *Diaries and Letters, 1939–1945*, p. 7; Macmillan, *The Blast of War*, pp. 53, 55, 59; A. P. Herbert, *Independent Member* (Garden City, N.Y.: Doubleday, 1951), p. 118.

34. Harold Balfour, *Wings over Westminster* (London: Hutchinson, 1973), p. 89; Foot, *British Political Crises*, p. 182.

35. Thirty-three Conservatives voted for the Opposition Vote of Censure and sixty Conservatives abstained (Gilbert, *Winston S. Churchill*, vol. 6, p. 299).

36. Butler, *The Art of the Possible*, p. 84; Humes, *Churchill*, pp. 181–82; Elizabeth Longford, *Winston Churchill* (London: Sidgwick & Jackson, 1974), p. 114; David Mason, *Churchill* (London: Pan Books, 1973), p. 42; Esmé Wingfield-Stratford, *Churchill: The Making of a Hero* (London: Victor Gollancz, 1942), p. 248; *The Memoirs of the Rt. Hon. The Earl of Woolton* (London: Cassell, 1959), p. 174.

37. Colville, *The Fringes of Power*, p. 312; R. W. Thompson, *Generalissimo Churchill* (London: Hodder and Stoughton, 1973), p. 64.

38. Thomas Jones, *A Diary with Letters: 1931–1950* (London: Oxford University Press, 1954), p. 457; Laurence Thompson, *1940*, p. 79.

39. Frank Owen, *Tempestuous Journey: Lloyd George, His Life and Times* (London: Hutchinson, 1954), p. 746.

40. Peter Rowland, *Lloyd George* (London: Barrie & Jenkins, 1975), pp. 769–70.

41. Colville, *The Fringes of Power*, p. 117; Macmillan, *The Blast of War*, p. 60.

42. Johnson, *Viscount Halifax*, p. 555.

43. Gilbert, *Winston S. Churchill*, vol. 6, p. 293.

44. Ibid., p. 943; Colville, *The Fringes of Power*, p. 310.

45. Tom Driberg, *Guy Burgess: A Portrait with Background* (London: Weidenfeld and Nicolson, 1956), p. 57.

46. Colville, *The Fringes of Power*, p. 406.

47. Lady Olwen Carey Evans and Mary Garner, *Lloyd George Was My Father* (Llandysul: Gomer Press, 1985), p. 158; A. J. P. Taylor, ed., *My Darling Pussy: The Letters of Lloyd George and Frances Stevenson, 1913–41* (London: Weidenfeld and Nicolson, 1975), p. 228.

48. Winston S. Churchill, *The Second World War: The Gathering Storm* (New York: Bantam Books, 1974), p. 589; Rowland, *Lloyd George*, p. 772; Ivor Bulmer-Thomas, *The Growth of the British Party System*, vol. 2 (London: John Baker, 1965), pp. 132–33; John Grigg, "Lloyd George," in *Great Britons* (London: British Broadcasting Corporation, 1978), p. 205; Kenneth O. Morgan, ed., *Lloyd George: Family Letters, 1885–1936* (Cardiff: University of Wales Press and London: Oxford University Press, 1973), p. 185; A. L. Rowse, *The Churchills: The Story of a Family* (New York: Harper & Row, 1966), pp. 522–23; Owen, *Tempestuous Journey*, p. 746.

49. Churchill, *The Second World War: The Gathering Storm*, p. 589; Wilson, *A Prime Minister on Prime Ministers*, p. 236; Kenneth O. Morgan, *The Age of Lloyd George* (New York: Barnes & Noble, 1971), p. 106. See also Brittain, *Testament of Experience*, p. 250.

50. Gardner, *Churchill in His Time*, p. 37; Humes, *Churchill*, p. 183; Wingfield-Stratford, *Churchill*, p. 249.

51. Gardner, *Churchill in His Time*, p. 37; Jones, *A Diary with Letters*, p. 458; Longford, *Winston Churchill*, p. 115; Cross, ed., *Life with Lloyd George*, p. 259; Churchill, *The Second World War: The Gathering Storm*, p. 589. Others agreed: Dalton, *The Fateful Years*, p. 306; Roy Douglas, *The History of the Liberal Party, 1895–1970* (Madison: Fairleigh Dickinson University Press, 1971), p. 241; Nicolson, *Diaries and Letters, 1939–1945*, p. 79; Rowland, *Lloyd George*, p. 772; Malcolm Thomson, *Churchill: His Life and Times* (London: Odhams Books, 1965), p. 300; see also A. J. Sylvester, *The Real Lloyd George* (London: Cassell, 1947), p. 261; Thomson, *David Lloyd George*, p. 452; Kenneth Young, *Churchill and Beaverbrook: A Study in Friendship and Politics* (New York: James H. Heineman, 1966), p. 138; Michael Foot, *Debts of Honor* (New York: Harper & Row, 1981), p. 102.

52. Colville, *The Fringes of Power*, p. 119; Morgan, *The Age of Lloyd George*, p. 106; Kenneth O. Morgan, *David Lloyd George: Welsh Radical as World Statesman* (Cardiff: University of Wales Press, 1963), p. 74.

53. Ivan Maisky, *Memoirs of a Soviet Ambassador: The War: 1939–1943*, trans. Andrew Rothstein (New York: Charles Scribner's Sons, 1968), p. 64.

54. John Evelyn Wrench, *Geoffrey Dawson and Our Times* (London: Hutchinson, 1955), p. 416; Stephen Koss, *Fleet Street Radical: A. G. Gardiner and the Daily News* (Hamden, Conn.: Archon Books, 1973), p. 305.

55. John Campbell, *Lloyd George: The Goat in the Wilderness, 1922–1931* (London: Jonathan Cape, 1977), p. 311; Colin Cross, ed., *Life with Lloyd George: The Diary of A. J. Sylvester, 1931–1945* (New York: Barnes & Noble, 1975), pp. 219–20. While the House of Commons was applauding Chamberlain after Munich, Lloyd George remained seated and made no sound (Frances, Countess Lloyd-George of Dwyfor, "Introduction" to Malcolm Thomson, *David Lloyd George: The Official Biography* [London: Hutchinson, no date], pp. 27–28. Prior to 1938, Churchill consistently voted to support Conservative foreign policy; only in that year did he begin to abstain on foreign policy questions, and only on those questions. During 1935–1938, he never voted against a Conservative cabinet (Richard Howard Powers, "Winston Churchill's Parliamentary Commentary on British Foreign Policy, 1935–1938," *Journal of Modern History* 26 [June 1954]: 179–82).

56. Birkenhead, *Halifax*, p. 452.

57. Welcomed: Paul Addison, "Lloyd George and Compromise Peace in the Second World War," in A. J. P. Taylor, ed., *Lloyd George: Twelve Essays* (New York: Atheneum, 1971), pp. 371–72; Pamela Brookes, *Women at Westminster: An Account of Women in the British Parliament, 1918–1966* (London: Peter Davies, 1967), p. 131; Cross, ed., *Life with Lloyd George*, p. 253; Gardner, *Churchill in His Time*, p. 37; *The Memoirs of Captain Liddell Hart*, vol. 2 (London: Cassell, 1965), p. 279; Nicolson, *Diaries and Letters 1939–1945*, pp. 74–75; Pelling, *Winston Churchill*, p. 438; Rowland, *Lloyd George*, p. 770; A. J. Taylor, "Lloyd George," in Lord Longford and Sir John Wheeler-Bennett, eds., *The History Makers: Leaders and Statesmen of the 20th Century* (New York: St. Martin's Press, 1973), p. 87. Tolerated: Donald McCormick, *The Mask of Merlin: A Critical Study of David Lloyd George* (London: Macdonald, 1963), pp. 285–86.

58. Trevor Wilson, *The Downfall of the Liberal Party, 1914–1935* (Ithaca, N.Y.: Cornell University Press, 1966), p. 383.

59. Colville, *The Fringes of Power*, p. 129; Cross, ed., *Life with Lloyd George*, p. 283; Gilbert, *Winston S. Churchill*, vol. 6, p. 332; Lord Morrison of Lambeth, *Government and Parliament: A Survey from the Inside*, 3d ed. (London: Oxford University Press, 1964), p. 170; Sylvester, *The Real Lloyd George*, p. 282.

60. Boothby, "War Lord of Parliament," p. 25.

61. Taylor, ed., *My Darling Pussy*, p. 245.

62. Lord Boothby, "Frustrated Autocrat," *Books and Bookmen* 18 (January 1973): 10; Lord Boothby, "Political Titans," *Books and Bookmen* 20 (August 1974): 18.

63. Countess Lloyd-George, "Introduction," p. 28.

64. Macmillan, *The Blast of War*, p. 52; Schoenfeld, *The War Ministry of Winston Churchill*, p. 8.

65. R. W. Thompson, *Winston Churchill*, p. 270; Gilbert, *Winston S. Churchill*, vol. 6, p. 293; Churchill, *The Second World War: The Gathering Storm*, p. 589.

66. Schoenfeld, *The War Ministry of Winston Churchill*, p. 8.

67. Macmillan, *The Blast of War*, p. 60.

68. Churchill, *The Second World War: The Gathering Storm*, p. 589.

69. Olivia Coolidge, *Winston Churchill and the Story of Two World Wars* (Boston: Houghton Mifflin, 1960), p. 128.

70. Macmillan, *The Blast of War*, p. 60.

71. Fleming, *The Churchills*, p. 191.

72. Butler, *The Art of the Possible*, pp. 30, 146; Colville, *The Fringes of Power*, p. 122. This was not Butler's first negative judgment of Churchill. He had earlier tried to execute Churchill, at least politically. In a 1933 Commons debate on India, speaking for the British Government, Butler warned Churchill that "there is waiting" for him "a sure and safe rifle to ensure his ultimate fate" (Butler, *The Art of the Possible*, p. 47). Many things proved impossible for the artist of the possible.

73. Brookes, *Women at Westminster*, p. 131; Tree, *When the Moon was High*, p. 176.

74. Schoenfeld, *The War Ministry of Winston Churchill*, p. 10; Lash, *Roosevelt and Churchill*, pp. 129–30.

75. Young, *Churchill and Beaverbrook*, p. 138; Nicolson, *Diaries and Letters, 1939–1945*, p. 85.

76. Cross, ed., *Life with Lloyd George*, pp. 261–62; Rowland, *Lloyd George*, p. 773; Sylvester, *The Real Lloyd George*, p. 264.

77. Gardner, *Churchill in His Time*, p. 43.

Chapter Eight

1. Roy Jenkins, *Nine Men of Power* (New York: British Book Centre, 1974), p. 169.

2. Thomas Jones, *A Diary with Letters: 1931–1950* (London: Oxford University Press, 1954), p. 222; A. J. P. Taylor, ed., *My Darling Pussy: The Letters of Lloyd George and Frances Stevenson, 1913–1941* (London: Weidenfeld and Nicolson, 1975), p. 12; Countess Lloyd-George of Dwyfor, "Introduction" to Malcolm Thomson, *David Lloyd George: The Official Biography* (London: Hutchinson, no date), p. 15; Kirsty McLeod, *The Wives of Downing Street* (London: Collins, 1976), p. 195; Peter Rowland, *Lloyd George* (London: Barrie & Jenkins, 1975), pp. 195, 305; Thomson, *David Lloyd George*, p. 69.

3. Jones, *A Diary with Letters*, p. 250.

4. E. T. Raymond, *Mr. Lloyd George* (New York: George H. Doran, 1922), p. 321. (E.T. Raymond was a pen name of E. R. Thompson).

5. Virginia Cowles, *Winston Churchill: The Era and the Man* (New York: Grosset & Dunlap, no date), p. 8; Harold Wilson, *A Prime Minister on Prime Ministers* (New York: Summit Books, 1977), p. 268; Howard Brenton, *The Churchill Play* (London: Eyre Methuen, 1974), pp. 78-79.

6. Childhood: Robert Payne, *The Great Man: A Portrait of Winston Churchill*

(New York: Coward, McCann & Geoghegan, 1974), p. 51. Old age: ibid., p. 376; Roy Howells, *Churchill's Last Years* (New York: David McKay, 1966), p. 184. Happy occasions: Arthur Bryant, *Triumph in the West, 1943–1946: Based on the Diaries and Autobiographical Notes of Field Marshal The Viscount Alanbrooke* (London: The Reprint Society, 1960), p. 356; Ivor Bulmer-Thomas, *The Growth of the British Party System*, vol. 2 (London: John Baker, 1965), p. 20; Anita Leslie, *Randolph: The Biography of Winston Churchill's Son* (New York: Beaufort Books, 1985), p. 49. Sad occasions: John Colville, *Winston Churchill and His Inner Circle* (New York: Wyndham Books, 1981), p. 155; Olivia Coolidge, *Winston Churchill and the Story of Two World Wars* (Boston: Houghton Mifflin, 1960), p. 250; Basil Liddell Hart, "The Military Strategist," in A. J. P. Taylor and others, *Churchill: Four Faces and the Man* (Harmondsworth: Penguin Books, 1973), p. 200; Lucy Masterman, "Churchill—the Liberal Phase—Part II," *History Today* 14 (December 1964): 827; Harold Nicolson, *Diaries and Letters, 1945–1962*, ed. Nigel Nicolson (New York: Atheneum, 1968), p. 237; Henry Pelling, *Winston Churchill* (London: Macmillan, 1974), p. 414; Soames, *Clementine Churchill*, p. 331; Christopher Sykes, *Nancy: The Life of Lady Astor* (London: Granada Publishing, 1979), p. 421; Philip Ziegler, *Diana Cooper: A Biography* (New York: Harper & Row, 1987), p. 279. In privacy: Walter Henry Thompson, *Assignment: Churchill* (New York: Farrar, Straus & Young, 1955), pp. 165, 202; Walter H. Thompson, "Guarding Mr. Churchill," in Charles Eade, ed., *Churchill by His Contemporaries* (New York: Simon and Schuster, 1954), p. 205. In public: Maxwell Philip Schoenfeld, *The War Ministry of Winston Churchill* (Ames, Iowa: The Iowa State University Press, 1972), p. 4. Before the powerful: Sarah Churchill, *Keep on Dancing*, ed. Paul Medlicott (New York: Coward, McCann & Geoghegan, 1981), p. 119; James C. Humes, *Churchill: Speaker of the Century* (New York: Scarborough Books, 1982), p. 199; François Kersaudy, *Churchill and de Gaulle* (New York: Atheneum, 1982), pp. 76, 376; Leslie, *Randolph*, p. 93; Elizabeth Longford, *Winston Churchill* (London: Sidgwick & Jackson, 1974), p. 143; Gerald Pawle, *The War and Colonel Warden* (New York: Alfred A. Knopf, 1963), p. 333; Wilson, *A Prime Minister on Prime Ministers*, p. 268. Before the powerless: Payne, *The Great Man*, pp. 240–41; Pelling, *Winston Churchill*, p. 644; Soames, *Clementine Churchill*, p. 398; Sykes, *Nancy*, p. 514. Ease: Robert Rhodes James, *Churchill: A Study in Failure, 1900–1939* (Harmondsworth: Penguin Books, 1973), p. 44; William Manchester: *The Last Lion: Winston Spencer Churchill: Visions of Glory, 1874–1932* (Boston: Little, Brown, 1983), p. 36; Robert Lewis Taylor, *Winston Churchill: An Informal Study of Greatness* (Garden City, N.Y.: Doubleday, 1952), p. 433.

7. Pawle, *The War and Colonel Warden*, p. ix; Piers Brendon, *Winston Churchill: A Biography* (New York: Harper & Row, 1984), p. 130; Martin Gilbert, *Winston S. Churchill*, vol. 6 (Boston: Houghton Mifflin, 1983), p. 909; Pelling, *Winston Churchill*, p. 82; Elizabeth Longford, *Elizabeth R: A Biography* (London: Weidenfeld and Nicolson, 1983), p. 161; Soames, *Clementine Churchill*, p. 360; James Stuart, *Within the Fringe: An Autobiography* (London: The Bodley Head, 1967), p. 110.

8. Kersaudy, *Churchill and de Gaulle*, p. 246.

9. *Churchill: Taken from the Diaries of Lord Moran: The Struggle for Survival, 1940–1965* (Boston: Houghton Mifflin, 1966), pp. 6, 446, 460, 472.

10. Heinz L. Ansbacher and Rowena R. Ansbacher, eds., *The Individual Psychology of Alfred Adler: A Systematic Presentation in Selections from His Writings* (New York: Harper Torchbooks, 1964), p. 288.

11. Randolph S. Churchill, *Winston S. Churchill*, companion vol. 2, part 3 (London: Heinemann, 1969), p. 1653; Schoenfeld, *The War Ministry of Winston Churchill*, p. 15; Moran, *Churchill*, p. 330.

12. Ronald Tree, *When the Moon Was High: Memoirs of Peace and War, 1897–1942* (London: Macmillan, 1975), p. 149.

13. Brendon, *Winston Churchill*, p. 153. See also Pelling, *Winston Churchill*, p. 456.

14. Moran, *Churchill*, p. 339.

15. John Grigg, *Nancy Astor: A Lady Unashamed* (Boston: Little, Brown, 1980), p. 164.

16. Humes, *Churchill*, p. 187; Elizabeth Nel, *Mr. Churchill's Secretary* (New York: Coward-McCann, 1958), p. 34; The Earl of Birkenhead, *Halifax: The Life of Lord Halifax* (London: Hamish Hamilton, 1965), p. 559; Malcolm MacDonald, *Titans & Others* (London: Collins, 1972), p. 92; Moran, *Churchill*, pp. 500–501.

17. Ansbacher and Ansbacher, eds., *The Individual Psychology of Alfred Adler*, p. 320.

18. Esmé Wingfield-Stratford, *Churchill: The Making of a Hero* (London: Victor Gollancz, 1942), p. 109. Ironically, this hagiographer himself described his hero's behavior as "disquietingly neurotic" (ibid., p. 139).

19. Anthony Storr, "The Man," in Taylor and others, *Churchill*, p. 213; Giovanni Costigan, *Makers of Modern England: The Force of Individual Genius in History* (London: Macmillan, 1969), p. 252; Malcolm Muggeridge, "Churchill the Biographer and Historian," in Eade, ed., *Churchill by His Contemporaries*, p. 293; Manfred Weidhorn, *Sir Winston Churchill* (Boston: Twayne, 1979), p. 30; H. G. Wells, *Men Like Gods* (New York: Grosset & Dunlap, 1923), p. 63; Moran, *Churchill*, pp. 112, 426.

20. Herbert Leslie Stewart, *Winged Words: Sir Winston Churchill as Writer and Speaker* (New York: Bouregy & Curl, 1954), p. 36.

21. Jones, *A Diary with Letters*, p. 465; Humes, *Churchill*, p. 120; A. J. P. Taylor, *Beaverbrook* (New York: Simon and Schuster, 1972), p. 465; Ferdinand Mount, *The Theatre of Politics* (London: Weidenfeld and Nicolson, 1972), p. 105; Muggeridge, "Churchill the Biographer and Historian," p. 296; Weidhorn, *Sir Winston Churchill*, pp. 27, 34.

22. Winston Spencer Churchill, *Lord Randolph Churchill*, 2 vols. (New York: Macmillan, 1906). See also: R. F. Foster, *Lord Randolph Churchill: A Political Life* (Oxford: Clarendon Press, 1982), p. 5; Wilson, *A Prime Minister on Prime Ministers*, p. 274; Kate Fleming, *The Churchills* (New York: The Viking Press, 1975), p. 162; Samuel J. Hurwitz, "Winston S. Churchill," in Herman Ausubel, J. Bartlet Brebner, and Erling M. Hunt, eds. *Some Modern Historians of Britain: Essays in Honor of R. L. Schuyler* (New York: The Dryden Press, 1951), pp. 311–12; Manfred Weidhorn, *Sword and Pen: A Survey of the Writings of Sir Winston Churchill* (Albuquerque: University of New Mexico Press, 1974), p. 55; Stewart, *Winged Words*, p. 6. What Churchill could not do was done, brilliantly, by Lord Rosebery (*Lord Randolph Churchill* [London: Arthur L. Humphreys, 1906]); Henry Green, *Nothing, Doting, Blindness* (New York: Penguin Books, 1980), p. 358.

23. Frank Brady and W. K. Wimsatt, eds., *Samuel Johnson: Selected Poetry and Prose* (Berkeley: University of California Press, 1977), p. 184.

24. Longford, *Winston Churchill*, p. 71.

25. Hurwitz, "Winston S. Churchill," p. 312; Storr, "The Man," p. 238.

26. Storr, "The Man," p. 244.

27. Anton Felix Schindler, *Beethoven as I Knew Him: A Biography*, ed. Donald W. MacArdle (Chapel Hill: The University of North Carolina Press, 1966), p. 291.

28. Lord Beaverbrook, *Politicians and the War 1914–1916* (London: Oldbourne, 1960), p. 284; Violet Bonham Carter, *Winston Churchill: An Intimate Portrait* (New York: Harcourt, Brace & World, 1965), p. 188; Moran, *Churchill*, p. 10; Taylor, *Beaverbrook*, p. 441; James, *Churchill*, pp. 122, 441; Moran, *Churchill*, p. 628; R. W. Thompson, *Winston Churchill: The Yankee Marlborough* (Garden City, N.Y.: Doubleday, 1963), p. 271; Arno J. Mayer, "Winston Churchill: Power Politician and

Counter-Revolutionary," in Kurt H. Wolff and Barrington Moore, Jr., eds., *The Critical Spirit: Essays in Honor of Herbert Mancuse* (Boston: Beacon Press, 1967), p. 330; V. G. Trukhanovsky, *Winston Churchill* (Moscow: Progress Publishers, 1978), p. 93; Cowles, *Winston Churchill*, p. 214; Payne, *The Great Man*, pp. 99, 121, 347.

29. Bonham Carter, *Winston Churchill*, p. 130; Brendon, *Winston Churchill*, p. 48; Ted Morgan, *Churchill: Young Man in a Hurry, 1874–1915* (New York: Simon and Schuster, 1982), p. 237; Pelling, *Winston Churchill*, p. 117; Lord Riddell, *More Pages from My Diary: 1908–1914* (London: Country Life, 1934), p. 1; Soames, *Clementine Churchill*, p. 66; Malcolm Thomson, *Churchill: His Life and Times* (London: Odhams Books, 1965), p. 103.

30. Moran, *Churchill*, p. 730.

31. *The Memoirs of Field-Marshal the Viscount Montgomery of Alamein* (Cleveland: World, 1958), p. 480.

32. Colville, *Winston Churchill and His Inner Circle*, p. 11.

33. Winston S. Churchill, *Thoughts and Adventures* (London: Thornton Butterworth, 1932), pp. 201, 206; Cowles, *Winston Churchill*, p. 3; Manchester, *The Last Lion*, p. 20; Stewart, *Winged Words*, p. 24; Philip W. Buck, *Amateurs and Professionals in British Politics, 1918–59* (Chicago: The University of Chicago Press, 1963), pp. 10, 79.

34. Edward W. Crowe, "Career Goals in Parliament: A Study of Their Influence on Voting Behavior in the British House of Commons" (Paper prepared for delivery to the British Politics Group at the 1979 Annual Meeting of the American Political Science Association), pp. 15–17; Charles Eade, ed., *Secret Session Speeches: By the Right Hon. Winston S. Churchill* (London: Cassell, 1946), p. 21; Ian Colvin, *The Chamberlain Cabinet* (New York: Taplinger, 1971), p. 232.

35. Lord Morrison of Lambeth, *Government and Parliament: A Survey from the Inside*, 3d ed. (London: Oxford University Press, 1964), p. 130.

36. Taylor, *Beaverbrook*, p. 44; Cowles, *Winston Churchill*, pp. 356–57; Stephen Koss, *Asquith* (London: Allen Lane, 1976), p. 265.

37. Sir Oswald Mosley, *My Life* (New Rochelle, N.Y.: Arlington House, 1972), p. 105.

38. Walter Bagehot, *The English Constitution* (London: Fontana/Collins, 1976), pp. 91–92; Arnold Bennett, *Lord Raingo* (New York: George H. Doran, 1926), p. 66; Vera Brittain, *Testament of Youth* (New York: Wideview Books, 1980), p. 479; Iris Murdoch, *The Black Prince* (New York: Warner Books, 1978), p. 48; Frank Brennand, *The Young Churchill* (London: New English Library, 1972), p. 37.

39. Pelling, *Winston Churchill*, p. 109; John Grigg, *Lloyd George: The People's Champion, 1902–1911* (Berkeley: University of California Press, 1978), pp. 250-51.

40. A. J. P. Taylor, *The War Lords* (Harmondsworth: Penguin Books, 1981), p. 72; Wilson, *A Prime Minister on Prime Ministers*, p. 240. Even other members of the British political elite assumed Churchill had served as foreign secretary (Riddell, *More Pages from My Diary*, p. 87). The closest Churchill came to that office was by filling in occasionally for an absent Anthony Eden. (John Colville, *Footprints in Time* [London: Collins, 1976], p. 238; Colville, *The Fringes of Power*, pp. 484, 667; Fraser J. Harbutt, *The Iron Curtain: Churchill, America, and the Origins of the Cold War* [New York: Oxford University Press, 1986], p. 68; Pawle, *The War and Colonel Warden*, p. 297). In this capacity Churchill ignored Foreign Office advice (Colville, *The Fringes of Power*, p. 667). In 1944, Churchill considered becoming foreign secretary while remaining prime minister and minister of defense (Colville, *The Fringes of Power*, p. 479; Colville, *Winston Churchill and His Inner Circle*, pp. 208, 225). That he never served as foreign secretary was not accidental. He had no use for the professional staff of the Foreign Office (Colville, *The Fringes of Power*, pp. 128, 275, 444; Colville, *Winston Churchill and His Inner Circle*, p. 201). Edward

Grey claimed Churchill knew nothing about Foreign Office work. (George Macaulay Trevelyan, *Grey of Fallodon* [London: Longmans, Green, 1937], p. 152). More importantly, no prime minister, including Lloyd George, ever asked him to become foreign secretary. In 1929, Neville Chamberlain blocked Churchill's possible appointment as foreign secretary in Stanley Baldwin's cabinet (Martin Gilbert, *Winston Churchill: The Wilderness Years* [Boston: Houghton Mifflin, 1982], p. 18). There may have been valid reasons for Churchill's absence from the Foreign Office. One of them, his "known hostility to America," is revealingly discussed by Clementine Churchill in a letter to her husband in the late 1920s. (Martin Gilbert, *Winston S. Churchill*, vol. 5 [Boston: Houghton Mifflin, 1977], p. 315n). That hostility was expressed over much, if not all, of a half-century. In 1899, Churchill referred to an Anglo-American alliance as "that wild impossibility" (Randolph S. Churchill, *Winston S. Churchill*, companion vol. 1, part 2 [Boston: Houghton Mifflin, 1967], p. 1012). Early in the First World War, Churchill ridiculed the significance of American opinion toward that war (Martin Gilbert, *Winston S. Churchill*, companion vol. 3, part 1 [Boston: Houghton Mifflin, 1973], p. 262). Later in that war, he hoped American merchant ships would be sunk by the German Navy (Ibid., p. 501; Cameron Hazlehurst, *Politicians at War: July 1914 to May 1915: A Prologue to the Triumph of Lloyd George* [London: Jonathan Cape, 1971], pp. 188–89). His lack of sympathy for American interests was communicated to President Woodrow Wilson by the United States ambassador in London, Walter Hines Page, and by Wilson's personal representative, E. M. House (Arthur S. Link, ed., *The Papers of Woodrow Wilson*, vol. 33 (Princeton, N.J.: Princeton University Press, 1980), pp. 255, 268). Shortly after the First World War, Edward Marsh told Churchill, "I'm in favour of kissing him [Uncle Sam] on both cheeks." Churchill responded, "but not on all four" (Christopher Hassall, *Edward Marsh: Patron of the Arts: A Biography* [London: Longmans, 1959], p. 484). Even two cheeks would have been difficult for Churchill then. In 1930 he told Prince Otto von Bismarck that after 1918 he had wanted "the debtor and creditor nations, including Germany" to form "a common front against America" (Gilbert, *Churchill*, vol. 5, p. 407). In view of Churchill's distaste for American economic policy, this was in fact probably his hope. In 1925, contemplating, as chancellor of the exchequer, a British return to the gold standard, he wondered whether that return would not be rewarding "selfish and extortionate" American policy (ibid., p. 93). In 1928, he saw the United States as arrogant and fundamentally hostile to Britain (ibid., p. 301). In that year, his "blood boiled" at the thought of American foreign policy, and he warned his cabinet colleagues against further "efforts to conciliate American opinion" (ibid., pp. 307–8). In May 1940, Churchill referred to the government of the United States as "those bloody Yankees" (Colville, *The Fringes of Power*, p. 136). Shortly after D-Day, he described the heads of the American military services as "one of the stupidest strategic teams ever seen" (Harbutt, *The Cold War*, p. 64). After the Second World War, Churchill's hostility to the United States was evident in his attack on the Labor party cabinet for accepting an American admiral as North Atlantic supreme commander at sea (Cowles, *Winston Churchill*, p. 6; Robert Rhodes James, ed., *Winston S. Churchill: His Complete Speeches, 1897–1963*, vol. 8 (New York: Chelsea House, 1974), pp. 8183–95).

41. James, *Churchill*, p. 7; Robert Rhodes James, "The Politician," in Taylor and others, *Churchill*, p. 55; Beaverbrook, *Politicians and the War*, p. 188; Ephesian, *Winston Churchill*, 2d ed. (London: Mills & Boon, 1927). p. 171 (Ephesian was a pen name of C. E. Bechhofer-Roberts.); Joseph P. Lash, *Roosevelt and Churchill, 1939–1941: The Partnership That Saved the West* (New York: W.W. Norton, 1976), p. 9; Manchester, *The Last Lion*, pp. 23–24; Robert H. Pilpel, *Churchill in America, 1895–1961: An Affectionate Portrait* (New York: Harcourt Brace Jovanovich, 1976), pp. 71, 76, 264–65; *Lord Riddell's Intimate Diary of the Peace Conference and After,*

1918–1923 (London: Victor Gollancz, 1933), p. 15; Storr, "The Man," p. 207; R. W. Thompson, *Generalissimo Churchill* (London: Hodder and Stoughton, 1973), p. 23.

42. Moran, *Churchill*, p. 180n. For a brilliant description in theatrical terms of Churchill's "black dog," see Brenton, *The Churchill Play*, pp. 73–79.

43. Taylor, ed., *My Darling Pussy*, p. 197; Morgan, *Churchill*, p. 50; Richard M. Dorson, *The British Folklorists: A History* (Chicago: The University of Chicago Press, 1968), pp. 145–46; Flora Thompson, *Lark Rise to Candleford: A Trilogy* (Harmondsworth: Penguin Books, 1984), p. 67.

44. Storr, "The Man," p. 235; Moran, *Churchill*, p. 130.

45. Colville, *The Fringes of Power*, p. 476; Moran, *Churchill*, p. 794.

46. Walter Henry Thompson, *Assignment: Churchill*, p. 21; George Malcolm Thomson, *The Prime Minister: From Robert Walpole to Margaret Thatcher* (London: Nationwide Book Service, 1980), p. xxii.

47. Frederick Woods, ed., *Young Winston's Wars: The Original Dispatches of Winston S. Churchill, War Correspondent, 1897–1900* (London: Leo Cooper, 1972), pp. 121, 186–87, 288; John Spencer Churchill, *A Churchill Canvas* (Boston: Little, Brown, 1961), p. 139.

48. Randolph S. Churchill, *Winston S. Churchill*, companion vol. 2, part 1 (London: Heinemann, 1969), p. xxvi.

49. Colville, *The Fringes of Power*, pp. 239, 482, 519, 578; Shane Leslie, *Long Shadows* (London: John Murray, 1966), p. 275; Soames, *Clementine Churchill*, p. 562; Randolph S. Churchill, *Winston S. Churchill*, companion vol. 2, part 1, p. xxvii.

50. Brendon, *Winston Churchill*, p. 225; Colville, *The Fringes of Power*, p. 341; Pelling, *Winston Churchill*, p. 116; Theodore H. White, *In Search of History: A Personal Adventure* (New York: Warner Books, 1979), p. 493; Mosley, *My Life*, p. 105.

51. Winston S. Churchill, *The Second World War: The Gathering Storm* (New York: Bantam Books, 1974), p. 286.

52. Thomas Jones, *Lloyd George* (London: Oxford University Press, 1951), p. 261; John Grigg, *1943: The Victory That Never Was* (New York: Hill and Wang, 1980), p. 15; Robert Brain, *Friends and Lovers* (New York: Basic Books, 1976), p. 18; Grigg, *1943*, p. 15.

53. Lady Olwen Carey Evans and Mary Garner, *Lloyd George Was My Father* (Llandysul: Gomer Press, 1985), p. 171.

54. Thomas Jones, *Lloyd George* (London: Oxford University Press, 1951), p. 261; Martin Gilbert, *Churchill: A Photographic Portrait* (Boston: Houghton Mifflin, 1974), photograph 332.

55. Robert Rhodes James, ed., *Winston S. Churchill: His Complete Speeches, 1897–1963*, vol. 7 (New York: Chelsea House, 1974), pp. 7136–38.

56. Moran, *Churchill*, p. 350.

57. William A. Sadler, Jr., *Existence and Love: A New Approach in Existential Phenomenology* (New York: Charles Scribner's Sons, 1969), p. 335.

58. Robert Rhodes James, *Lord Randolph Churchill: Winston Churchill's Father* (New York: A.S. Barnes, 1960), p. 369; Colville, *The Fringes of Power*, p. 55. For his comment to his secretary Colville, *Winston Churchill and His Inner Circle*, p. 30.

59. Sarah Churchill, *Keep on Dancing*, pp. 336–37; Payne, *The Great Man*, p. 377; Costigan, *Makers of Modern England*, p. 311.

60. Brendon, *Winston Churchill*, p. 220; Colville, *Footprints in Time*, pp. 253–55; Colville, *The Fringes of Power*, p. 703; Moran, *Churchill*, pp. 682–83.

61. Moran, *Churchill*, p. 838; Brennand, *The Young Churchill*, p. 37; Payne, *The Great Man*, p. 11; Beaverbrook, *Politicians and the War*, pp. 126, 307.

62. The Earl of Swinton, *Sixty Years of Power: Some Memories of the Men Who Wielded it* (London: Hutchinson, 1966), p. 120.

63. James, *Churchill*, p. 52; David Mason, *Churchill* (London: Pan Books, 1973), p. 35; Kenneth O. Morgan, ed., *Lloyd George: Family Letters, 1885–1936* (Cardiff: University of Wales Press and London: Oxford University Press, 1973), p. 160; Arthur Salter, *Personality in Politics: Studies of Contemporary Statesmen* (London: Faber and Faber, 1947), p. 97; Hazlehurst, *Politicians at War*, p. 195; Churchill, *A Churchill Canvas*, pp. 30–31; Gilbert, *Winston Churchill*, p. 53; Robert Rhodes James, *Gallipoli* (New York: Macmillan, 1965), p. 197; Robert Rhodes James, *Victor Cazalet: A Portrait* (London: Hamish Hamilton, 1976), p. 15; Hugh Martin, *Battle: The Life Story of the Rt. Hon. Winston S. Churchill* (London: Sampson Low, Marston, 1932), p. 217; Moran, *Churchill*, p. 794; R. W. Thompson, *Generalissimo Churchill*, p. 34.

64. H. H. Asquith, *Letters to Venetia Stanley*, eds. Michael and Eleanor Brock (Oxford: Oxford University Press, 1985), p. 399; The Earl of Oxford and Asquith, K.G., *Fifty Years of British Parliament*, vol. 2 (Boston: Little, Brown, 1926), p. 228; Winston S. Churchill, *Painting as a Pastime* (London: Odhams Press and Ernest Benn, 1949), p. 16; Cowles, *Winston Churchill*, p. 205; Harvey A. De Weerd, "Churchill, Lloyd George, Clemenceau: The Emergence of the Civilian," in Edward Mead Earle, ed., *Makers of Modern Strategy: Military Thought from Machiavelli to Hitler* (Princeton: Princeton University Press, 1966), p. 295; Martin Gilbert, *Churchill* (Garden City, N.Y.: Doubleday, 1980), p. 52; Sir Ivor Jennings, *Cabinet Government*, 3d ed. (Cambridge: Cambridge University Press, 1959), p. 59; Stephen E. Koss, *Lord Haldane: Scapegoat for Liberalism* (New York: Columbia University Press, 1969), p. 205; *War Memoirs of David Lloyd George*, vol. 1 (London: Ivor Nicholson & Watson, 1933), p. 234; Morrison of Lambeth, *Government and Parliament*, p. 54; Rowland, *Lloyd George*, p. 310; J. E. B. Seely, *Adventure* (London: William Heinemann, 1931), p. 228; James, *Churchill*, p. 111.

65. Brendon, *Winston Churchill*, p. 79; Soames, *Clementine Churchill*, p. 161; Anita Leslie, *Randolph*, p. 3; Bonham Carter, *Winston Churchill*, p. 330; Cowles, *Winston Churchill*, pp. 204, 214; Moran, *Churchill*, pp. 332, 521.

66. Coolidge, *Winston Churchill and the Story of Two World Wars*, p. 69; Robert Rhodes James, ed., *Winston S. Churchill: His Complete Speeches, 1897–1963*, vol. 3 (New York: Chelsea House, 1974), p. 2390; Soames, *Clementine Churchill*, p. 198; Brendon, *Winston Churchill*, p. 79; James, *Gallipoli*, p. 332; Alan Moorehead, *Gallipoli* (Baltimore: The Nautical and Aviation Publishing Company of America, 1985), p. 331; Bonham Carter, *Winston Churchill*, p. 333; Sarah Churchill, *Keep on Dancing*, p. 14.

67. Winston S. Churchill, *Painting as a Pastime*, p. 16.

68. Beaverbrook, *Politicians and the War*, p. 275; Lord Beaverbrook, *Men and Power, 1917–1918* (London: Hutchinson, 1956), p. 113; Coolidge, *Winston Churchill*, p. 75; Frank Owen, *Tempestuous Journey: Lloyd George, His Life and Times* (London: Hutchinson, 1954), p. 307; Stephen Roskill, *Churchill and the Admirals* (New York: William Morrow, 1978), p. 56; Cowles, *Winston Churchill*, p. 216; Gilbert, *Churchill*, p. 45; Storr, "The Man," p. 239. His comment on painting is from Sir John Rothenstein, "The Artist," in Sir James Marchant, ed., *Winston Spencer Churchill: Servant of Crown and Commonwealth* (London: Cassell, 1954), pp. 138–39. See also Cowles, *Winston Churchill*, p. 10.

69. Elizabeth Longford, *A Pilgrimage of Passion: The Life of Wilfrid Scawen Blunt* (New York: Alfred A. Knopf, 1980), p. 409.

70. J. D. Hoffman, *The Conservative Party in Opposition, 1945–51* (London: Macgibbon & Kee, 1964), pp. 22-23; Humes, *Churchill*, p. 221, Robert Rhodes James, *Memoirs of a Conservative: J. C. C. Davidson's Memoirs and Papers, 1910–37* (New York: Macmillan, 1970), p. 171; Taylor, *Beaverbrook*, p. 568; David Childs, *Britain Since 1945: A Political History* (London: Methuen, 1984), p. 1; Colville, *Footprints*

in Time, p. 200; Colville, *The Fringes of Power*, p. 609; Cowles, *Winston Churchill*, p. 355; Pawle, *The War and Colonel Warden*, p. 408.

71. Jennings, *Cabinet Government*, p. 202; Cowles, *Winston Churchill*, p. 355.

72. Moran, *Churchill*, p. 309.

73. Ibid., p. 179; Riddell, *More Pages from My Diary*, p. 29. Since the latter condition had been met, Churchill thought Adolf Hitler had chosen the right end. (Colville, *Footprints in Time*, p. 199).

74. Moran, *Churchill*, pp. 310–11.

75. Sarah Churchill, *Keep on Dancing*, p. 136; Guy Eden, "Churchill in High Office," in Eade, ed., *Churchill by His Contemporaries*, p. 92; Hoffman, *The Conservative Party in Opposition*, p. 227; James, "The Politician," p. 110; MacDonald, *Titans & Others*, pp. 122–23; Stuart, *Within the Fringe*, pp. 139, 145, 149–50; Weidhorn, *Sir Winston Churchill*, p. 22; Earl Winterton, "Churchill the Parliamentarian," in Eade, ed., *Churchill by His Contemporaries*, p. 69; Cowles, *Winston Churchill*, p. 356; Taylor, *Beaverbrook*, p. 581.

76. Cowles, *Winston Churchill*, p. 360; Hoffman, *The Conservative Party in Opposition*, pp. 241, 268; Stuart, *Within the Fringe*, p. 147; Elizabeth Longford, *The Pebbled Shore* (London: Weidenfeld and Nicolson, 1986), p. 242.

77. MacDonald, *Titans & Others*, p. 124.

78. Payne, *The Great Man*, p. 15; A. J. P. Taylor, "The Statesman," in Taylor and others, *Churchill*, p. 49; Wilson, *A Prime Minister on Prime Ministers*, pp. 265–66; Brendon, *Winston Churchill*, p. 203; Bulmer-Thomas, *The Growth of the British Party System*, vol. 2, p. 204; Colville, *Footprints in Time*, p. 253; Colville, *The Fringes of Power*, p. 653; Anita Leslie, *Randolph*, p. 110.

79. Storr, "The Man," p. 244.

80. Harold Dwight Lasswell, *Power and Personality* (New York: The Viking Press, 1969), p. 21.

81. Howard W. Cummins, *Mao, Hsiao, Churchill and Montgomery: Personal Values and Decision-Making* (Beverly Hills: Sage Publications, 1973), p. 50; Weidhorn, *Sir Winston Churchill*, p. 26; Trevor Wilson, ed., *The Political Diaries of C. P. Scott, 1991–1928* (Ithaca, N.Y.: Cornell University Press, 1970), pp. 48–49.

82. Mark DeWolfe Howe, ed., *Holmes-Laski Letters: The Correspondence of Mr. Justice Holmes and Harold J. Laski, 1916–1935*, vol. 1 (Cambridge, Mass: Harvard University Press, 1953), p. 341.

83. Bryant, *Triumph in the West*, pp. 214–15, 217.

84. Lasswell, *Power and Personality*, pp. 39, 53.

85. Alfred Adler, *Understanding Human Nature*, trans. W. Beran Wolfe (New York: Fawcett Premier Books, 1978), pp. 69–70, 137; Ansbacher and Ansbacher, eds., *The Individual Psychology of Alfred Adler*, p. 244.

86. Storr, "The Man," pp. 206, 221, 224.

87. Anthony Storr, *The Dynamics of Creation* (New York: Atheneum, 1972), p. 77.

88. Randolph S. Churchill, *Winston S. Churchill*, companion vol. 1, part 2, p. 793.

89. Brendon, *Winston Churchill*, p. 111; Colville, *Footprints in Time*, p. 96; Diana Cooper, *Autobiography* (New York: Carroll & Graf, 1985), p. 711; Gilbert, *Winston Churchill*, pp. 45–46; Manchester, *The Last Lion*, p. 781; Robert Gittings, *The Nature of Biology* (Seattle: University of Washington Press, 1978), p. 78; Peter Quennell, *Customs and Characters: Contemporary Portraits* (Boston: Little, Brown, 1982), p. 155; Christopher Sykes, *Evelyn Waugh: A Biography* (Boston: Little, Brown, 1975), p. 253; Moran, *Churchill*, p. 796.

90. Lash, *Roosevelt and Churchill*, p. 9.

91. Princess Bibesco, *Sir Winston Churchill: Master of Courage*, trans. Vladimir Kean (London: Robert Hale, 1957), p. 32; Bonham Carter, *Winston Churchill*, p. 12; Cummins, *Mao, Hsiao, Churchill and Montgomery*, p. 32; Humes, *Churchill*, p. 14; Malcolm Thomson, *Churchill*, p. 31.

92. Iris Murdoch, *The Flight from the Enchanter* (New York: Warner Books, 1975), pp. 159–60.

93. Brendon, *Winston Churchill*, p. 15; John Spencer Churchill, *A Churchill Canvas*, p. 161; Ted Morgan, *Churchill*, pp. 49, 57, 65, 221.

94. Randolph S. Churchill, *Winston S. Churchill*, companion vol. 1, part 1 (Boston: Houghton Mifflin, 1967), p. 469.

95. Ibid., p. 167.

96. Randolph S. Churchill, *Winston S. Churchill*, vol. 1, p. 43; Jonathan Gathorne-Hardy, *The Old School Tie: The Phenomenon of the English Public School* (New York: The Viking Press, 1978), p. 224; Colville, *Winston Churchill and His Inner Circle*, p. 29; James, *Churchill*, pp. 4–5; Pilpel, *Churchill in America*, p. 3; Storr, "The Man," pp. 221–23; Iremonger, *The Fiery Chariot*, p. 23; Robert Lewis Taylor, *Winston Churchill*, p. 93; Cowles, *Winston Churchill*, p. 28.

97. Pamela Horn, *The Rise and Fall of the Victorian Servant* (New York: St. Martin's Press, 1975), p. 66; Manchester, *The Last Lion*, p. 112; René Kraus, *Winston Churchill: A Biography* (Philadelphia: J. B. Lippincott, 1940), p. 26; Manchester, *The Last Lion*, p. 127; Woods, ed., *Young Winston's Wars*, p. xxiii.

98. Stephen R. Graubard, *Burke, Disraeli, and Churchill: The Politics of Perseverance* (Cambridge, Mass.: Harvard University Press, 1961), p. 180; Rosebery, *Lord Randolph Churchill*, pp. 2–3; James, *Lord Randolph Churchill*, p. 259; Humes, *Churchill*, p. 14; Foster, *Lord Randolph Churchill*, p. 387; Colville, *Winston Churchill and His Inner Circle*, p. 30.

99. Randolph S. Churchill, *Winston S. Churchill*, vol. 1, p. 93; Randolph S. Churchill, *Winston S. Churchill*, companion vol. 1, part 1, p. 144.

100. Bonham Carter, *Winston S. Churchill*, p. 14; Colin Coote, "The Politician," in Marchant, ed., *Winston Spencer Churchill*, p. 37; Cowles, *Winston Churchill*, p. 33; Weidhorn, *Sir Winston Churchill*, p. 13; Wingfield-Stratford, *Churchill*, p. 25; Brendon, *Winston Churchill*, pp. 5–6; Costigan, *Makers of Modern England*, p. 253; Fleming, *The Churchills*, p. 134; Foster, *Lord Randolph Churchill*, p. 383; Gathorne-Hardy, *The Old School Tie*, p. 224; Martin, *Battle*, pp. 10, 30; Ted Morgan, *Churchill*, p. 560; Storr, "The Man," p. 230; Manchester, *The Last Lion*, p. 135; Pilpel, *Churchill in America*, p. 9.

101. Randolph S. Churchill, *Winston S. Churchill*, companion vol. 1, part 1, p. 391.

102. Ibid., pp. 259, 515; Bonham Carter, *Winston S. Churchill*, p. 14.

103. *The Reminiscences of Lady Randolph Churchill* (New York: Century, 1908); Eileen Quelch, *Perfect Darling: The Life and Times of George Cornwallis-West* (London: Cecil & Amelia Woolf, 1972), pp. 54–55; Randolph S. Churchill, Winston S. Churchill, companion vol. 2, part 2, p. 717.

104. Randolph S. Churchill, *Winston S. Churchill*, vol. 1, p. 47.

105. Fleming, *The Churchills*, p. 110; Foster, *Lord Randolph Churchill*, pp. 18, 270; James, *Churchill*, p. 11.

106. Ibid., pp. 9, 11n; Peregrine Churchill and Julian Mitchell, *Jennie: Lady Randolph Churchill* (Glasgow: Fontana, 1976), p. 172; Fleming, *The Churchills*, p. 123; Foster, *Lord Randolph Churchill*, pp. 59, 96, 374; Humes, *Churchill*, p. 5; James, *Churchill*, pp. 9, 11n; Longford, *The Pebbled Shore*, p. 144; Mary Soames, *Family Album* (Boston: Houghton Mifflin, 1982), no pagination; Payne, *The Great Man*, p. 72; Pelling, *Winston Churchill*, p. 27; Storr, "The Man," p. 230. Although August von Wassermann did not devise his blood serum test for the diagnosis of syphilis

until a decade after Lord Randolph Churchill's death, the high quality of British neurology at the time supports his doctor's diagnosis.

107. Randolph S. Churchill, *Winston S. Churchill*, companion vol. 1, part 1, p. 531; Harold Wilson, *A Prime Minister on Prime Ministers*, p. 244.

108. Pelling, *Winston Churchill*, p. 28; Michael Bentley, *Politics Without Democracy, 1815–1914; Perception and Preoccupation in British Government* (London: Fontana, 1984), p. 274; Manchester, *The Last Lion*, pp. 89, 137.

109. Randolph S. Churchill, *Winston S. Churchill*, companion vol. 1, part 1, pp. 113, 127, 182, 184, 193; Manchester, *The Last Lion*, pp. 125, 134, 153.

110. Randolph S. Churchill, *Twenty-One Years* (Boston: Houghton Mifflin, 1965), pp. 15, 73; Riddell, *More Pages from My Diary*, p. 61; Moran, *Churchill*, p. 469; Fleming, *The Churchills*, p. 150; Gilbert, *Winston S. Churchill*, vol. 6, pp. 949, 1204; Colville, *The Fringes of Power*, p. 444.

111. Bibesco, *Sir Winston Churchill*, p. 50; E. D. W. Chaplin, ed., *Winston Churchill and Harrow: Memories of the Prime Minister's Schooldays, 1888–1892* (Harrow: Harrow School Book Shop, 1941), p. 18; Gilbert, *Winston S. Churchill*, vol. 6, pp. 948–49, 1204; Colville, *The Fringes of Power*, pp. 278, 282.

112. Chaplin, ed., *Winston Churchill and Harrow*, pp. 92–93; Brendon, *Winston Churchill*, p. 13; Randolph S. Churchill, *Winston S. Churchill*, companion vol. 1, part 1, p. 237; Manchester, *The Last Lion*, p. 154; Pelling, *Winston Churchill*, p. 33.

113. Ephesian, *Winston Churchill*, p. 23; Brendon, *Winston Churchill*, p. 13; Cowles, *Winston Churchill*, p. 33; Martin, *Battle*, pp. 15–16; A. J. A. Morris, *C. P. Trevelyan, 1870–1958: Portrait of a Radical* (New York: St. Martin's Press, 1979), p. 7.

114. Philip Guedalla, *Mr. Churchill* (New York: Reynal & Hitchcock, 1942), p. 44; Kraus, *Winston Churchill*, p. 29; Payne, *The Great Man*, p. 54; Robert Lewis Taylor, *Winston Churchill*, p. 100; Manchester, *The Last Lion*, pp. 154–55.

115. Bonham Carter, *Winston Churchill*, p. 15; Randolph S. Churchill, *Winston Churchill*, companion vol. 1, part 1, p. 268.

116. Chaplin, ed., *Winston Churchill and Harrow*, pp. 83–84.

117. Manchester, *The Last Lion*, p. 123; Gathorne-Hardy, *The Old School Tie*, p. 224; Randolph S. Churchill, *Winston S. Churchill*, companion vol. 1, part 1, p. 188; Cowles, *Winston Churchill*, p. 31.

118. Randolph S. Churchill, *Winston S. Churchill*, companion vol. 1, part 1, p. 101.

119. Ibid., p. 295.

120. Ibid., p. 294.

121. Weidhorn, *Sir Winston Churchill*, p. 13; This school was incorrectly identified as St. James' School by Cowles *(Winston Churchill*, pp. 29–30).

122. Manchester, *The Last Lion*, p. 22; Maurice Baring, *The Puppet Show of Memory* (Boston: Little, Brown, 1923), p. 71; Brendon, *Winston Churchill*, pp. 7–8; Winston S. Churchill, *My Early Life: A Roving Commission* (New York: Charles Scribner's Sons, 1963), p. 12; Humes, *Churchill*, p. 13; Anita Leslie, *The Marlborough House Set* (New York: Dell, 1975), p. 24; Longford, *Winston Churchill*, p. 18; John Lord, *Duty, Honor, Empire: The Life and Times of Colonel Richard Meinertzhagen* (New York: Random House, 1970), p. 68; Ted Morgan, *Churchill*, p. 32; Storr, "The Man," p. 231; Virginia Woolf, *Roger Fry: A Biography* (New York: Harcourt, Brace, 1940), pp. 32–33; Ephesian, *Winston Churchill*, pp. 19–20; Manchester, *The Last Lion*, p. 125; Martin, *Battle*, p. 12; Payne, *The Great Man*, p. 57; Pelling, *Winston Churchill*, p. 31; Gerhard Prause, *School Days of the Famous: Do School Achievements Foretell Success in Life?*, trans. Susan Hecker Ray (New York: Springer, 1978), p. 31; R. W. Thompson, *Generalissimo Churchill*, p. 25; Malcolm Thomson, *Churchill*,

p. 31; Jonathan Gathorne-Hardy, *The Unnatural History of the Nanny* (New York: The Dial Press, 1973), pp. 28, 74; Leslie, *Randolph*, p. 7.

123. Cowles, *Winston Churchill*, p. 28; Gathorne-Hardy, *The Unnatural History of the Nanny*, p. 26; Humes, *Churchill*, p. 28; Peter Stansky, ed., *Churchill: A Profile* (New York: Hill and Wang, 1973), p. xii.

124. Randolph S. Churchill, *Winston S. Churchill*, companion vol. 1, part 1, p. 284.

125. Winston S. Churchill, *My Early Life*, p. 73; Kraus, *Winston Churchill*, p. 25; Malcolm Thomson, *Churchill*, p. 31.

126. Colville, *Footprints in Time*, p. 20; Ivy Compton-Burnett, *A God and His Gifts* (Harmondsworth: Penguin Books, 1983), p. 46; Rosemary Haughton, *Love* (Baltimore, Md.: Penguin Books, 1971), pp. 41-42; Gathorne-Hardy, *The Unnatural History of the Nanny*, p. 26; Martin, *Battle*, p. 11; Payne, *The Great Man*, pp. 48, 50; Weidhorn, *Sir Winston Churchill*, p. 14; Randolph S. Churchill, *Winston S. Churchill*, vol. 1, p. xxxi; Randolph S. Churchill, *Winston S. Churchill*, companion vol. 1, part 1, pp. xiii, 207; Gilbert, *Churchill*, p. 11.

127. J. H. Plumb, "The Historian," in Taylor and others, *Churchill*, p. 125; John Spencer Churchill, *A Churchill Canvas*, p. 284.

128. Randolph S. Churchill, *Winston S. Churchill*, companion vol. 1, part 1, pp. 84, 116, 142, 144, 146, 167, 171, 174, 180, 185–86, 204; Manchester, *The Last Lion*, p. 157.

129. Adler, *Understanding Human Nature*, p. 43.

130. Randolph S. Churchill, *Winston S. Churchill*, companion vol. 1, part 1, p. 579.

131. Ibid., pp. 578–79; Randolph S. Churchill, *Winston S. Churchill*, vol. 1, p. 245; Ted Morgan, *Churchill*, p. 79; Cowles, *Winston Churchill*, p. 41; Manchester, *The Last Lion*, p. 215.

132. Randolph S. Churchill, *Winston S. Churchill*, vol. 1, p. 245; Manchester, *The Last Lion*, p. 215; Cowles, *Winston Churchill*, p. 41; Randolph S. Churchill, *Winston S. Churchill*, companion vol. 1, part 1, p. 579.

133. Randolph S. Churchill, *Winston S. Churchill*, vol. 1, p. 246; Manchester, *The Last Lion*, p. 216; Pelling, *Winston Churchill*, p. 41; Gathorne-Hardy, *The Unnatural History of the Nanny*, p. 30; Horn, *The Rise and Fall of the Victorian Servant*, p. 68; Humes, *Churchill*, p. 28; Bonham Carter, *Winston Churchill*, p. 13; Cowles, *Winston Churchill*, pp. 41, 273; Storr, "The Man," p. 222.

134. Winston Churchill, *Savrola* (London: Hodder and Stoughton, 1915), pp. 41-217.

135. Randolph S. Churchill, *Winston S. Churchill*, vol. 1, pp. 24, 207–8; Randolph S. Churchill, *Winston S. Churchill*, companion vol. 1, part 1, pp. 424–25; Horn, *The Rise and Fall of the Victorian Servant*, p. 165.

136. Bonham Carter, *Winston Churchill*, p. 13; Winston S. Churchill, *My Early Life*, p. 73; Longford, *Elizabeth R*, p. 27; Longford, *Winston Churchill*, p. 23.

137. Storr, "The Man," p. 241; R. W. Thompson, *Winston Churchill*, pp. 24, 51; Hugo Vickers, *Gladys: Duchess of Marlborough* (New York: Holt, Rinehart and Winston, 1980), p. 114.

138. Longford, *Winston Churchill*, p. 23; Stansky, ed., *Churchill*, p. xii; R. W. Thompson, *Winston Churchill*, p. 50.

139. R. W. Thompson, Winston Churchill, p. 11.

140. Paavo Talvela, *Sotilaan elämä: Muistelmat*, vol. II (Jyväskylä: Kirjayhtymä, 1977), pp. 133–35; R. W. Thompson, *Churchill and the Montgomery Myth* (New York: M. Evans, 1967), p. 25; R. W. Thompson, *Generalissimo Churchill*, p. 72.

141. Beaverbrook, *Men and Power*, p. 125; Gilbert, *Winston S. Churchill*, companion vol. 3, part 1, p. 191; James, *Gallipoli*, p. 22.

142. A. L. Rowse, "Churchill's Place in History," in Eade, ed., *Churchill by His Contemporaries*, p. 420.

143. Carlos Thompson, *The Assassination of Winston Churchill* (Gerrards Cross: Colin Smythe, 1969), p. 198; Brendon, *Winston Churchill*, p. 148; Payne, *The Great Man*, pp. 48–50.

144. Pelling, *Winston Churchill*, p. 379.

145. Randolph S. Churchill, *Winston S. Churchill*, companion vol. 1, part 1, pp. 283–84.

146. Cowles, *Winston Churchill*, pp. 28, 36.

Index